Fearful Odds

A Memoir of Vietnam and Its Aftermath

Charles W. Newhall, III

Chuck Newhall

Fearful Odds
A Memoir of Vietnam and Its Aftermath
by Charles W. Newhall, III

ISBN 978-1-63393-110-7

Published by
Bibliotheca Brightside
Owings Mills, Maryland
Visit: www.fearfulodds.com

in association with
Roxbury Road Creative, LLC
and

www.koehlerstudios.com

Printed in the United States of America

This book is dedicated to my wife Amy, who brought our family back to life and to Dr. Theodore Kaiser who guided us through the maze. Most importantly, it is dedicated to the brave men of the A Shau, living and dead, whose combat stories are told here.

Author near A Shau, Vietnam, 1968

Table of Contents

Prologue

Preface 11

1. The Crucible 13

2. Evangeline Abbott Newhall .17

3. Shattuck. 21

4. The A Team 32

5. Active Duty 39

6. Vietnam at Last. 44

7. In the Valley of the Shadow of Death 49

8. After the Guns. 58

9. Reconnaissance of Hamburger Hill 61

10. Top 76

11. My Captain 85

12. Back to the Field. 89

13. The Way of the Sword. 102

14. Scrounger 108

15. Christmas, 1968. 113

16. Curly and the Reporter 121

17. Medal of Honor. 127

18. Smitty and Ted Kennedy 129

19. The Bach Ma and Drugs. 132

20. Two Days and a Wake-Up 138

Picture Gallery 147

21. The Paths of Glory 166

22. Boston Brahmins 171

23. T. Rowe Price 177

24. NEA 185

25. The Ides of March .194

26. Guilt, Grief and Anger 205

27. Marsi's Diary. 211

28. Dr. Kaiser. 220

29. Another War 227

Afterword 239

Postscript 245

Letter from Dr. Solomon H. Snyder 246

Charles W. "Chuck" Newhall, III. 248

Acknowledgments. 250

"And how can man die better than facing fearful odds,
for the ashes of his fathers and the temples of his Gods?"

— Thomas Babington Macaulay, "Horatius"

Prologue

"It is well that war is so terrible,
or we should become too fond of it."

— Robert E. Lee

8 Aug 1968
I Corps
Republic of Vietnam—A Shau Valley
1000 hours

On the third morning in the A Shau Valley, my platoon is waiting in an open field for helicopters to pick us up. For the past three days we have searched for the North Vietnamese Army (NVA) in the draws and the stream beds and have found nothing. It had rained the morning before we move out, and we are wet and cold. Some colonel at headquarters decides we will have better hunting up the valley. He orders our company to conduct a combat assault into a new area.

When our helicopters land, the western A Shau ridgeline and Laos are behind us. We land in an open field facing a large bamboo grove. The bamboo is so dense it would take a half hour for five men to cut a five-foot path. How does our idiot captain expect us to find shelter in a wall of wood? Behind the open field toward Laos is a swath of densely overgrown, 10-foot, razor-sharp elephant grass.

Third platoon, my platoon, is the first to land and remains in the open field as we were ordered. The rest of the company arrives after us. Capt. Flattop, my company commander, has located his command post in a shell crater out of harm's way in the elephant grass. The 1ˢᵗ and 2ⁿᵈ platoons surround him in defensive positions in the heavy elephant grass. Third Platoon is in the open field. I think Flattop is nuts. The men are not spread out. One artillery shell would wipe out half the company.

There is a faint pop in the distance. It does not seem important at the moment, but seconds later there is a scream of incoming artillery and a deafening explosion as an artillery round explodes 100 meters away. Everyone hits the ground. I hear static electricity.

I feel this has happened before. It is all so unreal. Seconds pass and everything happens in slow motion. Other moments pass with the speed and jerkiness of an old silent movie. I feel strangely cold and clammy and cannot get my feet to move.

I experience real fear for the first time. Flattop yells at me, "Get the platoon to the wood line." Since the wood line is 200 meters away across open fields, I yell to him that it might be better to withdraw to the elephant grass and keep moving. The men would not be visible as targets to a forward observer. The captain is not in the mood to debate. There is another pop and Flattop's head disappears into the shell crater, but he keeps yelling at me to move to the wood line.

The NVA gun crews will soon be active again. It is difficult to move across the open field in front of us. My feet do not move, yet we must move fast to keep the NVA gunners from getting our range. I shout and half the platoon follows me. I scatter the platoon so we will be hard to hit. Sgt. Frank Dillon, my platoon sergeant, will follow me with the second half of the platoon when I reach the wood line. There are distant reports, the whiz of incoming followed by rounds exploding everywhere. Shrapnel whirls all around me. It is only a matter of time before the NVA gunners have our range. The vegetation is so lush: You smell and feel the jungle as if it is a living animal. The ground beneath you seems to be moving and alive. We still have 100 meters to go. I set a fast pace.

There are more pops. I shout, "Hit the ground." I dive and find myself looking at mud and grass. There is a wind-sucking explosion. My ears ring. My eyes bulge and my nose bleeds. I hear nothing. The sun is out and a wind blows across my body. It is like a lawnmower passing a half-inch over my head. Every molecule in my body has its own sensory system. The smell is awful. For a split second I think I'm going to vomit. The earth tastes like sugar. I inhale the pungent odor of scorched grass, burned intestines and flesh, and human excrement. My eyes water—or am I crying? I do not want to look up. I want to dig a hole, and my fingers claw the earth. I wish I were back in the bomb crater with Flattop. Amid the chaos of death, there is a still moment, a second in which I can actually reflect upon what is happening to me. When the first artillery round lands, I know life is no longer in my hands. I am breathless and alone, and so, too, is every man around me. God, let me live. Go left and die. Go right and live. I think life and death are arbitrary events. Survival is a matter of the odds, not skill, and in such a situation fear explodes. Sweat runs down my back. I have the urge to run, to shit in my pants, or to hide.

Then it dawns on me and I am awash with guilt that is palpable and immensely painful: My men are young instant soldiers with only six months' training. They did not benefit from being trained for four years by Col. Hess and Capt. Rose, my college ROTC instructors. They did not benefit from four years at Shattuck, my military boarding school, and two years in the Special Forces reserves. Not one of them hit the deck and there are body parts all around me. I am in the center of the shell blast; the grass around me is only one inch high, mowed by a shrapnel lawnmower. Why am I alive?

I see a corridor through the grass. Three feet in front of me is what remains of a man. Who was it? I am not sure, for there is nothing left of his upper body. I remember: This is the guy carrying ammo for the M-60 machine gun. His name was Cpl. Ronald Lee Noldner. He was an orphan raised by relatives. He was only 21. Will anyone mourn his passing? His legs are standing. What remains of his waist, chest and head has painted the grass blood red behind me. Seared flesh and roasted intestines covered with dirt and powder ooze slowly down his legs. I am conscious of the sickening smell. It seems to enter my pores. That scent remains with me to this day. If Noldner had not been in front of me to absorb the blast, I would not be alive.

It is quiet. I am intact. I know that I have escaped death. In front of me, someone is sobbing. It reminds me of the cries of a child. Everywhere my men are crying. My fingers clutch the earth. A voice yells out, "You bastards, you bastards. Where in the hell is the medic?" Then there is silence. I can hear again. The grass murmurs as the wind passes over me. I feel helpless. My arms and legs are wooden appendages.

I am an officer, a commander, but I do not know what to do or where to go. I have been in Vietnam two weeks, and I know that I may never again see my wife, my family or my home. How many days just like this have I stretched out on the ground back home in Maryland's Caves Valley and watched the white clouds go by in a blue sky? Clouds float in a slow motion over my head. At home, lulled gently by the sun, I slowly and peacefully fall asleep. I could do the same thing now. My body is at peace.

I hear a voice. It is Hess from my ROTC days yelling, "Artillery, Lieutenant!" I have to do something. The men who are my responsibility need help. They are around me. I feel their life's blood flowing into the soil. I yell, "Medic." There is no response other than the harsh panting of the wounded. I go to Noldner's remains. In shock and refusing to believe he is dead, I open a bandage. But seeing reality, I toss it away. I knock his legs over and they fall to the ground. I remember a sentence from a book I read in college. "If there is a god, he surely must be mad."

Where the hell is the medic? My men need more sophisticated first aid than I can give them. I crawl down the corridor of grass. The earth's sugar smell is mingled with burnt flesh. Explosions shake the ground. Grass falls over my head. I hear the shrapnel singing as it passes over my head. I cannot breathe. I crawl forward with my head down, trying to keep my body as close as possible to the earth. With my head down, I collide into the helmet of 2nd Platoon's medic, Spc. 4 James "Doc" McAllister. We crawl back along the path to our dead and wounded. It has taken only 10 seconds to find Doc but it seems like hours.

I find the wounded, and I start bandaging one of them. McAllister yells to me that the man is in shock. After treating him, I move to another man. The explosions rock the earth but I do not care enough to lie down. As the F-4s go after the guns, I stand and raise my fist, asking the gods of war to destroy my enemies. Some of my men are crying. I do not. I feel helpless. Again, my hands are wooden clubs, not alive. The NVA gunners fire for effect and rounds explode around us. I feel nothing. Why am I alive? It is a question that will haunt me forever. Did I fail my men? Is there something I could have done to force them to hit the deck?

There is silence when the barrage is over. Death is everywhere and I feel it envelope me. Sgt. Northcut has lost part of his leg. Northcut is my ideal squad leader. He never complains. He volunteers to take missions and accomplishes them. He represents the best of a long line of young men who have put their lives in harm's way for their country—the men who defeated Braddock at Saratoga, Lee at Gettysburg, the Kaiser in the trenches of France, and the Japanese at Iwo Jima. His men would follow him into the mouth of hell. He is handsome, 22 years old, fit and intelligent. He is 5 feet 9 inches tall with black hair. I count on him; he is a leader in our platoon. A few hours earlier, he had his whole life in front of him. He will now face life as an amputee. It is tragic that a young man with so much promise will have to carry that burden for a country that will never care. His war is just beginning and he will have to fight it with only his family to support him.

I make a tasteless joke and hand him a cigarette. He lights the filter with a shaking hand, but he doesn't notice the error. I work with the medic to stop the wounded from bleeding. The first aid regimen is to stop the bleeding, treat the wound, then treat for shock. Northcut passes out. Two other medics, Pfc. McNeal and Spc. 4 Thomas, arrive to help. I improvise a stretcher and get two men from my platoon to carry it. As I load Northcut onto the stretcher, the last sinews attached to his foot break. The foot falls to the ground. Stupidly, I pick it up and run to the stretcher shouting, "Don't forget Northcut's foot." Another wounded man breaks out in hysterical laughter.

Within half an hour of the barrage, the wounded and the dead are gathered around a landing zone waiting to be flown to a field hospital or Navy ship, depending upon the severity of their wounds. When the barrage ends, Flattop moves the rest of the company across the field into the wood line. His command post is 30 meters away, deep in a bamboo thicket. He had 35 men cut a place for him to hide. He even tossed a few grenades to speed up the process. His face is white when I report my casualties. His hands shake. He does not want to hear my report and he is talking frantically on the radio. Disgusted, I leave him. Still in the open field, I move among my men lighting cigarettes. I try not to show terror. Doc McAllister gives me a tranquilizer. Only three men of the 12 who moved with me to the wood line are not wounded or dead. In all, half my platoon is gone. Dillon got the remainder of them to the wood line safely. He had waited until the barrage was over before moving. I start searching the dead for their personal effects, which I put in marked bags to send home. It appears as if the NVA has left the area.

There is the sound of rotors overhead as the first Huey helicopter comes in. It hovers about a foot off the ground as I direct men to load the chopper, wounded first, then the bodies. The helicopter is on the ground for 90 seconds. It lifts quickly and takes off over the trees, as a second helicopter approaches. Again, an explosion rocks the ground 100 feet away. Shrapnel flies all around me, glancing off my helmet. The NVA gunners have not left; they open up again. Our wounded were the bait that would bring medevac helicopters to us. The man beside me, two feet away, screams. His left leg is cut in half; a vein shoots blood into the air. Again I am covered in blood, and again I cannot hear. I grab him by the waist and throw him onto the second helicopter, shouting to a medic to bandage him as his life spills upon the ground. This is the second time I have escaped death. After the helicopter leaves, Pfc. Ebert and I are alone in the landing zone, explosions surrounding us. Ebert, a freckled-faced boy from Texas, is the only member of my platoon who is with me in the field, as he will always be beside me in times of our greatest danger. The others fled into the bamboo. The smell of death is sickening. Jets arrive in support of the helicopters, having spotted the NVA guns. The first flight drops its load, pounding the fortified positions with bombs and napalm. I see distant fire on the hillside and hear the faraway explosions. A second flight approaches but I pay no attention, for the wounded are my concern. I feel only my heavy breathing as we load bodies on a Huey.

Artillery will not bother us again this day. My body shakes uncontrollably.

It is my third day in the field.

Everyone responds to death differently. I can be close to the man on my right, but if he dies standing next to me he becomes firewood. I toss mere logs of firewood into the helicopter. This is what I think while I am in the middle of it. I am an invincible warrior. It is a delusion.

I have lived a lifetime in the past hour. This war is now a part of me forever. My romantic ideal of war is destroyed with the deaths of men who were my responsibility. Is this what the crusaders felt? Or the Roman legionnaires? It is too early to say what I have done or not done. Questions like what are you doing, what will your future be, have no relevance for me now. A lifetime has passed in front of me and I feel old, exhausted and misled. There is nothing glorious or romantic about war. Violent death is a bloody phantom that tears the hearts from living men. I will never be the same again.

I look at the stoic soldier sitting near me, facing outward with his weapon pointed across the A Shau. He uses the lull to eat some C rations. If it were not for the blood on the ground I would not know anything had happened. I kiss a blade of bloody grass to gather strength from the warriors who have died. It will give me strength to avenge them. It is business as usual. I search to find strength within me and do not ask questions. The sun is warm and a gentle breeze blows across the open fields. I cannot cry.

I know I will not sleep tonight or the next night. The uncertainty of my life hangs in front of me, a black fog—evil and dark. Today and the next few days will be the most important of my life. For seconds, I fall into a private reverie trying to understand the last few hours. I give it up. You cannot understand that which is not understandable. War is not understandable.

Much to my surprise, I find that Flattop has left on the third helicopter with the wounded. The medic decided that Flattop had a hernia. I have a new company commander—pudgy Capt. Career. He seems to be the type of leader who would sacrifice the company to get a promotion. He greets me with a smile that quickly turns into a condescending smirk. I knew his type in high school. He was the type of boy who would trap flies between a window and a storm window, and pull off their wings so he could watch them die in the jail he constructed. Career orders me to bury the weapons of the wounded, and orders the company to empty their rucksacks into the same hole. I ask, why do we bury the weapons? It is stupid. The NVA will dig them up tomorrow and the next day we will be staring down our own barrels. Career says we will have to travel fast and can ill afford extra weight, but we could have called a helicopter to take the weapons. We are going after the NVA artillery tonight, and will have to cross the valley before daylight, probing our way through elephant grass and the abandoned minefields placed there by our allies, the Montagnards. A mist seeps over the elephant grass and night falls slowly. Will I be alive next week?

Career is medium height, with dark black hair with a cowlick that falls upon his forehead. His right arm is in the bottom of the fatigue shirt. Oh no, we have a self-styled Napoleon. I have an uneasy feeling that we were better off under Flattop.

I stop thinking. It is dark. In a few hours we will move out into the night.

Fearful Odds

A Memoir of Vietnam and Its Aftermath

"They say: Whether our lives and our deaths were for peace and a new hope or for nothing we cannot say; it is you who must say this."

— Archibald MacLeish, "The Young Dead Soldiers"

Preface

In Flanders fields the poppies blow
Between the crosses, row on row,
That mark our place; and in the sky
The larks, still bravely singing, fly
Scarce heard amid the guns below.

—Maj. John McCrae

F**earful Odds** is about a series of skirmishes in August 1968 during a reconnaissance in force of the Dong So ridgeline in the A Shau Valley. The Dong So was connected to the Dong Ap Bia or Hill 937, often referred to as Hamburger Hill. If anyone had listened to us, the battle of Hamburger Hill would have been fought in a different manner. It was there in May 1969 that three battalions from the 101st Airborne Division had 72 killed and 370 wounded. That bloody battle changed the war and led to Vietnamization—having the Vietnamese, supported by U.S. air power, do the bloody fighting.

This is a memoir, not a scholarly history. Some details are missing. I knew many of the men with whom I fought by rank and last name only. Or maybe just a nickname. So where first names are missing, it is because I never knew them or I've forgotten them and have been unable to track them down. Capt. Peter Quirin is the most important person in this book. For many years, I thought he was dead. Recently, I found him alive and well, living in Wisconsin, teaching young policemen to survive urban jungles where they fight for their survival. I thought Tiny Stanchfield died in my arms, but his name is not on the Wall of the Vietnam Memorial in Washington. The casualty figures I list are higher than the official history of my unit, the 1st Battalion,

327th Infantry Regiment, 101st Airborne Division. I wrote the names of those wounded and killed when I listened in on our battalion's nightly radio recap of the day's events. I believe my casualty figures are accurate. Figures of those wounded in action were often much higher than unit histories report.

"Fearful Odds" is a memoir of my experiences during my tour in Vietnam. It is about my lifelong struggle with post-traumatic stress disorder after the war. It is my hope that veterans with PTSD and their families will read this and know that it is possible to fight through the disease and lead a productive life.

This book represents all of the information I have been able to gather to date about the cause and effects of my own struggle with PTSD. I began writing when I started professional treatment in 1982. In the decades that followed, I have worked methodically to understand and articulate the defense mechanisms that I developed to cope with everyday life. The summation of all of these discoveries is represented here in conversations with one psychiatrist who has had the most lasting and meaningful impact on my life, the late Dr. Theodore Kaiser.

Most importantly for me, this is a book about universal truths: the nature of war, the nature of leadership, the band of brothers, and reflections about the nature of love between a warrior and his bride. It is about the damage war does to those who survive it. It is about how war destroys love and life. I have also tried to show the beauty of the camaraderie of warriors. The quotations beginning each section will introduce the topics covered there; the challenges I faced are nothing new. They have been faced by other warriors throughout time.

"Fearful Odds" is a book about the Vietnam War and its aftermath, but it also is a book about my family's long military history and the events that formed me. The force that created me created warriors who give up their lives and happiness for others who do not care nor appreciate their sacrifice.

In the end, there is nothing that can hide the devastation of war: the horror of man's inhumanity to man that takes place upon the battlefields of time and the wreckage it makes of all those who survive.

CWN OWINGS MILLS, MD 2015

1

The Crucible

"You could mark the path that they took by
the dead that they left behind."

—Stephen Vincent Benet

28 July 1968
Somewhere over the South China Sea
1400 hours

We took a commercial flight from Baltimore to San Francisco, and then boarded Tiger Air, a commercial subcontractor hired to take troops to Vietnam. The movie on the flight from Baltimore was "In Enemy Country," a World War II spy movie. I am wearing my first lieutenant's uniform and have orders for Vietnam.

It is an unusual journey. There is almost no air turbulence. Most of our flight has been in daylight over unusually tranquil seas. My orders state that I am to report to a replacement battalion, but I have been assured I will be assigned to the 101st Airborne Division. We are the replacements for troops lost during the Tet Offensive in January and February. The 101st as usual has been involved in some of the heaviest fighting during Tet. Along with Marines and MPs, troopers from the 101st assaulted and then recaptured the American Embassy in Saigon. After having spent late 1967 and early 1968 in heavy fighting around Pleiku, the 101st moved north to help re-secure Hue, the old imperial capital of Vietnam. There are rumors that the 101st is moving west into the mountains to prevent another surprise like Tet.

I am excited. I started wearing a uniform at age 8, and school is finally over. There will be no more playing soldier with blanks. My next year will be the real thing. I have spent nine years studying leadership, weapons, military history, tactics, first aid, navigation and self-defense at a military boarding school, ROTC and in the Special Forces Reserves. I have conducted some form of military exercise in every type of climate over all varieties of terrain, from Maine in the winter to Panama in the summer. My body is hardened and ready for what is to come. I have volunteered five times to go to Vietnam, and each time I have been turned down. My father asked his friend Gen. Howell M. Estes to get me this assignment and here I am. My alternative to Vietnam was a scholarship to the University of Edinburgh or Oxford, but I lost out in the finals. Vietnam was what I really wanted. At some point you must stop preparing for life and start living. I know instinctively that in war it is possible to become acquainted with your body and your soul. To be a warrior has been my dream since childhood. I pursue it to honor my grandmother's wish.

When we left San Francisco we were all talking and joking and trying to impress the pretty stewardesses on the plane. But now no one was talking. I am not even conscious of the plane engines' steady noise. Fear, excitement and the ghosts of my childhood do not let me rest. I remember what brought me to this flight and wonder where it will lead me.

The pilot's announcement interrupts my thoughts. We are 20 minutes from Vietnam, and we have started our descent. Suddenly I am cold. I wonder what my grandmother would have said to me at this moment. I had only a few minutes to see her before leaving the United States. She is the greatest influence on my life. As we descend, I can hear my grandmother asking me, "What is honor?" Her answer, drummed into me, is that honor is something all kings claim, but few have. Honor cannot be given, nor can it be taken. To gain honor may take years, but you can lose it in seconds. Honor does not necessarily lead to riches or happiness, and to have it means you carry the responsibility for the rest of your life. Remember to treat everyone with honor, even your enemies. We must all become used to death and not getting our heart's desire. What we do in life can last for an eternity. Your honor will live after your death in the minds of those who have known you and in the minds of those who remember what you have done. Honor is often gained in times of crisis, the crucible of fire, for that is where its steel is forged. My son—for you are as much my son as my grandson—come home with your honor.

That was what she said, but I knew what she meant: Come home with honor or do not come home. She was like Plutarch quoting what Spartan mothers told their sons as they headed to battle: Come back with your shield or on it. My grandmother told me that she did not envy the life I will lead. Her philosophy went like this: The gods torture only those whom they love. If you are one of fortune's favorites, as I believe you are, then you will win great triumphs but you will have to suffer more defeats than most men can bear. Defeat is God's way of telling you that you need a course correction. You will trust people who betray your trust, and each betrayal will take away a piece of your heart and your mind. But you must never stop trusting— 10 percent of the people you trust may betray you, but keep in mind the 90 percent who do not. You will dream greatly and suffer to make your dreams reality, only to see them vanish. Without a dream you cannot survive. Greatness is a vision, nothing more—an ephemera. Strive for greatness but never set your heart upon achieving it. Unhappiness is a sign of weakness. Do not forget that you may be a warrior of god whose mission is to cleanse the earth of evil, but you may need a little help from the devil.

In my last visit with my grandmother, she gave me a slender volume, a handbook of Epictetus sayings, the same book her father, Capt. Asa T. Abbott, carried with him during the Civil War. She said, "Read this on the plane. My father told me not to believe everything you will read in this book, but it will help a warrior who is a romantic at heart to cope with war. Good luck and remember all that we have talked about over the years."

I kissed her on the cheek. I left her room surprised by the formal austerity of her goodbye. Sometimes talking to my grandmother was like having an audience with the Delphic Oracle.

During the first few hours of the flight, I read and reread the book. My memories of Epictetus' stoic philosophy still resonate with me. "To survive as a warrior you must be baptized by fire and blood and come out steel. One of the most dangerous parts of war is what occurs in the minds of those that survive. Do not show emotions but preserve them; it is our emotions that bind us to humanity. Virtue is not happiness, wealth, or power; it is character and a way of living. To win virtue is the only real path to happiness. We compete throughout life, not with others, but ourselves. Continue to remember but cease to mourn. To be physically hardened, to endure separation from loved ones, and to face the horror without retreating is a warrior's fate. The brotherhood of arms is a tighter bond than that between husband and wife. Treasure it; for you will never find such intensity again even though it may only last for days. Anticipate evil at all times and prepare to deal with it. Free yourself from anger at individuals, but feel outrage against evil: torture, massacre, or rape. Without outrage against these acts we lose our humanity. If you want anything good, know that you can only get it from yourself."

My thoughts are interrupted by the lowering of the landing gear. In what seems like seconds, we land and start to exit the plane. Remember the past for what you have learned; live for today and tomorrow. I hope my grandmother is right; war will burn the fat off my soul.

As I come to the airplane door, I am blinded by the violent light and stunned by the fetid smell. Within a second of leaving the chill of the plane, I enter a cauldron of heat and fire.

Good morning, Vietnam.

2

Evangeline Abbott Newhall

By heaven, methinks it were an easy leap to pluck bright
honour from the pale-faced moon.

—William Shakespeare, "Henry IV (Part One)"

I was born Nov. 18, 1944, in Washington, D.C., the city that seemingly ran the world. The United States over the last four years had created the greatest war machine the world had ever seen. We had no doubts about our leadership of the world.

My father was an Army Air Corps colonel on Gen. Hap Arnold's staff. He was 38 and he helped manage development, production and allocation of fighter aircraft around the world. A small number of people ran America's war machine. They called themselves whiz kids. Father had no doubts about his destiny, for he was a whiz kid and the world was his oyster. My mother, Gladys Brantley Newhall, father and I lived in a modest two-bedroom apartment in a building called the West Chester.

After the war, my father became a struggling entrepreneur and venture capitalist who barely had enough money to pay for my tuition, as well as the membership fees of his 10 golf clubs. My mother came from Kite, a small town in Georgia that was sacked by Gen. William Tecumseh Sherman during the Civil War. It never recovered. Mother's parents were poor dirt farmers, but not sharecroppers since they owned their own land. Their house was made of smoke-blackened pine boards whose knotholes had all fallen out. The wind blew through those holes in winter. She left home at 16, never to return. When I look at pictures of her when she was young, I see one of the most beautiful women I have ever seen. She worked hard to finance her education. Before she married, she was an airline flight attendant in the days when that job required being both a pilot and a registered nurse. Father's mother always believed my father had married beneath him.

When I was 6 my parents sent me to camp for three months, hoping I would become self-sufficient. From the age of 6, I was forced to learn adult survival skills. At 10 I was sent to five-day boarding school for the same reason. I believe they regarded me as an inconvenience and wanted me out of the way.

Because of Father's job, my parents moved every six months. My father wanted his mother to raise me because he did not trust my mother to do so.

I was not aware of this decision until I was 15, at the end of my sophomore year at Shattuck. I was home for a few weeks. My father asked me what my proudest accomplishment at school that year had been. Shattuck had a competitive swimming program, one of the best in Minnesota. I had set the school record for the 400-yard freestyle that year, winning myself a spot on the board at the dining-room entrance that listed the best athletes in school history. My mother, who had been drinking, said, "Don't kid yourself. You are not an athlete, and in fact you are so skinny that you look like a girl." My father was not much better than my mother. He was always distant except when my grades arrived. At that time I was an erratic student at best. If I failed to get an A, which was often, he humiliated me. My parents' unwillingness to approve of my accomplishments hurt me, but I said nothing. I now realize they were just human. I cannot blame my mother; I can only imagine what forced her to leave her family at 16. I now understand my father's self-obsession, for in some ways I am like him.

After my mother's comment, my father took me aside and told me that I was going with my grandmother to visit cousins in Hawaii that summer. He told me his mother did a good job raising him and to trust her and learn from her.

My grandmother shaped my life. I spent weekends and summers with her. I visited my parents infrequently. My grandmother, Evangeline Abbott Newhall, encouraged me to be myself and to dream greatly. Beneath a man's exterior, there is always a little boy who never was. My grandmother's stories of heroism, stoicism and great deeds that made the world a better place sustained me.

She loved literature and encouraged my reading, rather than restricting it as my parents did. When I was with my parents, they told me I needed to sleep. I would reply, who needs sleep when there is something good to read? It was then that they took my books. My grandmother taught me that beauty is a hospital for the soul. She encouraged me to study science. Her particular interest was botany and plant breeding. But most of all, she was a hard, tough-minded woman. She was always available to help, but she herself never asked for help.

When I was 6, my grandmother was watching me ride a bike around the circle driveway at our New Jersey home when she stepped backward, tripped on a rock and broke her hip. At 85, she organized her own move into a nursing home, decorated her room, and then worked hard at rehabilitation. In time she recovered.

In 1957, when I was 13, we moved from New Jersey to Baltimore when Father became CEO of Flight Refueling. Flight Refueling was started by Sir Alan Cobham, a World War I fighter ace and pioneer of the British Overseas Airways Corp. (BOAC) round-the-world air routes. Flight Refueling provided a refueling system designed to support ground troops. In 1960, Gen. Curtis LeMay, Air Force chief of staff, said all wars would be fought from the air. Flight Refueling contracts ended and the company was sold. Yet the Air Force continued to use the equipment of the company my father ran, and Flight Refueling saved my life in Vietnam.

Two years later, when I was 15, my grandmother moved to join us in Baltimore and found an apartment so that she could again be close, but not dependent on us. My mother did not like my grandmother but respected her self-reliance. My grandmother always told me to do things for myself, whether it be packing a bag, moving across the continent, or fighting a war.

I remember the story she told me of shooting the hat off a burglar who was trying to enter her Minnesota home. My grandmother used to say that women need to know how to use firearms. She was taught by her mother, Fannie, who she said shot Indians in the Dakotas in the 1870s to save her family. She gave me a .22-caliber pistol for my 16th birthday. That pistol would come to haunt me for the rest of my life.

In her mid-90s, my grandmother again checked herself into a nursing home because she was too old to take care of herself. At 99 years and 11 months, she slipped and fell in her bathroom. The window was open. It was December. She did not use the call button. She chose to die because she did not want to put the strain of her care on her family when she was frail and senile. My father never recovered from his mother's death. No one was left who could solve his problems or rebuild his soul after the assaults of life. My grandmother made me an island unto myself so I would not suffer my father's fate.

When I was with my grandmother, I did not watch much television. She would tell me stories about the Civil War and her brave father's adventures. The Civil War was real to me. To some extent, my grandmother was an extension of her father and Shattuck School, where she had lived for most of her life.

She sent me there so the Lords of Discipline would govern my life for three years. In my fourth year, I would become one of those lords myself.

3

Shattuck

We few, we happy few,
We band of brothers;
For he today that sheds his
Blood with me
Shall be my brother.

— William Shakespeare, "Henry V"

My full immersion in our family's military traditions began at Shattuck School in Faribault, Minn. My great-grandfather, Capt. Asa Abbott, was military commandant from 1886 to 1901.

He was born in 1836. His mother and father died when he was 5; his grandfather and older sister raised him. His sister married, so Capt. Abbott took care of his grandfather until he died. At 16, he shipped out of New York on the brig Orilla and sailed to Georgetown, S.C. He traveled overland to Charleston and then to Memphis, where he got a job on a riverboat that went north to Minneapolis. When the Civil War broke out, he scrapped his college plans and enlisted in the 1st Minnesota Volunteers in April 1861.

Abbott received a battlefield commission at First Bull Run. He was wounded several times and received commendations for gallantry in action. He fought at First Bull Run, Edwards Ferry, Ball's Bluff, Cedar Mountain, Second Bull Run, Antietam, Shiloh, South Mountain, Fredericksburg, Chancellorsville and many other battles.

In February 1863, Abbott had to put down a mutiny in his company. Morale in the ranks was low. Some enlisted men were in the Army only because wealthier men had bribed them to take their places in the draft. Others had been conscripted against their will. Infantry conditions were bad, casualties were high, and the men revolted, threatening to shoot any officer. My grandmother told me how Abbott rode into their camp with two Army Colts blazing and a sheathed saber. He was fired upon so he shot seven men including the leader. When his pistols were empty, he drew his saber and wounded four more men. He told the remaining troops that they must obey orders or he would attack again. The mutineers surrendered. They gave Abbott the title "the fighting cock." He never punished the mutineers. Later, he turned down offers for promotion to field officer level because he loved the camaraderie and action that can be found only at the company level.

In July 1864, Confederate Gen. Robert E. Lee sent Gen. Jubal Early north with 15,000 men to take Washington. Early crossed the river at one of the forts above Washington and attacked Gen. Lew Wallace, later the author of "Ben-Hur," who commanded 5,000 raw recruits. Wallace was defeated and retired to Baltimore. Early's troops advanced to within 250 yards of Fort Stevens, only seven miles from Washington. Abbott was manning a signal detachment at Fort Stevens with five enlisted men. He was on the north parapet, communicating with Washington by flag signals. His parapet was the most important target for the Confederate Army.

President Lincoln arrived at the sally port and joined Abbott. Lincoln placed his foot on a gun chassis. He was dressed in a long frock coat and a plug hat, a conspicuous figure silhouetted against the sky. He almost seemed to be saying, "Take your best shot, Johnny Reb." Abbott and Lincoln watched the skirmish line of Confederates advance to within 100 yards of the fort. A colonel suggested that Lincoln retire, but he refused to move. Several officers clustered around him; two were hit by minié balls. Worried about more casualties because everyone clustered around Lincoln, Abbott, as the officer in command of the sally port, ordered Lincoln to leave the parapet. Lincoln got down from the parapet as deliberately as he had mounted it.

Abbott remained on the parapet sending signals despite a hail of bullets. A bullet struck the seat of his chair, throwing him to the floor. He rose and sent his message, "Rebels driving Union Cavalry down Tarreytown Road." The rebels were intercepted, stalling their advance.

If the Confederates had advanced that afternoon, they would have taken Washington. Abbott was on the parapet when the sun rose the next morning. Gen. Ulysses S. Grant sent reinforcements to the rescue. A wall of blue lay between Fort Stevens and Early's men. Abbott was ordered to wave the flag to signal the Union advance. The reinforcements jumped to their feet and charged Early. The enemy was driven back, and that was the last heard of Early in Maryland. Later Abbott interrogated a rebel prisoner who had been shooting at him. The man was delighted when he learned that he had shot Abbott's chair out from under him.

In December 1864, Abbott led several cavalry scouting missions toward Richmond, deep behind Confederate lines. On one of these trips he was picking an apple in an orchard. A young woman leaned around a tree and said, "Yankee, don't you steal my apple." Her name was Victoria Frances Cross—called Fannie by most. She had lost her father and brother in the Mexican War. She had been crowned Queen of Love and Beauty at the jousting tournaments held in Baltimore. Her mother moved her behind Confederate lines, where they found refuge with relatives. Abbott stayed for an hour talking to the friendly Southern girl. Whenever he led other scouting missions behind Confederate lines he would meet with her, and the visits became longer. By December, he was in love. Fannie had similar feelings for him.

Fannie and her mother were friends of Confederate Col. John Singleton Mosby, the Gray Ghost. They served coffee to Mosby and his troops after each raid. Mosby was the greatest irregular cavalry leader in the war. I was fascinated by stories of his raids against the Union Army. He was a tactical genius; his battle tactics would save my life in the years ahead. He always attacked at dawn in the mist where he was not expected. He would vanish before the sun was fully up, leaving behind a destroyed Army depot, spiked cannons and dead Union soldiers. He wore a broad hat with an ostrich feather similar to those his

Cavalier ancestors wore when they fought Oliver Cromwell's Roundheads.

On Dec. 23, 1864, according to a story often told in my family, Abbott rode through the Confederate lines carrying a rosewood and ivory jewelry box with an engagement ring for Fannie, but he was caught by Mosby and his raiders north of Richmond. Abbott was tied up and put at the end of the column as a prisoner of war. Mosby dropped back to talk to him as they rode through a dusty cornfield, and he whispered to Abbott, "Are you Fannie's young man?" Abbott said yes. Mosby cut Abbott's bonds and handed him his bundle. Mosby said, "Drop off the back of your horse and hide in the woods on the right. I will cover for you on the left. Merry Christmas." He waved his hat with the ostrich plume in salute. Abbott offered Mosby a salute in return and obeyed orders. Mosby drew his sword and galloped through the dense corn on his left, shouting, "Prisoner escaped!" He led his column on a wild goose chase and let Abbott slip away.

After the Civil War, Abbott was sent to command cavalry units fighting the Indian Wars in the Dakotas and Wyoming, which kept him in harm's way until he was 50. At that time he retired with his wife and daughters to Shattuck School to teach young boys the art of war, and the discipline it takes to master the art. Abbott retired before World War I. My grandfather, Dr. Charles Newhall, Abbott's son-in-law, was awarded an Army major's commission for Shattuck's expanded role in military training. During World War I, Shattuck graduated second lieutenants who went directly to war, skipping college. The names of those who died are flanked by suits of armor in the entrance hall. My grandfather had been a mathematics professor at Shattuck before becoming headmaster. He and my great-grandfather followed and fought the Great War on a large map in Abbott's home office.

At the end of the war, when a truce was called before the Allies entered Germany, Abbott was enraged. He pounded the map with his fist, scattering divisions. He ripped it off the wall, saying, "We will have to finish this job in 20 years." Fannie had been dead for four years. I believe Abbott suffered from PTSD after the Civil War, and eventually the black dog of depression stopped his heart. Abbott died a year later, deeply depressed by the loss of Fannie and our failure to end a war that he knew would recur. Life without Fannie was not worth living, even for a stoic. My grandmother told me Abbott had terrible dreams, and many nights he could not sleep. Because of my grandmother's stories, the Civil War is as alive to me today as the Vietnam War, the war I fought. Abbott's portrait is in my office. I always look to him yearning for advice. He stands at attention in front of me, his face gaunt but his body fit and trim. He is wearing the dark-blue uniform of a Union officer with its high, white, starched West Point collar, with his white hair and gold wire glasses.

My family and the family of my first wife, Marsi, have produced generations of Capt. Abbotts over 400 years. I read the books my ancestors have written about war and compare them to my own experiences. It has been my great pleasure to discover their histories, their victories, but most importantly, their defeats and how they overcame them as they practiced the art of war.

My grandfather started as a student at Shattuck in 1888. After graduating from Johns Hopkins, he returned to Shattuck, taught mathematics and coached football. He was headmaster from 1916 to 1936. He shepherded the school through World War I and the Great Depression. In 1933, he was awarded a Ph.D. by Dartmouth College for pioneering the use of small classes in the United States. Shattuck classes for juniors and seniors had the intimacy and the relaxed intellectual environment that encouraged debate and discussion similar to the tutorials at Oxford and Cambridge. He carried on the military traditions created by Capt. Abbott.

My father, the headmaster's son, graduated from Shattuck at the age of 16. Eventually, he earned an electrical engineering degree from MIT. My father thought my early years in school had been too free spirited. I pursued my own academic interests rather than the curriculum taught at my school. My father thought Shattuck would shape me up. My grandmother agreed that I should go to Shattuck—not because she thought I needed to shape up, but because she wanted me to be a warrior. I wanted to go to Shattuck because it was my family's home. I knew I would eat my meals in the school dining room surrounded by portraits of my family. I welcomed the pressure to excel and not disgrace myself in the presence of my ancestors. I would become a warrior so my parents and grandparents would be proud of me.

In September 1959 I reported to the cadet officer of the day dressed in a uniform of khaki pants, a starched cotton shirt and a solid-colored tie. I stood at attention and saluted: "Cadet Newhall is reporting for duty, Sir." Most of my classmates looked at me as if I had two heads; after all, they were still civilians. I was not. My family had been involved with the school for 77 years, and with the military forever.

Shattuck gave me an excellent education. It was a hothouse for my creativity, which exploded in my four years there. In an English class during my freshman year at Shattuck we read Milton's "Paradise Lost." We had just finished the King James Version of the Bible and would soon start Shakespeare's "Julius Caesar." Books became my escape. The magic of words became the hidden path to my world of make-believe. I allowed my world of books to become my reality. My imagination distracted me from the often-harsh military discipline.

Shattuck taught me so much and gave me my greatest gift: my own room, the room of my imagination. I could summon it at any time, any place—a ridgeline in Vietnam or a corporate boardroom in Massachusetts. No one can enter my room; it is a place of adventure, beauty and excitement. As a boy, when I first discovered this, my room was the field of battle where wars were won and lost. It gave me the strength to endure.

The value of my Shattuck education was soon proven. I had terrible Scholastic Aptitude Test scores as a result of my attention deficit hyperactivity disorder (ADHD). When, after Shattuck, I went to the University of Pennsylvania, I took achievement tests. I was exempted from the first two years of humanities courses and took graduate courses in my freshman year, for in graduate courses you could create your own curriculum.

As much as I liked Shattuck, it was not easy. I remember a hot day in September, at the end of the first month of my freshman year. Wearing sharply pressed wool uniform pants, a highly starched cotton shirt and a tightly knotted tie, I stood sweating in 90-degree heat. Somehow you were supposed to control your body so that you did not sweat, but few of us could do that. I knew then that I was expected to be in control under all conditions. For more than 102 years, Shattuck had been teaching stoicism to young warriors.

According to my grandmother, some of the money to build Shattuck's campus was given by Queen Victoria, at the request of the Shattuck family of Boston. Victoria wanted to establish an Anglican military boarding school in the West so that families moving there would have a place to educate their children, destined to be warriors, in a disciplined Christian manner. The school was started by Dr. James Lloyd Breck in 1857. In 1862, the Santee Sioux killed 800 Minnesota settlers, the highest civilian casualty toll prior to 9/11. Another 40,000 settlers in the region fled eastward in panic. In 1876, the Jesse James gang rode into Northfield, Minn., with guns blazing. Shattuck started as a tiny wood-plank building in an unfriendly wilderness, a pioneer school. The school's chapel would be built on ground that was once holy to the Indians. Indians had performed their war dances on Shattuck's parade grounds. The school must have absorbed some of the pagan wildness of Minnesota. By the time I got there, its meager beginnings had been transformed into a fortress of stone. It looked like Ivanhoe's castle, complete with crenellated towers.

As an impressionable boy raised in Ivanhoe's castle, I spent more time rehearsing the manner of my death than contemplating the future of my life. At Shattuck, I read the accounts of the Battle of the Nile where "the boy stood on the burning deck." I discovered the poetry of Byron and fantasized about being Lord Nelson on the decks of the HMS Victory, dying among his sailors, with the last words: "I have done my duty."

Early in the fall of my first year, I picked up a package from the mailroom and took it on the long walk back to my chilly dormitory at Breck Hall. The three-foot stone walls of the dormitory made the temperature 15 degrees cooler than outside. I ran up to my room on the third floor wanting to see what my parents had sent me.

Everything in the room was ready for inspection by our senior hall proctors. As a new boy freshman, only 13 years old, I feared the seniors. I had cleaned the joints on my iron bed with a toothbrush in preparation for a white glove inspection at any moment. If a senior said to do pushups, I did pushups. If a senior corrected a mistake I made and said run, I ran at high port for miles, carrying an M1 rifle over my head. I stood at attention when any senior entered the room.

Before I could open my package, my door was thrown open and slammed against the wall. Four seniors I did not know entered. They were sergeants, not officers. If you were still a sergeant as a senior, your aptitude for the military was questionable. One of them yelled at me: "Where is the package?" "Suck your gut in." "New boys are not allowed packages." "Why are you a fuck-up?" "Because you are the fourth generation of your family here, do you think you are special?" "Strip now!"

I removed my shirt, pants and underwear. I stood naked. I held the end of the metal bed with my hands, studying the dust that was caught in the sunlight on my Army-green blanket. One of them removed a wire coat hanger from my closet and straightened it. He twisted the tip and he beat me. I was too furious to feel pain. Finally, they picked up my package, laughing, and left. I never saw what it contained. I had bled a lot; my greatest concern was that blood did not stain my uniform or our room. A blood spot would have caused me to fail inspection. I did not cry or report their behavior so that our family honor was intact, and no senior bothered me again in that brutal way. Perhaps they were testing me. Would I rat on my comrades in arms? I learned an important lesson. Life is unfair. Deal with it and above all, never cry. Crying is weakness for a warrior.

Sunday was a special day in the new boy's week. We marched to chapel, held a parade and had an inspection. The inspection was the highlight of my week. I cleaned our room all during the week, dusting everywhere and shining what could be shined. Our floor usually passed inspection easily, but every so often we failed, no matter how hard we worked. Failure was a planned event.

Early in the year, we were standing at attention in our room waiting for inspection. The cadet officers entered our room, tearing mattresses off bunks and dumping dresser drawers on the floor. Their faces livid, they yelled at us, shouting that we were pigs and a disgrace to the school. We failed the inspection and were told we had the worst room in the school. My three roommates and I would pay the price. We did not know it but we were being taught a lesson. Life is essentially unjust. Catastrophe can happen at any moment. When bad things occur, you must overcome despair. Always have three alternate plans of action: one if the enemy comes from the front, one if he comes from the sides, and one if he comes from behind. Plan for all eventualities and act instantly. The seniors were changing us into warriors, creating in us the military mind. My motto in life became if it can go wrong it will, so be prepared.

This was my first exposure to the band of brothers, which has defined leadership for me ever since. A leader creates a band of brothers. A band of brothers can accomplish what most men believe is impossible. A band of brothers is the culture of we, not the culture of me. The mission and your comrades in arms come first. Your self-interest is secondary. It is why some soldiers jump on grenades. Being betrayed by your band of brothers is the ultimate humiliation. It is like being a cashiered cavalry officer in the Indian Wars. Your horse and pistol are taken from you and you are left in the desert alone to find your way to safety. When you strip away a man's pride, you strip away his life.

The day we failed the inspection was clear, dry and sunny, but the nights heralded the approach of a frigid winter and the heating system was not yet working. At lights out, around 2200 hours, taps was played around the campus. Our senior floor monitors told us to stand at attention outside our rooms. This was a Shattuck tradition. The temperature was 45 degrees, and after midnight, one of my classmates fainted. Over the next hours, two more freshmen followed. It was chilly and several of us started to cough. At 0100 the senior floor proctors came out of their rooms. We had a marshmallow race: We had to take off our pants, pick up a marshmallow in our buttocks and duck walk the length of the hall. It was quite a race; anything was fair, including an elbow in the face. The loser ate some marshmallows. That was the way the seniors initially encouraged us to behave. But we soon learned it was better to work together and confound the seniors. We crossed the finish line together. We turned the culture of me into the culture of we, which was what the seniors had sought.

My grandmother knew the Shattuck culture since her grandfather had created it. She sent me to Shattuck so that I might learn to survive. Capt. Abbott believed self-sufficiency was all-important for young men alone in the world of adults. An orphan and a warrior at the age of 16, he had to learn his lessons the hard way. This was the lesson of the band of brothers. I faced the Lords of Discipline at the age of 13 and lost my fear of them. I had a band of brothers, and together we could overcome anything.

My grandmother believed she had spoiled my father. He was self-centered and could deal with success but not failure. She would not make the same mistake with me. Maybe this treatment seems brutal today, but it prepared me for far worse trials in combat and in business.

At Shattuck my lifelong love affair with the military deepened as I studied history to learn battle strategies. In my childhood, my room had shelves of toy soldiers. I studied weapons, and convinced my grandmother and my father's friends to buy me weapons. I knew a hundred battle plans by the time I was 18. I arranged my toy cowboys and Indians into ancient and modern battle formations. I read Thucydides' "Peloponnesian War." I was fascinated by Leonidas, the general and master of terrain who selected a team of 300 Spartans and several thousand other Greeks to slow the march of Xerxes' Persian army of millions of men for five days. The Spartan phalanx was a tank; Leonidas located his tank in a narrow defile, the gates of Thermopylae. Three hundred men moved as one. Leonidas combined Olympic athletes with poets. Leonidas taught me teamwork and the fact that a good team needs all types of people, not just the strongest. The phalanx held the army of Xerxes until the Spartans were betrayed. The 300 Spartans covered the retreat of the other Greeks, and held the pass alone as long as they could, deadly until the last man fell with Persian arrows sticking out like porcupine quills from his chest.

Stoicism enables you to survive adversity. The men on your right and left become important when you are in danger, exhausted and scared. Will the soldiers around you, your partners, cover your back and not run? Will they stab you in the back? When you see a smile from a man who claims to be your friend, remember the hand behind his back may hold a dagger. What motivates me the most is keeping the respect of those around me, my platoon or my partners.

The final lesson I learned at Shattuck was leadership; Shattuck was a laboratory for it. By my senior year, I was one of 10 cadet officers who ran the school. As such, we were responsible in high school for the other students' futures. If we found a student breaking the honor code and reported him, he would be expelled after a trial. It was a heady experience to stand in front of the 400 young men of the cadet corps, order the company commanders to report to you, and order the battalion to march to church. Whenever I walked before them, my classmates stood at attention. As cadet officers, we took our responsibilities seriously. If we failed in our duties, we were relieved of command—as one of my classmates, a company commander, found out. When I left Shattuck, I was a leader of men.

I look back on Shattuck with thanks for the three lessons I learned outside the classroom: the military mind, the band of brothers and leadership.

My grandmother's training and Shattuck prepared me for life. I could face great trials without succumbing to fear. Control yourself. Conquer yourself. Jump school, escape and evasion training, and all the other military adventures I would experience were pieces of cake after my childhood. Shattuck training saved my life in battle but left me ill-suited for marriage and civilian life.

When we graduated from Shattuck we would be scattered across the United States. I never again have seen the brothers of my youth; I have been too busy fighting new battles with new comrades in arms.

4

The A Team

"I am clearly in sentiment with you that every man
who is in the vigor of life ought to serve his country
in whatever line it requires and he is fit for."

—George Washington in a letter to David Humphreys,

June 25, 1797

In 1963, I graduated from Shattuck and enrolled at the
University of Pennsylvania—the next step on the path to
a ridgeline in Vietnam. I was in the ROTC program and in the
2nd Special Forces, an Army Reserve unit. I was allowed to start
a Special Ranger detachment at Penn.

The second in command of the ROTC department was Capt.
Rose, the first of my three captains and a positive influence
on my life. He was about 6 feet 1 inch tall with a blond flattop.
He was in excellent shape. He was the supervisor of the Penn
Ranger unit and we worked closely together. In my sophomore
year at a training exercise at an Army base in Indiantown Gap,
the Rangers were ordered to ambush the rest of the battalion.
We started on the mission at 1600 hours and spent the night
and the next morning climbing one of the worst mountain
ranges I have ever seen. Every one of us with a full pack fell and
sprained something. We were all exhausted when we finished
the exercise in the afternoon. When we returned to the barracks,

I went to my private room and lay on the bunk. The rest of my men prepared for an inspection. Rose entered my room. He was furious with me. "You lead from the front. Never ask your men to take a risk that you are unwilling to take. Eat after they have eaten and go to bed after they are in bed. In the morning, rise and dress before they wake. Being tired is no excuse. In war the tired die first." He was giving me the best advice and I was ashamed of my actions. This was not the only time I would make this mistake, but Rose led by example and taught me how to be a warrior.

Because I had graduated from military school, at Penn I commanded juniors and seniors in my freshman year. It was awkward for a freshman English major to walk around the campus in camouflage fatigues, jump boots and a green beret. I always carried a foot-long commando knife strapped to my waist. I would later use that knife to kill a man. I knew I was going to Vietnam after graduation and would be determining which of my men lived or died. I was convinced I would write the Great American Novel after that experience. The knife gave me comfort as I walked among other students who felt I was the personification of evil in America.

It made me furious to walk past a campus protest where students were trying to occupy the university president's office. "Ban the bomb" signs were painted on the campus walls, protesters spat at me and women laughed at me. I did not date often in college or anywhere else. Women considered me odd.

As a freshman, I was fascinated by graduate courses in Greek history. I read the texts in English while the rest of the class read in Greek. It was a courtesy to me because I was young. Those courses changed my life.

As an English major, I was drawn into a world of Hemingway, Faulkner, Fitzgerald, James, D.H. Lawrence, and, of course, Conrad. One of my favorite classes focused on Henry James. It was taught by Professor Nancy Leach, a beautiful, statuesque, dark-haired woman who looked as if she should be wearing a sidesaddle riding habit. For me, she was Isabel Archer in Henry James' "Portrait of a Lady," married to a man 30 years her senior. She carried herself with exquisite grace. I dreamed of taking Nancy to Venice to a beautiful bedroom in the Gritti Palace on the Grand Canal. In the moonlight overlooking Santa Maria del Salute, I would place a 1930s diamond Van Cleef choker around her neck. She would not notice because she was staring at the marble beauty of the Santa Maria del Salute Church that seemed to be the path to heaven. I touch her. I revel in the scent of her hair, which cascades over luminescent diamonds that float in a sea of shimmering chestnut beauty. I want to kiss her all over. Professor Leach would have been shocked had she known that I was sitting in class not listening, but dreaming about her neck, the sparkle of diamonds, and a night of passionate lovemaking.

My Army Reserve duties included flying around the country on weekends to conduct Special Forces training exercises. In North Carolina we were pitted against an active-duty Marine battalion. Our mission was to complete a combat jump into a heavily defended area, establish base camps, and take out the Marine battalion headquarters. After the successful jump, we broke into teams. Each team took a separate route to our objective. Our weapons were loaded with blanks. My team was ambushed shortly before midnight as we moved through the woods. We separated and ran alone. I ran for 15 minutes and then lay flat on the ground in a pile of leaves. Two Marines pursued me, firing their weapons. The night was cloudy and the clouds blocked the moon. Soon, the Marines stood above me. Although they stood on my boots, I felt safe. They did not see, hear or smell me. They did not feel me. "Idiots," I thought. Never lose the sense of feeling, especially in your toes. Sense everything always ... if you wish to survive.

The exercise lasted 48 hours. We had no sleep for two days, with no food and little water. Eventually, I found the Marine command post. With a stolen Marine uniform, I entered the compound, tossing a smoke grenade into the command bunker.

Unfortunately, the exercise had ended an hour earlier. But I still remember the thrill of escaping the ambush and lying still for hours thinking of Isabel Archer and Nancy Leach.

Several months later, during an ROTC exercise at Indiantown Gap, I was leading the Ranger platoon across a field when I saw Lt. Col. Hess, my ROTC commanding officer.

At Penn, Hess never said a word; unusual for a highly experienced combat officer. Rose, his executive officer, told me the stories of Hess' exploits in World War II. Hess had parachuted into a hot landing zone at Normandy. The paratroopers were easy targets as they floated to Earth. When they landed, companies and platoons were intermingled so they fought with strangers. Hess was at Bastogne as a platoon leader. At Bastogne, platoon leaders had less than a 1 percent chance of surviving. In desperate straits, a combat platoon leader's principal job is to die well.

When we were about halfway across the field, Hess pulled out an artillery simulator, basically a big firecracker. There was a pop followed by a shrick and an explosion. He was busily pulling out others. Artillery equals shrapnel. It was time to leave the area quickly. I signaled the platoon to run for the wood line. In an instant, Hess was in front of me, two inches from my face, and in his mind he must have been reliving an artillery barrage in Normandy. His face was bright red. His neck muscles bulged; his arms and chest seemed to be bursting from his uniform. He was obviously in good shape for a 50-year-old man. "Cadet, you have killed your platoon. When you hear the pop of an artillery round, hit the deck. If you are standing when the gunners have your range, you are dead. Cadet Smith, you are now in command. Newhall is a rifleman." I was mortified; my face turned crimson. Hess seemed to shrink in size as his anger subsided.

In my imagination, my reading fused with my military experiences. As my study of English literature progressed, Joseph Conrad's "Lord Jim" captured my imagination. Why did Jim, an officer, jump from his old cargo ship that was carrying pilgrims to Mecca? Was it a lack of courage? How could Jim leave the Indian pilgrims who were his responsibility, afloat in the ocean, while he fled with a group of drunks? Wasn't his code death before dishonor? Later Jim, despite his best efforts, failed to defend the village he chose as home. What caused him to leave his wife, Jewel, the love of his life, to make the final pilgrimage of honor to the village chieftain, Jewel's father? It cost him his life; Jewel's father shot him in the forehead. It doomed the family he loved to loneliness and the charity of others.

His focus on an abstract code of honor probably caused him to ignore what the consequences of his actions were to others. It must be as the gentle collector of butterflies, Jim's friend Stein, said: "Jim held honor above love because he was one of us."

But to his credit Jim did not hide from the rawness of life and followed Stein's advice: "In the destructive element immerse."

Live life, do not hide from it. Romantics live life with such intensity that life often consumes them and those around them. Many romantics use stoicism as a shield. I envisioned myself as a romantic and a stoic. My goal at the time was to write literary criticism that was itself an art form, like Cleanth Brooks' "Well Wrought Urn." My sculpture course and independent study devoured my mind.

"How to Be" became the title of my senior-year independent study thesis—an analysis of the romantic hero in modern British and American fiction. My thesis was much more than a paper for me; I was seeking a solution for the rest of my life. How can I as a romantic pursue a dream in the destructive element without destroying family and all that is around me? Vietnam became my portal to Lord Jim's world.

At that same time I was going to debutante parties. In Baltimore there is the custom to have debutante balls to introduce young women to "society." Suitable college men are invited to these events that occur over every holiday during the school year. The parties are beautiful and provide just the proper setting for a young romantic warrior to meet his bride.

I met Mary Washington Miller, known to everyone as Marsi, at such a party in the summer between my junior and senior years. She was the 12th direct descendant of Mary Ball Washington, the mother of George. George Washington, William Augustine Washington, Sam Smith, Robert E. Lee, and many other heroes were her ancestors. She made her debutante debut at the Bachelors Cotillion in Baltimore. She was photographed for an article in "Town & Country" called "Sex and the Deb." In addition to the debutante parties, there were a host of other functions—cocktails, small dinners, horseracing, sailing, ski trips and other pleasures. This was Marsi's world. At the time it seemed like another planet to me, and although I despised some of its values, it attracted me. I felt at those parties the way I thought Nick Carraway felt when he encountered Daisy Buchanan in Fitzgerald's "The Great Gatsby." The WASP social circuit in the '60s was a world of languorous beauty in refined settings, a world where art and architecture were the background for parties and what seemed to me a lifetime of leisure devoted to sports or travel. All of this was a far cry from the life I knew in a military boarding school, or living with my grandmother.

My mother tried to prepare me for this world by giving me a striped gray seersucker tuxedo jacket with one-inch-wide lapels. It would have been the appropriate dress for a weekend in Las Vegas with the Rat Pack. Most of the young men who attended the parties were graduates of Lawrenceville, Choate or Andover. They wore elegantly tailored black or midnight blue dinner suits, as the English call their tuxedos, with high starched collars. They were tall and slim and could foxtrot to Lester Lanin or Peter Duchin with the grace of Fred Astaire. Conversation revolved around the best hotel to visit with a young lady when staying in Gstaad or spring vacation in Sea Island or summer in Newport. The women were from the best schools: St. Timothy's, Foxcroft and Garrison Forest. Their mothers took them to New York to buy designer ball gowns, and their jewels had come down through the family and were real.

In my seersucker tuxedo, having barely mastered the box step, I remained a wallflower at most of the parties. Instead, I played the role of the young bohemian—a Hemingway in the making. My table conversation centered on "Lord Jim," D.H. Lawrence, the merits of the '61 Bordeaux, the many meanings of a haiku verse, and my desire to become a warrior. If a good party consists of many diverse ingredients, I added a little spice to the mix. For me it was a world of flowers, perfume, multiple bands, silk gowns—and sublime moments like watching the moon rise over the Caves Valley covered in a sea-like mist. We danced beneath illuminated tents in front of houses that resembled Scarlet O'Hara's Tara. I learned phrases such as lounge lizard and parlor snake, and I thought all summer nights were "de-lovely" and cool, accompanied by the music of Cole Porter.

Somehow Marsi picked me out from among all those swirling young men. She loved my stories of Faulkner's Sartoris and his wife, the beautiful Drusilla, fighting in the Civil War to save a doomed way of life. She loved the fact that I was a warrior who was ready to fight and, if necessary, die. For her it was romantic to think of knights in armor on battlefields of honor. She honored the sacrifice of her ancestors and saw the same values in me. She also loved that I gave her the keys to the world's libraries, and together we explored the world of the imagination. But she did not realize how far apart our worlds really were, and she would soon have to live in my world with all its inherent violence and dangers. We were married after I graduated, just after her first year at college. She was barely 19. In our generation it was not unusual to get married young and then have the husband go to war. That was what all of our parents had done.

I did not know when I married Marsi that my violent world would contribute to her death.

5

Active Duty

But I've a rendezvous with Death
... And I to my pledged word am true,
I shall not fail to meet that rendezvous.

— Alan Seeger, killed on the Somme, July 4, 1916

In October 1968, Marsi and I headed for our first home, and my first active-duty assignment as a basic training officer with the Army at Fort Polk in Louisiana. For Marsi, this must have been like a voyage to the far side of the moon. Our first home was a platoon barracks. We had a bathroom with 20 shower stalls and we made love on a granite floor with a warm shower running over us, oblivious to the emptiness around us, or the deaths of the soldiers who had showered in the place where we joined our souls. We next lived in a converted chicken coop. It had linoleum on the runway, and the sides and the top were enclosed in plywood. I decided to move when I found out our neighbors on either side ran whorehouses.

We found safer accommodations 20 miles away in a small town called Leesville. We rented a house on L.C. Lee's large ranch and were adopted by the Lee family. Marsi bought a horse called Kickapoo and was happy riding during the days. We had a house of our own with two bedrooms, a living room and a kitchen. It was wonderful, although the drive added two hours to my already long day. One of my most precious memories is coming home from work in a sweaty uniform and Marsi racing Kickapoo up a narrow dirt road trailing clouds of dust toward me. She pulled in the reins, and Kickapoo's nose was six inches from my face. The sun created a halo behind her and her smile illuminated my life. I thought such love was my birthright; I was a fool.

Capt. Holt, my company commander, was a Korean War veteran who had won a battlefield commission. At his house he showed us his proudest possession, a Bronze Star awarded for valor. The citation that came with the Bronze Star described the reason for the award: As a private in Korea, he had held a line of defense for days while the Chinese attacked in human waves. His stories made the mindless violence of the attack as real as if I had lived through it. If he had been an officer at that time, he would have been given the Distinguished Service Cross. He entertained us with his war stories of Korea, about the allies and the Chinese hurling themselves at each other's elaborately entrenched positions. It was a war fought in foxholes, bunkers and no man's land, like World War I. Holt had already served two tours in Vietnam. Fort Polk was to be his last tour of duty. He did not make field grade, being held back by the lack of a college education, but he was a true warrior.

My life was focused on the company. I awoke at 0330. It took me an hour to get to the post. I drove, half awake, along a narrow Louisiana back road that twisted like a black snake in front of me. After reveille came physical training and breakfast and then we ran to classes. I learned a lot about life at Fort Polk, a lot about people. It was a good tour of duty, but each day became more frustrating. I should be in Vietnam fighting, using what I had learned over the past nine years rather than training kids to fight the war that was my destiny. During my year as a basic training officer I volunteered five times for the 101st Airborne Division's 1st Brigade in Vietnam. Each time I was rejected. Despite my training and readiness, the Army wouldn't let me go. Most of my contemporaries were putting their energy into beating the draft and protesting in the streets. Yet I could not get to Vietnam, my destiny.

I'd spent years preparing for this moment: military boarding school for four years, two years in college ROTC, three years in the Reserve Special Forces unit while at college, and one year

on active duty. I went to jump school at 18. I was Special Forces
trained, light weapons qualified and a Jungle Warfare School
graduate. My training was equal to West Pointers' and I had an
obligation to serve my country in combat and not let my training
go to waste. I was a warrior who wanted to fight, stuck training
boys to be warriors. There is a critical difference between a
soldier and a warrior. A warrior's job is to kill the enemy face
to face, to accomplish a combat mission, or to die trying. The
soldier's job is to support the warrior. In Vietnam, it took nine
soldiers—intelligence, division staff, quartermaster, engineer
and others—to keep one warrior in the field.

Since I could not get to Vietnam by volunteering, I asked
my father for help. He had been on Gen. Hap Arnold's staff in
World War II. Many of my father's friends from that time were
now senior officers in the four services. Gen. Howell M. Estes
Jr., a West Pointer who commanded the Military Air Transport
Service, was a close family friend. A call from Estes to his old
West Point roommate Gen. O.A. Barsanti, commander of the
101st Airborne Division, was all that it took. I received orders
for Vietnam within a week. But my orders did not give a unit
assignment, which is unusual.

I felt deep in my soul that I belonged to the 101st. My
commanding ROTC officer at the University of Pennsylvania,
Col. Hess, served with the 101st in World War II. I liked the
elegant patch: the famous black eagle with a white patch on his
head. Hess wore it on his right arm. I intuitively knew the bald
eagle was my spirit animal. A spirit animal is a force that adopts
you. It chooses you, not the other way around. American Indian
braves had spirit animals that they identified with. To this day
when I am out West, eagles fly with me.

The origins of the 101st go back to the Civil War, to a
volunteer unit of the Wisconsin militia whose mascot was a
large bald eagle nicknamed Old Abe. Whenever the unit went
into battle, Old Abe would be released. The eagle would fly
high over the battlefield, screaming, and then dive a few feet
above the Confederates' heads. The unit's unofficial motto was
"No quarter."

A Southern general hated the eagle and he issued orders
to his men to shoot it, but the eagle remained unharmed. The

general then offered a reward to any sharpshooter who could hit the eagle. Old Abe was wounded twice but survived and he flew when his Wisconsin unit fought, low and angry over Confederate heads, screaming his war cry, "No quarter." The Wisconsin warriors would see their eagle overhead as they drove their bayonets home without remorse. No quarter is a warrior's religion unless there is valuable intelligence to be gained. It was my religion in Vietnam. Old Abe lived to be 21; he spent his declining years in the Wisconsin state capitol. After his death, he was mounted on a perch and placed in a memorial hall. In 1904, fire destroyed the hall and Old Abe. But his legend has lived on for those who seek to fly with eagles. In July 1939, another eagle with identical markings to those shown in photographs of Old Abe was found in the Wisconsin wilds. Naturally, the eagle was named Young Abe.

In August 1942, Major Gen. William C. Lee was given the task of organizing the 101st Airborne as an elite strike force. The 101st would be first on the ground in Operation Overlord, the Normandy invasion. The paratroopers were dropped behind enemy lines June 6, 1944, and disrupted enemy reinforcement to the beaches of Normandy. The mascot of the 101st was Young Abe, the screaming eagle.

Gen. Maxwell Taylor commanded the division. They jumped again at Arnhem, and from there the division moved to Bastogne and was surrounded by Hitler's counterattack in the Ardennes during the Battle of the Bulge. Their orders were simple: "Hold Bastogne." Brigadier Gen. Anthony McAuliffe commanded the unit in Bastogne; he was surrounded by two German divisions and running out of food, ammo and medical supplies. The Germans gave McAuliffe an ultimatum: Surrender or die. His one-word reply: "Nuts." The 101st was the first division in American history to receive the Presidential Unit Citation, the highest award for a division in battle. The 101st fought its way through France and Germany, all the way to Berchtesgaden.

The 101st is the unit described in the book "The Band of Brothers." I wanted to be a part of this history. My spirit animal, the eagle, will be with me for the rest of my life.

When I was a child, my grandmother told me stories of the Sioux. She gave me an insignia of the 7th Cavalry that had been worn at the Battle of Little Big Horn. She told me that when Crazy Horse charged Custer, he inspired his warriors by saying: "It is a good day to die." I have experienced many such days in peace and war but somehow I am alive.

Before leaving for Vietnam, I shook hands with Holt and said goodbye. He had a wistful look. Perhaps he wanted to go with me. Holt, like Capt. Rose at Penn, taught me an enormous amount about being a leader: If you want to lead men, you lead by example. Run beside them, eat what they eat, and lead from the front.

My goodbye to Marsi was different, because we were both children and naive. She drove me to the airport as if we were going to a movie theater. We kissed and said goodbye. As I walked into the airport, I looked back to wave goodbye, but she was gone.

I realized the next year was mine alone, and no one would kiss me or care whether I was alive or dead, because they were caught up in their own lives—my parents, my in-laws, and my child bride. At least my grandmother would think of me often because she knew what I would be facing; she sent me there to face it.

6

Vietnam At Last

You have thought no doubt of sacrifice,
the great word that sustained you in the mud,
and of all those decent girls in your pockets
who married others when the grief had ebbed,
you have thought perhaps and reconsidered
since what you died for now is dead.

— Stephen Plaice

28 July 1968
Bien Hoa, Vietnam
0900 hours

The Bien Hoa airport stands out in two colors, tan and green. Sweat runs between my shoulder blades before I can walk down the exit ramp. The sun reflects from the runway. The ground is a shimmering wasteland, pockmarked by artillery and mortar craters. The highest points in the terrain are the circular family graves that dot the Vietnamese countryside. Are these graves recent or centuries old? Ironic— my greeting when I arrive in Vietnam is a field of graves.

A sergeant in jungle fatigues directs me toward a tin-roofed waiting area. Everyone is there: Special Forces, 1st Division, 199th Light Infantry Brigade, 4th Division, the 173rd Airborne Brigade and, of course, the 101st Airborne Division. Everyone is off the plane. We are sorted and shuffled like a deck of cards. We are picked up by buses and driven to the 90th Replacement Battalion at the largest Army base in Vietnam—Long Binh. Vietnamese are everywhere. The women, clad in brightly colored silk ao dais, are beautiful. The ao dai is a high-collared long dress slit to the waist with pants underneath. It is enchanting. All is enclosed, yet all is revealed by implication. On the ride to the replacement battalion, we see Vietnamese manning machine gun bunkers at each intersection. The beauty of the women is at odds with the beasts of war. In war one of the things that keeps you alive is the memories of the woman you love and the women you could have loved.

It takes only 10 minutes to check in at the replacement battalion. There are no lines, no shouting clerks. Everything is bright and efficient. Then I am alone, alone in Vietnam. I am surrounded by people, but I do not know a single person. Helicopters are in the sky. The noise of rotors is deafening. I spend two long days at the replacement battalion wondering what will happen and feeling lowly. Something has gone wrong. At noon on the second day, I hear a loudspeaker: "Lt. Newhall, report with your equipment to the reception desk. Your transport is here for the 101st." I breathe a sigh of relief.

Eighteen lieutenants arrive at the 101st Replacement Battalion and I make friends with Dave Meiggs, an infantry platoon leader, and Bob Stein, a quartermaster lieutenant. The first person we meet is Spc. 4 Davidson. He is a company clerk who manages the administration of the replacement battalion. He is a college dropout and quite smart. The senior NCOs and a few officers teach and spend time with the new replacements. Davidson takes care of everything else.

Capt. Creple, Sgt. Batista and Sgt. McGrove are our principal instructors. They are all paratroopers. I have never heard so many creative ways to swear. Despite my long exposure to the military, cursing has never become part of my language. Creple describes his career: six Purple Hearts, two Silver Stars, five Bronze Stars for valor, and innumerable other awards. He tells stories of taking the hill that is now Firebase Bastogne and many other 101st Vietnam War stories. When a private falls asleep, Creple puts him in a push-up position over a pool of slimy water.

Thirty minutes later the private collapses into the pool. Creple tells him to jog for one hour with gear at high port.

Creple turns over the rostrum for first-day orientation to Batista. The enlisted men like the sergeant more than Creple. Batista combines madness and sex. We are sitting in the sun on bleachers at the 101st Replacement Battalion and his opening line is: "You men are now Airborne—the 101st. Yea, though you walk through the valley of the shadow of death, you will fear no evil because you are the meanest motherfucker in that valley. Let me tell you about the Tet Offensive a few months ago; it was such a rough show even the lieutenants had to fight. (All the enlisted men laugh.) If I see a chicken shit he won't be coming back from my patrol, since I shoot a fuck-off. If you don't believe me, visit the 2/502 at Camp Eagle and ask about Batista of 2nd Platoon, A Company. If they don't remember Batista, ask them if they remember Batman. I had been in Nam 30 months and had $8,000 in the bank. When I got back to the world for leave I went to a car dealer—"Give me a car, a new red one." The car dealer calls me "Sir." That's the way it is for the 101st—nothing but the best."

Batista's next subject is R&R. "R&R is what they call rape and rampage. You stay here six months, and you have a CIB (combat infantry badge), pretty ribbons and money. Go anywhere you want—Hawaii, Bangkok, Hong Kong. I like Sydney, Australia— that's where the pussy is. You go to your bank man and get $2,000—you say, "Give me all of it." Go to the best hotel. Pay cash. Get a car and driver. Go to dinner, order a steak, lobster and a bottle of scotch. Call for a girl. You get a different one every night and they all got big tits."

Batista is followed by Sgt. McGrove, and our first-day orientation is almost over. McGrove is well over 6 feet tall, about 230 pounds, and very black. To get everyone's attention, McGrove gives a private a live fragmentation grenade and pulls the pin. The private has to hold it to keep it from going off, and he sweats profusely. McGrove continues, "Go to Bangkok. Cost me $135 for six days—$30 for a car and driver; $35 for a woman, a classy one with her hair piled on top. Six days of good pussy. The girls have cards. The government inspects them—no clap. They even buy their own drinks. Don't sweet-talk Saigon dollies.

You think you got a line. You don't. I been here three years—never got it free. Cash on the barrelhead—they want cash. Put two rubbers on your dick when you fuck one of them—powerful clap. Take a shower when you get back to the base. Don't stay overnight for another two bucks. I knew a sergeant who did that. Next day they found him with his head chopped off."

Platoon leaders get two principal lessons from the speakers. First, don't assault fortified positions with M-16s. Use air strikes and artillery. Second, tired is careless. Careless is dead. Officers are left alone in the evening. The men do physical training.

Tired is careless—careless is dead. This is not the first time I have heard this lesson.

After a week at the replacement battalion, I am ready for war. The night before I leave, I get myself to Saigon, 20 miles southwest of Long Binh. I spend the evening at a hotel with a panoramic view of the city. I eat a steak, drink bourbon, and watch a firefight somewhere in the city—the tracer rounds look like tiny shooting stars.

The next morning I pick up my equipment. We are pack mules in the world's largest sauna humping a compass, maps, a claymore, 20 M-16 magazines, a beer can opener, five two-liter water canteens, a poncho, a poncho liner, a rappelling D ring, dog tags, toothpaste, a razor, a sewing kit, a P38 can opener, C4 heat tabs, a wristwatch, mosquito repellent, five days of C rations and long-range patrol rations (LRPs), jungle boots, socks, fatigues, four grenades, toilet paper, an entrenching tool, a fingernail clipper, two smoke grenades, a knife and a helmet. My most important possession is a photo album with the pictures of my life with Marsi and our dreams—especially a picture of a mansion on the eastern shore of Maryland that belonged to her family. The mansion had a 280-degree view of the Chesapeake Bay. It is filled with antiques and art; we dream of owning it. It represents a refined world of beauty that is my life's mission to create. My foremost goal in life is to have an antique-and-art-filled place by the ocean, where I can sit on a shaded porch and listen to the ocean's serenade. I have a picture of a quail plantation with hanging Spanish moss where I shot a quail and looked into Marsi's eyes waiting for approval. The plantation is owned by Jason Meyer. He is the husband of Marsi's godmother. I have a picture of Marsi in a miniskirt, a picture of her lounging in bed—her nakedness covered by sheets; pictures of my parents; a picture of her family; and a picture of her throwing me a kiss. I will eventually burn the album because if I die, I do not want it falling into enemy hands. I believe my death is certain.

The following morning, packing 120 pounds of gear and clutching a handbag with my teeth, I arrive at Phu Bai near the Demilitarized Zone—the border with North Vietnam. The U.S. has divided South Vietnam into four corps, I, II, III and IV. Phu Bai is in I Corps, pronounced eye corps. I'm on my way to the 1st Battalion, 327th Infantry Regiment, at nearby Camp Eagle.

I remember the gladiator's toast: "Morituri te salutamas"— "We who are about to die salute you."

7

In The Valley of The Shadow of Death

The sarissa's** song is a sad song.
He pipes it soft and low.
I would ply a gentler trade, says he,
But war is all I know.

— Steven Pressfield

**Sarissas were 18-foot fighting spears used by Alexander's pikemen. When his
army camped the spears were arranged in long rows facing the wind. When the
wind blew the sarissas sang.

6 Aug 1968
I Corps
A Shau Valley
1000 hours

O ur chopper lifts off from Camp Eagle and I have been in Vietnam for 10 days. Our route takes us past Firebase Bastogne and Firebase Veghel, named after battles the 101st fought in World War II. The helicopter engine noise makes it next to impossible to think. Looking below, I see hilltops devoid of vegetation covered with bunkers and barbed wire.

The A Shau Valley is the North Vietnamese infiltration route into South Vietnam. The 1st Cavalry Division lost scores of helicopters when it attempted an airborne assault into the valley.

The valley borders Cambodia and Laos, and connects Hanoi to its army in the south. The A Shau had been the center of the logging industry during the French occupation of Vietnam. The center of the valley is crisscrossed by streams. Fields of elephant grass wave in the wind. The valley is ringed by mountains, covered with forests. In times of peace, herds of Indian elephants roam the valley; tigers hunt here too. We hear them roar in the night. Orangutans move silently in the trees above. If it were not the central infiltration route of the NVC, the A Shau would be a magnet for tourists because of its garden-like beauty. The days are hot and humid. The nights are cold as monsoon season approaches. On some mornings, you see your breath.

After what seems like an interminable flight, my helicopter finally lands. Dust catches in my nostrils, and I'm assaulted by a smell I'll never forget as long as I live: rotting vegetation and jungle flowers.

I take my first steps in what will be a six-month-long walk through hell. I walk up the path from the landing zone (LZ). The slick brown earth has been walked over long before this place was an LZ. We look out on a valley that stretches before us. The shadows cast by the wreckage of the 1st Cav's assault litter the valley. Crashed helicopters, the tails and the blades scattered at odd angles. An old U.S. Special Forces and Montagnard camp— what remains of it—stands in the far distance. At last, I am here in the place of dreams—in the valley of the shadow of death.

At our chopper, men are working quickly to unload the supplies: rations, mail and ammunition. They must get the bird airborne as soon as possible because a sitting chopper is a target for rocket-propelled grenades (RPGs). I move away from the LZ at a run. I am a replacement for the third platoon leader of Delta Company, 1/327th Infantry. The last officer was wounded one month ago and in the meantime Sgt. Dillon, a platoon sergeant new to combat, has led the platoon. The path I follow is narrow, like a dragon's spine. The dragon sleeps but is ready to awake, so I tread softly. Fifty feet in front of me the trail twists and turns. My rucksack weighs more than I do. It cuts deep creases in my shoulders. In future years my back will complain of the abuse it received on those ridgelines and I will be partially crippled. Today I walk with severe back pain, a reminder of the price a warrior pays.

On the way to the company CP, I turn a corner and in front of me is a North Vietnamese soldier. There are flies around his head and he has a bullet hole in his forehead. Pictures of his wife and children lie at his feet, taken from his wallet. He is scalped and rivulets of blood have dried on his face. An ace of spades is lodged in his mouth. When the 101st kills, some of our soldiers leave our calling card, the ace of spades, in the corpse's mouth. Mutilation of the dead is sport for both sides of this war. The NVA believe a man is damned to hell if his corpse is mutilated. The 101st never leaves a body of one of our own behind. Occasionally, we lose a body for a while. When we find it, it is always booby-trapped with a grenade underneath. The goal is to regain the body without getting blown up.

The 1st Brigade of the 101st is called the Hatchet Brigade, and our enemies know if they face us they could face mutilation, which will deny them access to heaven. To scalp someone, use a hatchet designed for the purpose. You use the hatchet blade to cut a horizontal gash across the hairline, and a knife-like pick to cut two parallel strips in the front and the rear of the scalp. You grab a forelock of hair, and with a vigorous jerk you have yourself a scalp. No scalpings occur in D Company for the rest of my tour. When discipline is slack, bad things can happen. I never scalp anyone but I know it occurred. I remember Epictetus and get a firm grip upon my emotions.

In war, fear is my companion and death is beside me. Some of my men mix bits of their enemies' ears in their rations—or so they claim. Perhaps this is only a tall tale meant to scare lieutenants, but I believe them since I have seen them toss scraps of raw meat into their LRPs. The memories created by these transgressions never disappear. The price of bravado is high. This practice will stop when we get a new commanding officer.

Oh yes, someday I will leave Vietnam thinking I am normal, but it will be an illusion. The fear and the violence will remain hidden inside me only to erupt when a memory is triggered. For the rest of my life I will react to some family and business crises as if I were on the floor of the A Shau Valley. Small problems for me will become life-and-death situations. The good news is that my Army training will help me overcome most challenges in my life. The bad news is that I never can get relief from the anxiety of the battlefield. That will damage those whom I love.

In the valley our rules of engagement are simple: Kill or be killed.

I walk the highway to heaven or to hell; it is only a step to the right or the left. In the days ahead we patrol along narrow ridgelines amid mahogany forests. The military term for this vegetation is triple canopy. It has a layer of mahogany trees that grow 150 feet, a second layer of trees that grow to 60 feet, and a layer of scrub trees that grow in dense shade up to 30 feet. The trails, one to two thousand feet above sea level, that we follow are 36 inches wide and if you were to ski off the side of the trail, the slopes would be what skiers call black diamond runs. We march in a single file. My normal order of march is point man first, slack man (M-60 machine gun), me, my radio telephone operator (RTO), the ammo bearer for the machine gun, and then the rest of the platoon. Most other lieutenants chose to stay farther back, but the only way to inspire men is to lead from the front and share the risk of death.

The five men at the front of the line are like Wyatt Earp and his brothers walking into the O.K. Corral—single file. Like the Earps, as we march we know that some of us will soon be dead. Wyatt, the platoon leader, should always be third. The point man and machine gun go left and right when action occurs. The platoon leader faces the enemy. The point man immediately fires at the enemy to keep him from firing at you. The platoon leader directs the traffic by maneuvering his squads. The machine gun, like Doc Holliday with a sawed-off shotgun, pins the enemy down with 750 rounds a minute.

Action occurs often because the North Vietnamese send out continuous patrols of 20 men to keep the highway to South Vietnam open. When an NVA patrol meets our company on the aerial highways above the jungle, the quick live; the slow die. If you do not have a quick draw you are dead. Of the 28 confrontations on the trail in the three weeks before I arrive, we have won 25. It is great for the ego, and like all deceptions of success it breeds overconfidence. I am excited, not scared, for when I hear the stories of all this it is just like a Hemingway novel. I have not yet seen the true face of war. It is still my first week in the field.

We are not seen by the press and we live in the isolation of the jungle as young gods of war. There is no political correctness in our war. It is unlike the war fought along Highway 1 and in the Mekong Delta.

About 100 feet from the corpse is the company's perimeter. Two-man defensive positions are set up about 20 feet apart. Claymore mines are placed in front of each position so that if we are attacked we can send a meteor shower of steel balls into the enemies' faces. Most of the men eat before sunset and the meal is cold C rations. Mostly I eat the fruit and crackers and throw away the rest. A few brave souls will try the spaghetti C rations, but we suspect they are all Korean War vintage. A bottle of Tabasco sauce sells for $75 in the field and makes the C rations palatable. Seventy-five percent of the food sent out to us is thrown away except for the LRPs. LRPs are the steak dinner of the 101st. I use a heat tab to boil water. I pour boiling water into a plastic sack and, behold, I have chicken con carne. LRPs, fruit and crackers become the staple diet– forget the rest.

I meet Capt. Flattop, our company commander, for the first time at the command post (CP). His RTO is on the horn with battalion. The nightly family chat with the battalion commander is about to begin. Flattop is in his mid-30s, old for a captain. He is an Officer Candidate School graduate. He asks me to pick a radio call sign. I choose Sartoris, but no one around me catches the allusion to Faulkner's "Absalom, Absalom!" They think it is a strange choice. They do not know Sartoris is the call sign of a warrior.

You can tell Flattop is much admired by the men. This is not always a good thing. I will later hear stories about how Flattop will not let the battalion commander push our company around, seeking his men's approval, and some are on a first-name basis with him. In war you have to make decisions that kill your men. Personally, I think it is best to keep some distance by addressing them with their rank: "Sgt. Sizemore, can you set up a listening post." Flattop may be captain but he runs a loose ship.

He moves at his own pace, even when the battalion orders him to make haste. He should have made a career running his own gas station because he is not fit to lead warriors. The men are cocky. The company has won many gunfights at the O.K. Corral. New officers are a worry to everyone: Are they strong enough to lead a platoon? Stupidity or arrogance in an officer can mean unnecessary death. School is out. At night, I do not put up ponchos to keep off the rain. Poncho tents obstruct night vision and setting one up makes too much noise. If it rains, I throw my poncho around my shoulders. There is no smoking or talking.

Nasty Naylor, a corporal and my RTO, has been the unofficial platoon leader. He's a drowned rat of a man, maybe 5 feet 8 inches tall, 120 pounds. His pack and radio weigh 160 pounds. He looks 100 years old and stands like Gollum in "The Lord of the Rings." His face is defiant of authority. I think little men make the best warriors. They don't come tougher than Nasty. I am convinced that his Army career started as a way to keep him out of jail. Appearances deceive. He has one of the best sarcastic senses of humor that I will ever encounter. His career before the Army could have been hubcap stealing, but when someone is wounded he is Mother Teresa. If I had to fight for my life, I would rather have three Nastys beside me than 100 football players. He helped me become a platoon leader as much as my three captains, but best of all he knew how to leave and let me lead by myself.

He's good at locating the machine guns for me and tells me why they have the right fields of fire. To illustrate his importance, he tells me how 3rd Platoon discovered 68 two-and-a-half-ton trucks on a camouflaged jungle road. Nasty helped blow up the trucks, seriously damaging the NVA's attempts to resupply its units in the south. In a combat unit, organizational charts count for little.

Our platoon is a few feet from an enemy bunker that was occupied the night before. Overhead fly B-52 bombers. Their engines seem a long way off. There is a slow scream as bombs drop. They explode and the ground beneath me shakes. To untrained ears the air strike seems close. Later that night I hear the plunk of mortar tubes. Everyone in the company scatters from their sleeping positions to the steep sides of the mountain, placing their faces in the wet earth. False alarm: I return to my sleeping position. An hour later, the NVA starts to mortar the 1st Army of the Republic of Vietnam (ARVN) troops in the valley below; they are supporting the 101st in this operation. Insects buzz. The wind rustles the leaves of the jungle. I am cold and wet. Eventually I sleep—sort of.

At first light, everyone is awake. The trip flares and claymore mines are packed up. The air is crisp, like a Maine morning, and I shake myself to get the blood flowing. Our mountaintop is one of a chain of islands in a sea of dense fog that fills the A Shau Valley. I lift my rucksack. This 120-pound bag on an aluminum frame is my mobile home. Some of our soldiers will die fighting behind the rucksacks, using them as shields. But rucksacks cannot stop bullets.

I shiver—is it the cold or am I afraid?

7 Aug 1968
I Corps
A Shau Valley
0900 hours

Morning is the time to move, find an enemy position and attack it. Flattop signals for 1st Platoon to be first in line and take the point. First Platoon is led by Sgt. Herman, who is near the end of his third tour. The skill of the man on point is critical. He can prevent an ambush and save lives. A new bunker is spotted. We check it out. There are fresh human feces beneath the brush. Someone had our position under observation last night. That is normal on a resupply day since we have to make so much noise cutting an LZ with chain saws. The NVA watch us closely, hoping to plan an ambush when the company moves out.

It seems to come out of nowhere—an M-16 opens up on rock and roll, full automatic fire. Two others join it. I hit the ground as two hand grenades detonate nearby. The fire is from behind me, somewhere in the middle of the column. Everyone takes cover. Machine guns maneuver to cover the paths. I yell for my men to hold their fire since there is no return fire. I see nothing except vegetation. One of the men saw movement in a tree. This is real trouble because an enemy advance through the middle of the line could cut our company in two. Leapfrogging teams in front of

me, I move forward to check out the area. Nasty, my RTO, keeps
the captain, in the middle of our column, abreast of everything
by radio. A bloody mess is on the ground in front of us. It is a
dead orangutan. I feel like an idiot when I call the captain to
tell him of our mistake. His only comment: "At least you hit the
monkey." But for now our position is compromised and the NVA
again know where we are. We walk down the hill to the plain,
having learned that a day in the jungle passes slowly. My jungle
fatigues are soaking by the time the sun burns off the mist.

Vietnam is different from many wars. Relationships are
fleeting. Men are wounded and medevaced, never to return.
Men die. Men go on R&R and are reassigned. Men leave
Vietnam when their tours are up. Replacements come and go.
Men get sick and disappear in hospitals. Years later, I will visit
the new Holocaust Memorial behind the Albion Hotel in Berlin.
You enter a field of granite slabs. They are different in size and
shape. It has rained and the water reflects on their polished
granite surfaces. You enter the field with 50 other people and
wander separately through the field of slabs. You look left and
right to get glimpses of people but ultimately they all disappear.
The memorial is meant to simulate a concentration camp where
you make acquaintances that you will know only for the briefest
of time, for all of your lives will end in the gas chamber. That is
what my relationships were like in Vietnam. On my second day
in the A Shau, I had barely mastered the names of my platoon.
The rest of the men in the company are strangers.

About 1730 we break out into the elephant grass of the valley.
It is about 10 feet high and razor sharp. We stumble around
for an hour before linking up with Charlie Company at the
abandoned Special Forces base camp at Ta Bat. It grows dark.
Rain has started. My men fix their night positions and clean
weapons. I establish the order for sentry duty and try to force
down a can of C rations. The mist and night make it impossible
to see. I wrap a poncho liner around my shoulders and nod off
in a fitful sleep.

I hope that it will be dry by day when we are marching. I
want rain at night so I can catch rainwater in my poncho. Potable
water is scarce. Streams in the valley are covered with a slime
that is the same color as the fer-de-lance, a deadly lime-green

snake with an arrowhead-shaped head. I keep a sharp lookout. They say the fer-de-lance is a three-step snake: After it bites you, you walk three steps then die.

In August, the northern tip of South Vietnam is ending its dry season. Our operation Somerset Plain is the last before the monsoons arrive. If this is what war is like, I am disappointed. Each day teaches me a new lesson about the terrain. One afternoon I take a break by what I learn is an ant bush. Fire ants crawl over my equipment and from there to my back. I have never disrobed so quickly. I use a precious canteen of rainwater to wash off the ants and recover my clothing.

The next day I notice a small sore on my hand. This is my first exposure to jungle rot. It's a lot like leprosy. It eats away the flesh leaving throbbing, sensitive wounds. I learn to live with it, but each time I bump into a tree or am hit by a tree limb, I feel pain.

Jungle rot leaves scars that last 10 years on the flesh but longer in the soul.

8

After the Guns

"A warrior's job is to face adversity and erase it."

—Victoria Duval, Haitian-American tennis player

8 Aug 1968
I Corps
A Shau Valley
1800 hours

It is almost dusk as I stare across the A Shau Valley, silent now after the NVA artillery barrage that shattered my platoon and me. Something snaps within me and I focus on the details of war that will haunt the rest of my life. Is the defensive perimeter set up correctly? Are claymores out? Has ammunition been passed out? Our future is uncertain; nothing but the present matters. The next few days will be among the most important of my life. Crossing the A Shau Valley at night after death in the afternoon is hell. The night is shades of gray and black. Clouds obscure the moon but occasionally moonlight illuminates the landscape through an opening. Everything I see has a sinister appearance. Is it a bush or a bunker? A night move is our only alternative since we have proven that trying to cross the fields during the day is suicide. I hear that the company RTO has picked up a Russian radio transmission. It must be the Russian advisers who are across the border in Laos. We know the NVA does not expect we will move at night across a minefield. At least the new company commander allows what is left of my platoon to move in the middle of the column. Sweat is washing away the blood of the afternoon. My rucksack bites into my shoulders and fatigue gets the best of fear. We move slowly through the old Montagnard minefield around the ruined Special Forces base camp. Sgt. Herman of 2nd Platoon is on point.

Herman is a soldier's soldier. He is just under 6 feet tall with the body of an athlete. He is all business with no time for useless conversation. His dark hair and deeply tanned face make him look as if he put on camouflage for a night patrol.

Every few feet we stop and wait so Herman can probe the ground with a bayonet. My bones complain that they are being pulled from their joints. We move again. Around 0200 we hear running water on our right. The company must cross a small river. The current is slow and it is difficult to see the other side. A message is sent down the column with each soldier whispering to the man behind him. The silence is deafening. It seems an enemy boat is moored in the river.

Herman will deal with this problem. He is a survivor. Officers come and go for 2nd Platoon; only Herman remains. The officer of the week is killed or wounded; Herman resumes command of 2nd Platoon. He is a great noncommissioned officer. An officer may give the orders, but it is up to the NCO to do the dirty work and carry them out. Now Herman must swim to the boat and toss grenades into it. You hope the cat has one more life left. A quiet ripple of laughter passes back through the column of soldiers. Herman's camouflaged boat seems to be a pile of rocks with some shrubs eking out a meager existence on top of them.

We ford the river. The water is up to my chest and the rocks on the riverbed are slimy. My old lesson about kit comes back to me. If I slip now, will I be able to release my rucksack? How can I survive without it? The company must move quickly. If the sun rises while we are still on the valley floor, the NVA gunners will be even deadlier at closer range. The last few feet to the riverbank are soft mud. My boots sink 18 inches into it. Each step is a tug of war. I am up to my neck in water now. It is dark as the clouds block out the moon. The wind rustles in the elephant grass, which towers over me. I cannot see the man who has climbed up the bank in front of me. He has disappeared into the heavy grass.

It takes all my strength to climb the slippery bank. I feel my leg; a slimy leech falls off. I see streams of blood running down my legs, so I drop my pants and squirt myself with mosquito repellent because it kills leeches as well as repelling mosquitoes. They drop off, writhing in what seems like pain. It is almost as if I am squirting acid on them, and I enjoy their agony. They have a clammy, headless ugliness. They are not harmless—leech bites lead to jungle rot.

Hours pass as we continue to march. We are a part of a slow-motion dance of death. I just follow the man in front of me. Although light means death, I am unaware of the sun slowly rising.

9

Reconnaissance of Hamburger Hill

"Courage, my comrades, war is near!"
I hear afar its hateful drums;
Its horrid din assails my ear:
I hope I die before it comes. ...
Yet as into the town I go,
And listen to the rabble cheer,
I think with heart of weary woe:
War is not coming—WAR IS HERE.

— Robert William Service

9 Aug 1968
I Corps
A Shau Valley
0700 hours

With no time to spare, the sky turns from black to blue and our company arrives at its destination—the base of Dong So, an 1,100-foot hill connected by a horseshoe ridgeline to another hill, Dong Ap Bia. Overnight, we have crossed the valley floor and now we will climb the hill to look for the NVA artillery. When the division re-enters the valley next spring, Dong Ap Bia will become known as Hamburger Hill. Our fight on Dong So will become essentially reconnaissance in force for the much larger battle of Hamburger Hill. The trees overhead have been defoliated by Agent Orange. The earth beneath me is charred by fire. Dead leaves caught by the wind skitter across the ground.

Even in this wasteland, the smell of death is omnipresent. Capt. Career signals a halt. We establish a hasty perimeter and I lean back against a fallen tree, falling asleep quickly. I awake a half hour later to find the sun beating on my face. We may have had two hours sleep at most in the last two days. I do not remember the last time I ate something. An insect buzzes in my face. Whenever anyone moves, a cloud of dust is kicked into the air. It is difficult to breathe. Ever so slowly, D Company starts ascending the ridgeline. My platoon is the last in line.

An explosion amid the point platoon breaks the silence. Two more explosions follow. Have the NVA forward observers found us? Are they calling in artillery fire from Laos, from guns that two weeks ago the New York Times claimed did not exist? Someone swears: "It is a fucking accident." Second Platoon is commanded by Sgt. Curly, since they lost their officer a month ago. I have already encountered Curly. He seems obsessed with trying to stay away from the point he now occupies, while somehow maintaining his record of outstanding efficiency reports. I hear from my men that he delayed his field assignment for months by feigning ailments. Making this more pitiful—he is both Airborne and Ranger qualified. Those schools were supposed to wash out trash like him.

He is close to 6 feet tall, reasonably fit, with short, curly, reddish-brown hair. His shoulders are stooped and he has big lumpy muscles like the trolls in "The Lord of the Rings." Both his jaw and his nose protrude. His face is meant for yelling sadistic demands at new recruits. His orders are meant to humiliate them rather than to build them into soldiers. When Curly is around superior officers he is an unctuous model of efficiency and proper military comportment.

Word is passed down the line—one man is dead. Curly had a man carrying a grenade launcher with a high explosive round walking point, which is unusual. I always put a rifleman on point followed by a machine gun because in an ambush we need a high volume of fire at close range, not a big bang 50 meters away. The point man of 1st Platoon thought he saw movement and asked Curly if he could fire. The fool said yes, and the range was too close so the point man caught a sliver of shrapnel in the chest, a harmless wound—but he died of shock a minute later. In war, imagination kills some people as effectively as a bullet. As his limp body is carried back down the ridge, his head rolls lifelessly to the side. He is a black man and his tongue is now white rather than red, giving his face a macabre appearance.

Curly is trying to talk the captain into letting him go with the medevac. He seems to have been nicked by a piece of shrapnel. This wound will earn him a Purple Heart, a good efficiency report, all that he seeks in his tour of duty. Career says yes. He walks among his platoon trying to get sympathy. I am disgusted by cowardice. A young buck sergeant, Sizemore, now commands 1ˢᵗ Platoon, and it is better off for the change.

My platoon sergeant, Frank Dillon, is a black man from New Orleans. I could not serve with a better man. The Army is his life. When he arrived he was 30 pounds over prime weight. He has lost the weight and is in top shape. He has a round face that is brightened by his smile. He works hard to see that his platoon is well treated—food, proper equipment, and when needed, medical care. He isn't disrespectful to officers but he does stand his ground. Yes, he is afraid, but he hides his fear and is learning to survive in this new country. He is a soldier. It must pain him to see another NCO disgraced like this. An officer who does not realize that NCOs determine his fate is a fool. NCOs lead face to face. Officers lead but must maintain distance.

Career calls his platoon leaders over to his position. He is a squat, pudgy man with a receding hairline. He wears a jungle sweater of World War II issue. His white flesh peeps through the sweater's moth holes. He has a two-week beard and he always smokes a pipe carved in the shape of a human skull. A captain with a pipe like that thinks he is Douglas MacArthur. Career commands from the last platoon in our order of march. When we assault Dong So, his command post is at the very rear of the company. It gives him the chance to deploy the maneuver elements, which is what the other two platoons are called. Career tells his platoon leaders that in college he had been an ROTC general and had a staff that catered to his every need. In his mind he is just marking time until he will be a general again. He loves the Army and is convinced he will be the architect of great military victories.

10-13 Aug 1968
I Corps
A Shau Valley

"Let me die rather than prove unworthy of their name."

—Lt. George Croghan, 1813, Lake Erie Campaign

The next days are long. The sun is shining, and the slope we are climbing is devoid of life. If you look right or left the jungle looks like a beautiful, peaceful garden. Only our barren ridgeline shows the potential destructive violence hidden beneath the trees. We hear the distant pop of enemy artillery, but the rounds pass over our ridgeline. We dig foxholes in the rock-hard soil. It takes three sun-scorched hours.

The next day, from a clearing, we see the entire A Shau Valley. One of my squad leaders spots several camouflaged trucks below. Spotting them is like finding the key parts of a jigsaw puzzle. I count six trucks and start to call in an air strike on top of them, but my command is interrupted. Tiger Force has contact and paratroopers are in danger. Tiger Force is the battalion's independent reconnaissance platoon commanded by Lt. Fredrick Raymond, the Tiger.

Raymond is a pro. When sitting he looks like a good old boy, but he can move like a cheetah. His Vietnamese camouflage fatigues, black and green, make him look as if he should star in a John Wayne movie. In certain lights, his eyes look reptilian and you know he is a killer. His men would follow him into hell. In later life, he will be a National Guard general. The Tigers have encountered a platoon-size NVA force. Raymond pops smoke to mark his position as he calls in an air strike and a gunship on the NVA. In moments, a jet streaks over and drops a load of bombs. I see NVA soldiers dying far below me. I know how they feel.

Seeing the NVA trucks move in broad daylight across the A Shau, along with remembering Naylor's story of finding 68 trucks in a camouflaged highway, makes it clear to me why we are here. The A Shau is the supply route the NVA uses to support its troops in South Vietnam.

Before the Tet offensive six months earlier, the NVA moved large numbers of men and materiel within easy striking distance of the large population centers near the coast or in the central highlands of South Vietnam. They caught us by surprise, since we had incorrect intelligence about their strength and armament in the South. For the 101st it was a personal and costly lesson. The unit lost many paratroopers during Tet, on the rooftop of the American Embassy, in the highlands around Pleiku, and in the streets of Hue.

That is the reason we are wandering over this beautiful, forgotten A Shau Valley. The 101st cannot again allow the North Vietnamese Army a staging ground close to our bases. We remember friends lost, the paratroopers, and have a reason to be here. We find ourselves in a valley out of our artillery range. We must share our air support with the Marines at Khe San. The net result is that whoever is losing the most men gets air support. Marines are known for going "high diddle diddle, right up the middle" and seem to take pride in taking casualties. They get most of the air support. Air support consists of Air Force, Navy and Marine Corps fighters that drop bombs and napalm, and Army Cobra gunships armed with rockets and machine guns. It is great when you have it.

In a valley ringed with .50-caliber Chinese machine guns, air support is hazardous at best. We get air support half of the time we ask for it. The NVA have Russian artillery guided by Russian and Chinese advisers located a mile away across the Laotian border. They fire at will from the safety of Laos. From my experience yesterday, they have fire superiority. I know from intelligence briefings that our two battalions, broken down into companies and scattered across the valley, are outnumbered by division-strength NVA forces only two miles away in Laos.

On our current mission, my company is like a minnow on a fishhook, being dangled in front of a vicious pike. We tempt the pike to commit to a fight at the time and place of the 101st's choosing. It is a good strategy to catch a pike. Minnows are expendable.

This is not what Vietnam is supposed to be. I read the accounts of the war in the American press, where our enemy is depicted as the Viet Cong, poorly armed freedom fighters, defending their homes from French dictators and baby-burning Americans. We never see the Viet Cong; instead we fight against a well-trained and well-equipped North Vietnamese Army. Vietnam is three countries: Tonkin, Annam and Cochin, joined by the Chinese long before the time of the Manchu emperors. There are three distinct cultures, languages and worldviews. The North does not have the racial diversity of the South. The North is trying to conquer the entire country and impose its form of government.

I look toward Laos from my perch on the Dong So and see a country that is a safe harbor one mile away. There should be no place to hide. Laos should not be a safe haven where the North Vietnamese can train, resupply and launch combat operations. It violates all the rules of war formulated by Von Clausewitz.

It is a sunny day. No clouds are in the sky. I imagine the NVA units in Laos sipping tea, fishing, enjoying their French cuisine and laughing at us as we stumble around, covered in leeches, in the A Shau Valley. The U.S. troops are bleeding. We are winning battle after battle, but every night our deaths are shown on TV sets across the United States.

The war is fought on TV and in the newspapers. I remember the famous North Vietnamese leader Trung Kien's words: "They do not have the will to fight a war of attrition." Vietnam is the guerrilla war of the future, but someday in the future we will have a total war in which nuclear weapons will be used and we will have to destroy our enemy or be destroyed ourselves. Such a war will probably not be started by the major powers but by the impoverished rogue states that want what the major powers have. A country that is used to fighting in the news media and is governed by political correctness will have a hard time adapting to a total war. A country that despises its warriors will soon have no warriors. What will happen if the warriors refuse to serve when their civilian masters send them to die—but not to win—a war for the sake of political expediency?

The next morning we leave the barren slope. In addition to using Agent Orange, the Air Force had dropped 500-pound bombs and napalm, burning all that remained. At least under the jungle canopy again we are away from the merciless sun and throat-parching dust. However, we are short of water, having thrown away most of our water and food before we crossed the valley at night. We are lucky, for we have been trained to go without food for days.

The day passes uneventfully, as our trail twists and turns following the edge of the ridgeline. Sometimes the ridgeline is 50 feet across, other times it is five feet. The slope falls off at a 70-degree angle. Rock formations and twisted masses of vegetation are below us. Occasionally through the trees we catch a glimpse of the summit ahead of us. It is foreboding, surrounded by high trees. The sky is clear, bright blue. We usually hear constant noise in the jungle—birds, small creatures scurrying in the bush, or insects buzzing.

Today, the jungle is silent.

14 Aug 1968
I Corps
A Shau Valley
1400 hours

> Sing, Goddess, Achilles' rage,
> Black and murderous, that cost the Greeks
> Incalculable pain, pitched countless souls
> Of heroes into Hades' dark,
> And left their bodies to rot as feasts
> For dogs and birds.
>
> — Homer, "The Iliad"

When we arrive at the base of the summit, it is 3rd Platoon's turn to lead. We must cross what seems like a small dip in the ridgeline before we can reach the summit of the Dong So. Soon we will find out if the NVA artillery is located here.

Dong So's summit stands before me, a great stone staircase of upright boulders, 30 feet high, with a path twisting through the boulders. The rest of the company is in a defensive perimeter 200 meters behind us. Career says he will call in an air strike to support our platoon if it is needed but we are not high on the priority list for air strikes. We are told the machine guns will support us, but they do not have clear fields of fire. On our right flank is a steep incline covered with trees and underbrush. The top of the Dong So seems to be a rock fortress.

I keep the 2nd Squad with me at the base of the great stones and call Sgt. Dillon to maneuver the 1st and 3rd squads in leapfrog motion. I remember how Hannibal fooled the Roman commanders Paulus and Varro at the Battle of Cannae. Hannibal feigned retreat, led the Roman army into a confined area and attacked from all sides. This staircase is a similar trap. I wish my squads had 11 instead of seven men. Even with reinforcements, my platoon has only 20 men.

Pfc. Ebert caught my attention during the artillery barrage, when the NVA caught us in the open in the valley plain. He stayed with me to load the wounded onto the medevac choppers. He stood beside me as the shrapnel cut down others who were not as fortunate. His eyes during the barrage fascinated me. We were both afraid, but he made fear work for him. Others are not like that. I see it in their eyes.

I move my machine gun back 50 feet to provide fire support for the platoon and tell Sgt. Stephenson and 2nd Squad to take positions in three abandoned foxholes. I signal Ebert to move forward with me through the staircase. Ebert is 15 feet ahead of me. Peering around a corner, he sees something that upsets him. I peer around that corner. Holy shit! We have walked up to a fortified enemy defense perimeter. It is an NVA trap. They want us to advance in force. They then will surround us and cut us off from the rest of the company. They are protected by fortified bunkers and mortar positions. Two squads of NVA are setting up mortars. The Chinese have sent the NVA small 60 mm mortars that the Chinese captured from an American unit during the Korean War. They are great jungle mortars that can be handheld if necessary. You can identify them instantly by the sound they make when fired. I pray the NVA do not have 82 mm mortars somewhere in the bunker complex. Ebert and I open fire on the mortar crews. We count four men down. Ebert throws a grenade. Ebert covers for me as I talk to Dillon. On our right, the bunker complex opens up on Dillon's squads. Two steep rock slopes provide cover for my men. But we are 20 against what may be an entrenched NVA platoon of 40 to 50 men reinforced with heavy weapons. Career is too far removed to provide effective support—what a surprise. We see North Vietnamese infantry leapfrogging down the slope toward us.

How do we find our way back down that twisting stairway? It will soon be hell's alley. A reinforced platoon is firing at us from a rock fortress. AK-47 rounds are ricocheting everywhere. We are as likely to be killed by a ricochet as by a direct hit. An RPG explodes somewhere. The bends in the staircase are our salvation. I fire a magazine while Ebert withdraws 15 feet. He shoots over me as I withdraw in a crouching position. We take turns being first. Moving 50 feet takes us less than a minute, but it could have been a day.

I signal Ebert to take one of the platoon's two machine guns and make sure anyone who shows his face at the staircase door is dead. I guess the NVA are now moving through the staircase and on the rocks on the left and the right. The NVA will likely try to get machine guns on those rocks so they can open up on Dillon. I position myself in a spot away from the staircase entrance where I can see both parts of my platoon and prevent an NVA machine gun from getting on top of the staircase. One of Dillon's men is slightly wounded. Nasty, my RTO, joins me. I call the captain on the radio. Where is the air strike? Career says he needs someone on the ground to call it in. He is too far back to help. I have done this in exercises on the flat plains of Fort Benning, but this is different. We are hanging on the edge of an axe blade. The slope is so steep, the air strike must be precisely dropped. Because of the slope, a 30-foot error could put the bombs on my men.

Career tells Spc. 4 Lural Lee Blevins III to join us to call in the air strike. Blevins, from Philadelphia, was accused by police of stealing hubcaps. He calls everyone dude and gives them a Black Panther salute. It seems like an hour, but it is only minutes later that Blevins arrives. Blevins shocks my reality. He is a black, muscular, hard man with close-cropped hair. He calls me "Lieutenant Whitey." I am wary of him. It was just last year that Baltimore had race riots. I missed the point. Blevins is Herman's best friend, and half his friends are white. His Black Panther salute is just his way of saying I am your equal, and I will die to save you just as you will die to save me. Remarkably, Blevins has only two days left on a year-long tour. He should be in the rear packing his duffle bag. But he's here, fighting beside us. Even though Blevins taught me not to make premature judgments, I have made the same mistake 100 times since.

He gives me a Black Panther salute and I think, "What an asshole." I am the asshole, an asshole of the environment in which I was raised. Until I joined the Army, I had never been around black people. The only black person I knew was the maître d' at the Green Spring Club, Mr. Plumb. He fascinated me. He was so kind, and one of the few adults who could talk to children as if they were adults. Mr. Plumb was 70 years old and bald with a smile that could bring sunshine into a room. He was an old warrior and my friend, especially when he served me a rum southside when I was underage. I asked him why he did it, and he said if you are old enough to die for your country you are old enough to have a drink. When you are 20 years old, that is the definition of a friend. My one regret is that I never thanked him for his service. I bet he was the Nasty Naylor of his days.

Dillon signals me that 2nd Squad has only half its ammo left. Blevins and Nasty, who has joined him, move about 30 feet to the rear; a squadron of F-4s is on station overhead. Career called them a half hour earlier in case they should be needed. Blevins shouts into his radio, "Falcon 1, this is Panther, do you read me?"

"Panther, this is Falcon 1, it's a Roger."

Blevins is all business as he calls in the coordinates. He yells to Stephenson, "Hey man, how about a couple of Wilson Pickets," or white phosphorous rockets used to mark enemy positions. There is a scream of jet engines and machine cannons as the F-4s approach our position. All I can hear are explosions. Dillon's men are throwing grenades. The NVA are still maneuvering down the hill. A great explosion seems to suck air out of my lungs. Blevins called the strike too high. It goes over the ridgeline to explode on the downhill slope. Well, better over than on us—Blevins is good after all. "Falcon 2, this is Panther."

"Panther, this is Falcon 2, over."

Blevins calls the corrections to the pilot. The cannons of the F-4 open up again and this time it comes from behind us. Then I hear an awful sound: one, two and then three .50-caliber machine guns open up on the F-4 as it screams overhead. It is trailing smoke. The bombs remain on board. The pilot does not respond to Blevins' calls. There is a sickening shriek as the plane spirals to the valley floor. The plane crashes with a deafening explosion and a great cloud of smoke. The pilot does not eject.

"Falcon 3, this is Panther."

Blevins does not wait for a response but calls more coordinates over the radio. Two jets approach with their cannons firing, making it impossible for anyone in the bunkers to move. A third jet drops the bombs. There are secondary explosions; shrapnel passes overhead through the trees. I yell to Nasty to have Dillon haul ass off the mountainside. First Squad's machine gun opens up to provide cover for Nasty and Blevins' withdrawal. I move to the right, toward Dillon, to help with the wounded. Two grenades land in the middle of 3rd Squad. Cpl. Colledge, who has been behind a rock, runs out, and with the skill of a rugby player, kicks the grenade off the ridge. If he had acted a second later, 1st Squad would have been wiped out.

The F-4s dive overhead, dropping their bombs on the Dong So and shooting their rockets at the NVA bunkers. Blevins is in continuous contact with the pilots. I see the fighters overhead withdraw from their station. In the clouds above, a large airplane is flying slowly toward them with a long rubber hose dangling from its tail. On the end of the hose hangs something shaped like a funnel. The planes drink from this funnel like hummingbirds from flowers. This in-flight refueling means they will be back on station in 20 minutes, not the 90-minute round trip to be refueled at an air base or on an aircraft carrier. We would have been without air support during that time. This is the irony of ironies. My father's last company, Flight Refueling, pioneered the technology that has just saved our lives.

Blevins is back in action after the refueling and the F-4s start a strafing run. Blevins has courage. Courage is when you shit your pants and can still charge an enemy machine gun nest with grenades. For someone who is short, one day and wake-up, to join us on this hill is the definition of courage. He does it because he is the best man in the company to call in close air support.

I move further to the right. I am in an exposed position. There is a moment's silence and then I hear that awful sound again. It's not the pop of an artillery piece, it's the plunk of a mortar, and then my old ROTC commanding officer, Col. Hess, is there beside me yelling, "Hit the deck." And again I hear, "What are you waiting for, Lieutenant?" I collapse face first into a mound of rotting jungle vegetation. Explosions are all around me. There are 60 mm mortars, but I think there is an 82 mm explosion as well. Next I hear a funny sound, as if someone has thrown a water balloon into a bathtub. I look up. Twelve inches in front of me is a 60 mm mortar shell. Smoke comes from its tail. I hear a sound like someone spitting tobacco into an empty tin and then, pop—it is over. The round is a misfire. For the third time, I have escaped death. But at this rate I will need hundreds of lives to survive in Vietnam.

It was a misfire, but this is an established defensive position. It is pre-registered so the mortar crew can fire quickly at the positions that are the logical routes of advance. After pre-registered, the next command is fire for effect. I am a dead man in a killing zone. I hear the plunk of a half dozen mortars. I move to a nearby rock formation and take shelter between some rocks, but my left side is exposed. More 82 mm mortar shells explode. Another 60 mm shell falls near me. The round that failed to explode explodes with the new shell. I am covered with dirt. My side explodes in pain. Fireworks go off in my head, I cannot hear, and then darkness.

How long am I ineffective? My men move past me, a wounded man is carried by one of my troops. I look to my left, down at my side. Blood stains my uniform, my sleeve and my left leg. Thank God it was not an 82 mm mortar but a 60 mm. There's nothing left in my stomach to vomit so I dry heave. At least I have not shit myself. I open my first-aid pouch, remove a bandage and stop the worst bleeding. Tying the bandage on my right hand, I force myself toward Dillon. He has one wounded. The captain orders withdrawal.

I want the hill. It belongs to us, but we start to move away from the staircase. An NVA .30-caliber machine gun opens up and rock dust covers me. I am gray—only my blood adds color. Gunships scream overhead pounding the NVA bunkers. We later learn that the bunkers have been dug deep and have two levels. When the gunships and jets arrive, the NVA go to the bottom level. When the gunships and jets leave, the NVA re-emerge and resume their steady firing. What a price we paid for two feet of nothing.

Now I help withdraw the machine guns. Their barrels are searing hot. I help with the wounded and my blood mingles with the blood of my men. Colledge, helping to move back 1st

Squad's machine gun, is shot in the same foot he used to kick the grenade off the ridgeline. Eventually he is medevaced to Japan and we hear he loses the foot. Sgt. Skilaski helps to carry Colledge off the hill. I am the last man off the hill. I back off. The NVA are not following. It is 1800 and it will be dark soon. I am conscious of my wounds. Minutes ago, I felt nothing. Now there is a pounding in my ears and my left arm and leg throb with pain. I move with frantic energy making sure that what remains of my platoon is off the hill. One of the older squad leaders, a man who fought at Pleiku, a man who has seen a lot, says, "Good job." That makes me feel as if I accomplished something. I am no longer a cherry lieutenant.

Lural Blevins taught me a life lesson. Before, I looked at him and saw only a man with a chip on his shoulder and an attitude toward young white officers. Now I think I can see into his soul. The best way to see the soul is in actions. Men may cheat or be disloyal—or they may risk their life on a hillside to protect people they barely know. I hope to thank Blevins, but he is already back with Herman. Before he joined us on the hill, I had never spoken with him. He saved my life. But I never see him again.

I am in a daze now. I do not know where or who I am. I do know that my platoon, or more realistically my squad given our reduced size, needs to tie into the company defensive perimeter. A medic tells me to sit down. I tell him to fuck himself. I locate two machine guns to cover the trail down from the hill. Will the NVA attack tonight? Not likely, in my mind. If I were they, I would sit in those damned two-level bunkers and say, "Come and get me, sucker." The NVA have artillery support, which we lack, and as events have shown, air support on a hill is difficult at best. The day seems like a dream. Career shows up with the medic and orders me to sit still. I am poked and prodded. I am bandaged, given pills and an injection of Darvon. I cannot eat. Lights dance in front of my eyes.

Career has ordered me to be medevaced in the morning. I start to argue but soon stop talking. I recline on the hillside, and I float in light. I hear the crackle of NVA artillery and jump. The B-52s return as they did several nights ago to the valley and the ground shakes as bombs strike NVA positions. I float in my ball of light as the world fades away.

My life unfolds before me. I see my eagle circling above. I see doors not opened, paths not taken, love unspoken, battles not fought, and gifts not given. I swear war will be my fate no matter the risk to my soul. I float in peace, oblivious to the war around me.

From my golden globe I can look down and study my body below me, but I am not part of that body and no longer feel its pain or fear. My body is immobilized, with legs curled under, floating free, warm, and in peace with the world around me. My body seems to be healing itself, the bleeding is stopped, and I am conscious of my flesh knitting itself back together. Time is suspended and the night is dark, but all I see is golden light. My wounds are open so the shrapnel can be removed, but the edges of the wound will knit and will close immediately after the shrapnel is gone.

My eyes close as sleep claims me.

15 Aug 1968
I Corps
A Shau Valley
0700 hours

> They perished in the seamless grass,
> No eye could find the place;
> But God on his repealless list
> Can summon every face.

— Emily Dickinson, "The Battlefield"

The next day it takes six hours for my platoon to cut an LZ about 1,000 meters from the enemy position. Before I leave I hear reinforcements arriving in the NVA bunkers. I worry about my men, especially Dillon and Ebert. They are still very much in harm's way. I grab my rifle and empty rucksack and limp toward the LZ. I remember that I have hardly had anything to eat since the artillery attack in the A Shau Valley four days ago. I am lucky, for I learned that food is irrelevant for a mind properly prepared.

The helicopter arrives to evacuate the wounded. I hop on. Dillon waves a salute and I nod an acknowledgement. I feel guilt:

Twice under my leadership my platoon has been decimated, and I alone bear responsibility. As the bird rises, Dillon's face gradually diminishes in size. My men watch as I disappear. The command of the platoon now rests on Dillon's shoulders. His shoulders are bent and he turns and walks back into the jungle toward the enemy.

I have lived an eternity in the past week, facing violent death every day. I feel as if I have been hugging a giant palm tree during a tidal wave swirling around me, as the bodies of my friends and enemies pass by. Their mouths hang open and their eyes glance at me accusingly.

I am short of breath, and I feel as if I am suffocating. Each nerve in my body is electrified. The A Shau Valley is a place worse than hell that I am condemned to revisit for the rest of my life. Worse, these returns will come as a total surprise. I'll be in a business meeting one moment, and on the hill above the valley the next.

When I was climbing that hill, I thought we looked like Spartan warriors with chiseled faces. When I look back on pictures taken in the valley, I see only warriors who still have the softness of youth. But their eyes tell you they are killers.

10

Top

"Far better it is to dare mighty things, to win glorious triumphs, even though checkered by failure, than to rank with those spirits who neither enjoy nor suffer much, because they live in grey twilight that knows neither victory nor defeat."

— Theodore Roosevelt

15 Aug 1968
Firebase Bastogne
1000 hours

The medevac lands at Firebase Bastogne. No one meets us to help the severely wounded. I help the other wounded off the chopper. D Company cannot win the battle on the Dong So. In the back of my mind I realize that we are not there to take the hill. We are there to pin down a large enemy force so that it can be pummeled by bombs and napalm and then surrounded. You realize you performed your mission, but looking at the wounded and dead you wonder if the cost is justified. Using bait to attract an enemy is a tactic as old as warfare itself.

Another chopper arrives to take me and the other wounded to the field hospital 20 minutes away. I am flown to the 326th Medical Battalion. Within an hour, they have removed most of the shrapnel from my arm, leg and side, and my wounds are stitched and bandaged. They want me to stay to prevent any infection, but I refuse. Capt. Career is the only officer left in my company and that worries me. I need to return to the Dong So where my men are. A captain tells me that leaving will be impossible. I tear off the medical tags and sneak out a side door. The 326th is too busy with the seriously wounded and dying to miss me. When you are dead, you are supposed to report to graves registration. Perhaps another time. I catch a ride on a jeep and return to my company.

At the company headquarters tent, sitting at the first sergeant's desk, is an old man. He must be as old as my father, 50-something. He waves a salute to me and says, "Lieutenant, I am Top Hantsen." Where the hell did they find this fellow? 1st Sgt. Robert M. Hantsen is 6 feet 2 and about 280 pounds, most of it concentrated in an enormous beer belly. He is not a military man by appearance. His uniform looks like pajamas that he has been wearing for a month. He has gray stubble on his chin and his hair has streaks of gray. I notice his left hand is partially paralyzed. I later learn this is a memento from the Korean War.

He is a crafty fellow, firing a rapid stream of questions at me, continually testing me. He wants to know about the condition of the company's men. He wants to know about Career. He wants to know what weapons the NVA are using. He scowls when he hears about the artillery, the .50-caliber machine guns and heavy mortars. We have a lot to talk about. To my surprise, Top is heading out to the field to serve as first sergeant. I know of no other first sergeant who spends time in the field except maybe a few minutes to bring the mail on resupply day. Most senior NCOs manage the paperwork that is part of the military system; they do not fight. Most of them manage the company HQ in the rear and spend their evenings in NCO clubs. Hantsen is different. He is a true warrior and wants to be where he can make a difference, accomplishing the mission and saving lives. Over the next few days as we wait for the return of D Company, I will gradually come to understand him. He is an old friend of the battalion and division sergeants major who often stop by to see him, drink beer and tell stories. They greet each other with the name of a forgotten Korean hill where they all once served together.

Top has had quite a career. As a soldier in World War II, he was promoted to staff sergeant in six months. It takes most soldiers 10 years to make that rank in peacetime. As Gen. Douglas MacArthur moved up the chain of islands in the South Pacific, it was Top's job to cross enemy lines and spy on Japanese command posts. He told me a story of being trapped in the attic of a hut that the Japanese had made into a temporary command post. He understood some Japanese and while he was there, he learned of a planned offensive.

After World War II, he fought Communists in the hills of Greece in the late '40s. This was not a war that I had even known about, but it was a bloody fight. In Korea, he served with the 187th Airborne Regiment. Few members of this elite unit survived the war. They were used on impossible missions, often suffering 90 percent casualties. Top had been shot up badly and was lucky to be alive. The Rangers were eventually disbanded because volunteer replacements were too hard to find. During the '60s, Top spent time in South America chasing Che Guevara.

This is his third tour in Vietnam. The first two were with the 1st Division. I asked the battalion sergeant major why Top did not have a higher rank, and was told that Top and the peacetime Army did not have an affinity for each other. He had been broken in rank several times only to be promoted again in the next war. But rank is of no interest to Top, as I would soon learn. He spent the last three years before Vietnam in Germany, which was his third tour in Germany. He owns a German cab company and plans to retire there after his last tour of duty. He had purchased a house in Munich and was decorating it when he received orders for Vietnam. He collects Japanese armor of the Edo period and antique German country furniture. He is addicted to German opera and sings Wagnerian arias when he has had too much to drink. He loves Mumm's Cordon Rouge champagne for breakfast. He has a son from a failed marriage, and no longer wants a woman in his life. Top sent his son to an English boarding school to study engineering. The boy is now finishing college at MIT but will stay on for a doctorate.

15 Aug 1968
I Corps
A Shau Valley
2100 hours

"Despite three hours of air and arty prep the volume
of enemy fire increased rather than decreased and
the 3rd Platoon was hard hit by .50-caliber, RPD, AK-47,
RPG, Chicom grenades, M-26 grenades, command-
detonated explosive, 60 mm and 82 mm mortar fire.
U.S. artillery, TAC air and gunship support were called
in as close as 25 meters from friendly troops."

— Official battalion history

It is about 2100 the day after I was wounded, the sergeants
major have left, and Top and I remain drinking. At 2100, all
company commanders of 1/327th radio in to the battalion
commander and report on the day's events. This group
conversation is called family talk. Top and I use our radio to
listen to the day's events. We heard Career's report.

Following the same path I had used the day before, 2nd Platoon
moved up the mountain around 1400. The 2nd Battalion, 502nd
Infantry Regiment, was working the valley below. The 2/502
was in heavy contact and receiving mortar fire from somewhere
below us. Cobra gunships walked a wall of fire in front of 2nd
Platoon. Spc. 4 Lucey from 2nd Platoon walked point. Pfc. Stewart
was the slack man. Tiny Stanchfield, 2nd Platoon's best squad
leader, was third in line followed by platoon leader Sgt. Herman,
RTO Cpl. McGrew and of course Blevins, back for his second day
on the stone staircase. Ebert volunteered to go with 2nd Platoon
and show them the way. Herman's plan was to go through what
the men now called the Devil's Staircase, walking gunships in
front of him. He found the charred remains of the mortar crew
and some riflemen we had killed yesterday. The gunships ceased
their fire, and 2nd Platoon heard the clatter of rocks rolling down
the hillside, as the NVA moved back from their ventilated safe
areas into the bunkers with open fields of fire.

When Stanchfield spotted four NVA moving on the right,
he and Blevins, Herman and McGrew took cover behind a rock

formation. The rest of the platoon tried to enter the staircase, but they were stopped by NVA heavy machine gun fire. The NVA had moved a .50-caliber with a perfect line of fire down the staircase. Chunks of heavy rock flew through the air. The point man reported seeing four NVA moving into a bunker, and he dropped three of them. The NVA bunkers opened up then, and 2nd Platoon's lead element was trapped. Blevins had an M-79 and fired the grenade launcher, taking out the bunker with the machine gun. Last night the NVA moved more ordnance into their fortress. Now the extra firepower was being used against 2nd Platoon, and it was overwhelmed by 82 mm and 60 mm mortar barrages, automatic weapons fire and RPGs.

Herman spotted a command bunker. He crawled toward it to get a shot, but a grenade landed too close, exploded and wounded him severely. We all thought Herman's wife and children, whom he talked about all the time, would have to learn to live without him because we were certain he would die. He didn't, but 2nd Platoon will have to go on without him. I am not sure who has the harder task since Herman fought with a streetwise battle sense that saved lives. Blevins and Stanchfield had opened up and pulled Herman back. In doing so, Blevins received grenade fragments in his head. Lucey and Stewart had covered the withdrawal. An AK-47 burst shot up McGrew's radio. Spc. 4 Boswood crawled to the staircase entrance to give Blevins a radio. Blevins had reported the situation and called in the gunships. The F-4s were supporting Khe San, so 2nd Platoon had air support only from Army Cobras. Second Platoon suffered its final casualty around 1600. They had encountered a reinforced company. The Dong So backs up on Laos. The NVA can keep two divisions in Laos and reinforce their positions with men and ammunition simply by marching them up the back of the hill. It is not a good day for D Company.

Blevins was supposed to have left Saigon for the U.S.—but he stayed to keep the band of brothers safe.

16 Aug 1968
I Corps
A Shau Valley
1600 hours

> Here let their discord with them lie
> Speak not for those a separate doom
> Whom fate made Brothers in the tomb;
> But search the land of living men,
> Where wilt thou find their like agen?
>
> — Sir Walter Scott, "Patriotism"

This is D Company's last day on the mountain. Top and I listen on the company frequency throughout the day. In late afternoon yesterday, the company had withdrawn several hundred meters down the ridgeline to the knoll that 2nd Platoon had cleared for my medevac extraction. Career was aware of the mortars below him that fired on the 502nd. He heard movement on the left and he thought the enemy was trying to encircle him. At 0100 this morning, D Company's abandoned position was attacked. Herman, severely wounded and suffering, could not be medevaced until the next day.

Around 1000, 1st Platoon starts its move up the hill and attempts to reach the summit. Blevins goes wild with air support. He is a god of vengeance for his friend Herman. Thirty-six tanks of napalm fry the summit to a crisp. The bunkers are no longer camouflaged; the jets drop 250-, 500- and 750-pound bombs, and gunships bombard the fortified positions with rockets. The fighters report that the napalm has taken out 50 NVA moving to reinforce their positions. The NVA are taking heavy casualties but they still outnumber 1st Platoon 8 to 1 with their reserves.

Lt. Copeland, the new 1st Platoon leader who arrived when I was extracted, walks point with an M-79 loaded with canister rounds. Dillon commands the remains of 2nd and 3rd platoons in fire support; 1st Platoon moves up the ridgeline, choosing to scale the sides of the staircase instead of walking through it. The point element consists of Copeland, Spc. 4 Breland, Pfc. Jose Antonio Graniela, Sgt. Greg DeLaurentis, Pfc. Colhoun and Spc. 4 Boaz. Blevins, back for his third day, sits on top of the staircase adjusting air support. First Platoon walks into a classic ambush and receives heavy fire from NVA waiting for them on top of the rocks. Heavy mortars launch a barrage. RPGs and heavy and light machine guns fire at the men continuously. NVA sniper positions are using our own metal bomb fragments as shields. Recoilless rifles open up. Judging by the sound of the weapons, 1st Platoon faces a force that according to Career was larger than yesterday, perhaps now two companies.

Dillon's support group takes out five snipers but heavy fire renders our M-60 machine guns useless. Spc. 4 Sanchez crawls into a tree and takes out two or more snipers. But things are not going well for Copeland's command. A blast cuts off Graniela's leg. Pfc. David Chisum, 21, of Salinas, Calif., running to get Graniela, is hit by RPGs in the face and chest and there is little left of him. All of the medics in the company move in to help the wounded. Satchel charges the NVA had buried explode, wounding several men.

As usual, Blevins is in the middle of the action. He has an M-16 and is taking up slack for the machine gun on the top of the stairway. Ammo links on that machine gun are breaking continuously, interrupting fire, so Blevins covers the gun as it reloads. At the same time he brings in Cobra gunships, directing white phosphorous rounds to mark the bunkers for the gunships. The gunships start to fire, but snipers and an NVA machine gun target Blevins. He is shot in the forehead. He dies instantly. Blevins' body falls from the staircase to the NVA's side of the summit. The men couldn't recover his body.

Blevins was supposed to leave for home yesterday. Blevins, who four days ago was a dude, is the true hero dying for the man on his right and left. I am devastated, but it would be unmanly to cry. I will later learn that Blevins' body is recovered the next year. At least he will have a grave somewhere in the United States.

Copeland, on the other side of the staircase, drops his pants and moons the NVA bunkers. This is about all he can do to insult the NVA in their bunkers, since he clearly could not take the hill. They shoot him in the ass; his legs are crippled. He is carried off the hill and is soon on his way to a Japanese hospital with Herman.

Spc. 4 Murphy now commands Copeland's platoon and directs the evacuation of the dead and wounded. An F-104 is hit on a bombing run and crashes into the Gulf of Tonkin. Twenty to 30 men of D Company are wounded or dead, and many who are wounded are medevaced out of Vietnam. We have received 15 reinforcements. There is no way an understrength company can take out several companies reinforced by heavy weapons in stone bunkers. My unit, the 1/327th, has suffered 100 casualties. D Company has been under heavy attack for five days. During that time we moved 1,200 meters with little food and less sleep.

I am drunk by now. Top has had much more to drink, but he is stone cold sober. I am trying to follow Top's analysis of the Inchon landing. He has a truly intimidating knowledge of military history and current events. He and I discuss Truong Kien's book on NVA strategy, "The Resistance Will Win." He gives me his copy and expects it to be read by the next evening. He says it will explain what the Dong So is about.

In the mid '30s, Truong Kien wrote the systematic outline of Indochina's guerrilla doctrine. Truong saw a protracted war. Barbarian war was not new for the Vietnamese. Under the Tran Dynasty, Vietnam fought the feared Manchu Hordes (the Qing Dynasty of China) for hundreds of years. For 31 years, the war Truong Kien planned, the Vietnam War, will be a war without fronts, fought by both militia and regular army units. The people are the water; the people's army are the fish. Soldiers are disguised as civilians. In this war, winning battles and defeating the enemy are not important. What is important is outlasting the enemy. Body bags sap the superpower's strength. Do any of today's generals remember Washington's secret for victory? He defeated the English in the Revolution by winning only three of 38 battles. On the Dong So, we tricked the NVA into fighting at a time and place of our selection. It cost them heavily, but they will fight again tomorrow and the next day until we lose our will to fight and withdraw.

We stop talking at 0100, and I stagger off to my empty bachelor officer's quarters. There are no other officers, even replacements. In the distance, flares illuminate the bunkers, the defensive perimeter of the division. A gunship flies overhead, its machine guns firing. One of the cherries on the bunker line must have seen a shadow and called for help. As I fall asleep, hearing the gunships' rockets explode in the distance, I realize I am now a combat veteran.

The 101st strategy has worked. An initial NVA reinforced platoon was reinforced by a company and then reinforced again to contain D Company. Other NVA battalions were brought in to contain A, B and C companies and the 2/502. It had been a killing field for jets and helicopter gunships. How many NVA died—perhaps 500? That is what we are told. But they are body count figures and I am skeptical of them. The higher the body count, the faster an officer's career is advanced. The 1/327 had 100 casualties, and their wounds and deaths will never be reported in American newspapers as dying for a worthwhile cause—closing the A Shau staging area. The American public will remember our casualties and forget we killed 500 of the enemy. With 20 dead we had a 25-to-1 kill ratio, but who really knows? The NVA retained the ground but it cost them dearly. As we listen to our radio, we hear that the decision has been made to withdraw from the A Shau. The oncoming monsoon season makes resupply too difficult. The division has found the NVA's highway to the south: It will return in the spring with the intention of making the A Shau our valley. The men of 3rd Platoon who are my responsibility are coming home to Firebase Eagle.

The extraction from the Dong So occurs at first light. The helicopters look like dragonflies on the ridge, hovering in place for a few seconds, extracting what is left of the company. Capt. Career is on the first chopper, probably comparing his withdrawal from the Dong So to Lee's retreat from Gettysburg. I am sure he believes it to be an equal accomplishment. Because of weather, had we continued the advance we would have been cut off without jets and without gunships. We could have been outnumbered 20 or 30 to 1. Without a resupply of ammunition, we would have died fighting with entrenching tools.

As the last helicopter leaves, it starts to rain, washing away the few remaining puddles of blood.

11

My Captain

O young Lochinvar is come out of the west,
Through all the wide Border his steed was the best;
And save his good broadsword he weapons had none,
He rode all unarm'd, and he rode all alone
So faithful in love, and so dauntless in war,
There never was knight like the young Lochinvar.

— Sir Walter Scott, "Young Lochinvar"

19 Aug 1968
I Corps
Camp Eagle
0900 hours

As 1/327 returns to the LZ at Camp Eagle, I await my platoon—or what is now a reinforced squad. I clap the men on their backs as they jump off the helicopters. I shake hands with Sgt. Dillon. These men are the heroes of the A Shau and they deserve the best stand-down party the Army can provide. When I see my company area, I am amazed by how much it has changed; it is impeccably neat and the ground is freshly raked. Top is standing at the entrance. His pajamas are gone. He wears a crisp pair of freshly starched jungle fatigues. He has no rank insignia, just a T-shirt. I find it hard to believe that this is the man I drank with last night. He is all business, shouting at the men. The heroes of the A Shau are given latrines to be cleaned, tents to set right and various other duties. Somehow Top's physical presence alone has everyone jumping. A few of the men knew him in Germany, so they know Top never comes out a loser in any argument. Top's arguments are resolved behind the tents after hours. I watch Top move men around the camp faster than they moved for Capt. Flattop, yet he is a stranger to most of them. Top passes by me and says, "It's the private; he's what's happening." Why does he do this? Why is he raising hell with my men? This is not the way to treat the men who have walked to hell and back.

An unfamiliar man steps out of a tent. He is not wearing a shirt. He is about 5 feet 10 and has the body of a Greek wrestler. When I see him, I think of Achilles. Like me, the men wonder who the hell this man is. Top salutes him. He's our new captain. I turn around, the captain looks at me, and I salute. He waves his hand at his forehead. He looks at the men in the street and shouts, "D Company, I am Capt. Peter Quirin, your new commanding officer." Top shouts, "Fall in. Attention." These are my men. They have just fought for their lives and the honor of their country. Now they are standing at attention like they are at a parade ground. Capt. Career was hard, but at least he would be at the officers' club by now, not conducting an inspection.

Quirin goes through the ranks slowly. He is inspecting weapons and asking questions. One man is carrying a damaged rocket launcher. It could have exploded by accident where he stands, killing those around him. Then there is Pvt. Moron from my platoon. Moron is the man who somehow always manages to be at the back of the line. His uniform resembles pajamas and he always fails the personal hygiene test. He is slightly overweight and continually stares at his shoes. I doubt he has a friend in the platoon. He did not help load wounded on the helicopters after the barrage. I do not remember seeing him on the Dong So ridgeline. Why? Because he is invisible. Quirin stands before Moron, and Moron apologizes. His M-16 is inoperative. Quirin asks him how a weapon that was used in combat can be inoperative. It turns out the gun has never been cleaned and never fired. The obvious question was, how can he never have fired his weapon when the enemy overwhelmed his platoon? Quirin gives him an Article 15, a form of nonjudicial punishment that can be handed out at the company level without the bother of a court-martial. Top escorts Moron to the stockade for five days' detention, the length of our stand-down. Quirin walks over to me and says, "See that that does not happen again, Lieutenant." I feel as if he had just pissed in my face.

I have served under Capt. Flattop, who sang "Kumbaya" with the men but hid in a bomb crater when the shit hit the fan. I have served with Capt. Career, the great leader far removed from danger, and now we have this asshole Quirin, who acts like John Wayne impersonating a drill instructor. It is one hell of an army. Top sees I am having trouble and he saunters over. He asks, "Lieutenant, what's the matter? Why don't you go with these two sergeants and help them organize our stand-down. It will cheer you up."

It doesn't seem necessary to know the sergeants' names. We drive off for half an hour to a village. A medic from division headquarters joins us in our jeep as we leave the base. When we arrive at the village, he hops off and goes to the headman. He speaks Vietnamese and there is a spirited conversation. He keeps saying, "Beaucoup." A number of young women appear in a line. Several are beautiful, and my heart skips a beat. The sergeant takes the headman into a hut and pulls out a wad of money. The medic goes into another hut and emerges from it after 20 minutes with four of the young women walking behind him. The sergeants sit in the jeep. Another jeep appears out of nowhere for the young women. We return to Camp Eagle.

On the drive back, I wonder what has happened to Capt. Career. Top had seemed so interested in my description of his command on the Dong So. The NCOs are like the voodoo doctors of the Army. Their drums beat all night and things happen, like reassigning officers. I later learn Career has been assigned to be some quartermaster general's aide; he will finish his tour as a "decorated" combatant with his nose up a general's ass.

Our jeep rumbles back to our company camp. Four tents are in place and there are lines of men in front of each tent. The four girls each walk into their own tent. The sergeants take the money at the door of each tent. The medic vanishes after he makes sure the girls don't have V.D. Top stands on the porch in front of the company HQ and nods to a soldier when it's his turn. Each enlisted man is allowed five minutes. I bet many of those young men will fail to get an erection, and leave by the back of the tents embarrassed. I am confused. I would like to join that line and know a woman's touch, but I cannot.

Steaks are grilling on 50 half-gallon oil drums turned into barbecues. How did anyone get steaks so quickly? Quirin and Top must have connections. A truck filled with iced beer arrives, and soon Company D is a party in the making.

I sit with Ebert and have a few beers. A bunch of the men start talking about how great Flattop was. Under his command many gooks were blown away on that ridgeline, without casualties. Someone gets the idea that the company should give Flattop a Silver Star. A pad of paper is brought out and signatures are solicited for Flattop's Silver Star. Soon there are 30 signatures. Top sees there is something going on and walks over. His belly is bigger than I remember. He looks at the sheet and grabs it, crumpling it into a ball and tossing it into the fire. He tells us, "Medals are for bravery, not popularity. We do not vote on medals."

Top scowls and slowly walks away.

12

Back to the Field

"In war, there are no unwounded soldiers."
— Jose Narosky

The four days after the party lack women, steaks and beer. I am immersed in details: filling sandbags, briefing replacements, issuing new equipment, maintaining orders and writing letters to the parents of the dead. I check what I will need for the field countless times. The stand-down is almost over. We learn that our battalion commander, Maj. Duane Cameron, call sign Black Hawk, is going to have a Prop Blast Ceremony. Cameron is a soldier's soldier and looks the part.

When a company is involved in a firefight, Cameron will sometimes try to join them. His commands are usually only one sentence long and his fatigues are often pressed. He is of average height but he seems much larger when you are around him. He would have done well as one of Patton's tank commanders. Even Ebert says Cameron has balls.

The Prop Blast is an Airborne tradition. The dinner is nice—steaks. Officers toast their men who were killed or injured. Twenty pairs of their boots, accompanied by their M-16s with bayonets and helmets on their stocks, are stuck in the ground by the entrance. All the young lieutenants stand at attention and are given a drink to swallow rapidly. The drink is scotch, bourbon, vodka, brandy, creme de menthe, or any other alcohol that can be found. All of this is dumped into a recently fired 105 mm artillery shell. The new lieutenants like me are supposed to drink this gallon and a half of filth—alcohol mixed with burnt powder. Fortunately, Top has warned me about what will happen. "This is an intelligence test," he said. "Don't do something stupid." As a result, I take a spot in the back, well away from the senior officers. Several lieutenants fight to be in the front so they can show their stuff. We are ordered to drink the contents of the whole 105 shell. I find that if I lean forward and hold the shell at a certain angle, most of the liquor falls on the sandy floor without spilling on my T-shirt. No one is watching the sand. Time passes slowly—I pretend to gulp and gulp. Several men in the front rows pass out, and the medics are ordered to pump their stomachs. Our battalion commander yells, "Dismissed." We salute and stagger back to our tents. Cameron and the company commanders continue to drink, tell jokes and laugh. Thanks to Top, I am back to my tent safely, well away from the Prop Blast.

The stand-down is over on the fifth day. We are driven to an empty plain close to Camp Eagle. My arm and leg are bandaged, but with luck I will not get an infection. Quirin gives me a complete briefing. Flattop never bothered to explain the complete mission to me. Career gave me a description of his role in influencing division strategy. Quirin tells me that our mission is to break into small units and continuously patrol the areas around fire support bases Eagle, Veghel, Berchtesgaden and Son. We are to establish contact with the NVA as often as possible and prevent any massing of troops that might enable an attack on the firebases. As always, we are minnows on a fishhook.

On the morning of Aug. 25, I am on the first helicopter into the landing zone as an NVA machine gun and two RPGs open up from the wood line. Quirin, on the first helicopter with me, signals to hit the ground. He has pre-registered artillery and calls in the guns to fire for effect. The wood line erupts with a massive artillery barrage and gunships finish off the work. We examine the remains of several NVA bunkers, finding a few bodies and several blood trails. We also find four caves with two 12.7 mm antiaircraft machine guns. Tiger Force, our reconnaissance platoon, discovers three 55-gallon drums of powdered riot control chemicals. Quirin is everywhere on the field working with the new 1st and 2nd platoon leaders to deploy their men. I move 3rd Platoon to the company's point, ready to move out on command.

I hear stories about Quirin when he served with the Military Assistance Command in Vietnam (MACV). I am told he saved an ARVN firebase and has been nominated for the Distinguished Service Cross (DSC), the second-highest U.S. award for valor. He always runs to the fire, which is good for the men's morale. But if anything happens to him, I am the senior platoon leader and next in line to command a company. I have been in country only one month and I am one bullet away from command.

Quirin gives the order to move out. We now have to cover distance at twice the speed we moved with Career and Flattop, and Quirin orders everyone to wear a helmet rather than a cloth boonie hat. The helmet seems heavier with each hour that passes. I come to a steep ravine that is about 200 feet deep and 100 feet across. It is an ideal spot for an ambush: A squad moving across the ravine would be dead if camouflaged NVA occupy the other side. Ebert volunteers to secure the other side, and moves quickly across the ravine.

Then, at the rear of the company, 10 explosions shatter the afternoon. I am with two machine guns covering Ebert and I send a squad across to reinforce him.

Quirin, of course, leaves our area to go where the firing is. The rear of the company opens up with heavy firing, but there is nothing moving across the ravine. Quirin reappears carrying a wounded man. The rear of the company was ambushed while we were crossing the ravine. The same two squads of NVA that met us at the LZ have been following us. Carelessly, the men took off their helmets when we stopped and did not put out claymore mines, or a listening post. The NVA got within 30 meters before firing and then unleashed a barrage of RPGs. The RPGs exploded in the trees and shrapnel ricocheted off the canopy, driving deadly hot metal downward. The result is devastating— four serious head wounds. Quirin calls all the platoon leaders and is apoplectic. Platoon leaders are responsible for helmets to be worn at all times, claymores out, and a listening post must be established 20 yards in front of the perimeter whenever we stop. He is furious that our carelessness could have cost lives.

The men are cutting an LZ. During the stand-down, I got to know several men from 2nd Platoon, my favorite being Sgt. Tiny Stanchfield. He leads 1st Squad with 11 months in country and was one of Sgt. Herman's best men. Stanchfield is like Nasty Naylor. He is short, wiry and tough. Stanchfield has a head wound; he wants to talk to me. As I hold his head against my shoulder, my uniform is covered in blood. He is bleeding heavily. There are two half-inch holes in his head and he looks at me and says, "Wear your helmet, Lieutenant." There is a strange gray substance oozing onto my fatigues. The medic tells me it is Stanchfield's brain. He passes out. I believe he dies in my arms before the helicopter arrives but I could be wrong. Quirin shouts at me to get my fat ass over to my squad across the ravine. On my way over, I take my anger out by punching the rocks. It is a stupid thing to do; bloody knuckles are just another thing that can get infected.

After moving with Quirin for five days, I am dead tired. Quirin has a love affair with his rucksack and helmet, and he is never far from either. He looks like a Hemingway figure carrying a CAR-15, a short-barreled M-16 carbine. Each time I get to a hilltop, I am told to move to the next one. My platoon is always on point, which is not fair to my men. I have never been so tired in my life and I do not give a damn if an NVA company pops out of the brush and blows us away. I hear my men swearing about Quirin when he is not around and I do not chew them out, since I feel the same way.

I never thought Top could keep up with the younger men but he has been shedding weight and probably has lost 15 pounds in a week. He will soon be 190 pounds. He not only keeps up with 20-year-olds, but marches them into the ground. With one hand, he will pick up a young soldier who is slouching. The young soldier never slouches again. But today even Top is tired, although he never complains.

I think Quirin is a fool to push the company so hard. So when the men say, "The old man is a hard-ass," I don't care even though he is only 10 feet away. That night Quirin calls me over. He quietly explains to me why the whole battalion has to push: We are trying to catch up with the NVA force. It is a different battalion than the one who attacked the Dong So. All the companies in the 1/327th are commanded by officers like Quirin; A, B and C companies have West Pointers.

Quirin says, "Your performance is disgusting. Officers are many things but they are not tired or weak, for when a platoon leader acts like a spoiled child and starts complaining because the going is tough, the platoon is vulnerable. Lives like Stanchfield's will be lost and the platoon leader is accountable. When a man dies under your command, you are forever accountable." He asks me if that is what I want. The past few days have pushed me to the limit, but that is exactly when it is important for me to act like a leader. I notice that both Quirin's arms are covered with open jungle rot sores oozing puss. They must hurt like hell. He is right, just like Capt. Rose, my ROTC mentor, was at Penn. But just like then, the truth hurts. I do not like being told the truth by him. His delivery is not vindictive, but it seems as if he was explaining my weakness to me as if I were a child. My pride is hurt and worse—I have failed the men on my left and right, Top and Quirin.

The next day I do not complain. I start checking the men at random for all manner of things—weapons, helmets, rucksacks, food. In the next three days I become a hard-ass. I know I cannot make the tour of duty less dangerous. I do not control our mission. But perhaps I can keep my men alive and accomplish our mission. Sometime in the future I will have to order men to certain death. If I start to care too much, and try to save lives only to endanger more lives, I cease to lead. That is why being a leader is so lonely. Oh yes, underneath I do care, especially when I write the letters to their families; I just cannot show it. Never show your emotions.

Because I am curious, I start asking questions about Peter Quirin. Where did he come from? What made him into the man he is?

As it turns out, Quirin had a typical American childhood. His parents were hardworking middle-class Americans. They gave Quirin his work ethic and a sound moral framework. They lived in an old house on a lake where he spent most of his free time in the water, the woods and the swamps, exploring and adventuring. He went to a strict Catholic school but he hated it and was never a good student.

At 11 he joined the Boy Scouts and stayed active until he was 19 or 20. The Scouts were his thing. He excelled in leadership and ascended to Eagle Scout. At 15, he was hired as a Scout summer camp instructor and served five years in that capacity. In high school, he was taught under the guidance of the Christian Brothers Academics. He excelled in running and wrestling, not academics.

With his family's encouragement, he started at Kent State University and enrolled in the ROTC program, in which he excelled. After three years, he dropped out and enlisted in the Army. He applied to the Infantry Officers Candidate School in 1964 and was accepted. Inspired by his roommate, Herb Lloyd, he volunteered for Ranger School and a Vietnam combat assignment. Instead, he was sent to the 7th Infantry Division in Korea.

In 1966, he received orders for Ranger School and then to Vietnam as an adviser to a Vietnamese Army battalion. He learned to speak Vietnamese and think like the NVA. He fought with this unit extensively over Tet. His time with the Vietnamese taught him lessons in survival and what good and bad leadership were about. After a year in country, he was assigned as the commanding officer of Delta Company 1/327, and that is where our paths crossed.

It is morning, about seven days after landing on the hot LZ, and the company is tired but not as tired as the week before. A helicopter flies over, and someone kicks out salt tablets to prevent heat stroke. The other platoons have lost several of their men in the past few days to heat stroke and broken limbs. I move around the platoon methodically checking to see that the men are awake, alert and wearing their helmets. I notice most of the men in 2nd Platoon are dozing in their positions. Ever since the platoon lost Herman in the A Shau, it has not been the same. Second Platoon has lost its pride. The platoon has a new commander. I call him Lt. Sorry Ass. He does not give a damn about what he is doing. He does not give a damn about the men.

He reminds me of a Florida State ROTC fraternity boy with whom I served in basic training. He moved slowly and spoke with a Southern drawl. While pretending to be my friend, he tricked me into taking his time on the duty roster for five months so he could party. I cared only about making the company win the competition as the best basic training unit and really did not notice that he was never in the field. He probably joined the ROTC only because it was a sure way to get into some girl's pants. Capt. Holt found out what he did and frat boy never had a chance at making the Army a career.

Quirin gives the order to move out on Sorry Ass' second day in the field. As usual, 3rd Platoon is on point. Second Platoon brings up the rear. Without warning, a machine gun opens up and I hear cries for the medic. A man from 2nd Platoon staggers toward our position. He collapses, shot in the gut, and passes out. I call our medic to give him first aid. Quirin is in the middle of the action. Eight men are wounded.

Quirin is furious, since Sorry Ass at the time of the ambush was not with his men but was at the command post slinging shit with Nasty Naylor, who is now Quirin's RTO. Quirin had moved Nasty to the command post to give me a chance to lead a platoon without being second-guessed. Nasty is good, but I will always be a cherry to him. Later, I berate Nasty for not kicking Sorry Ass back to his platoon and Nasty admits he has made a mistake. Quirin is now in the front with what is left of Sorry's platoon. Top is right: The war is about men. For a squad leader, a platoon leader, or a company commander, softness kills. I have to admit that a week before, the same thing could have happened to my platoon. It is easy for two NVA squads to follow us and launch a surprise attack when men are careless. Sorry Ass collapses on the third day, is medevaced out and does not return. Before Vietnam, he helped run a company at Officer Candidate School. Let him go back there and terrorize the candidates with tales of Nam. Top takes over the platoon and within a day, 2nd Platoon has found its pride. In business and war you are only one leader away from victory.

Darkness comes early on the day of Sorry Ass' departure. At night I am cool, if not cold, although during the day, my blood was boiling. As my soaked fatigues cool, I shiver in my own sweat. But tonight we have a treat awaiting us: LRP rations, my favorite spaghetti and meat sauce. I cook a cup of cocoa in a canteen cup over a heat tablet and think that days in the jungle take on a unique rhythm. Taking care of jungle rot takes time, looking for fer-de-lance snakes before turning in at night takes time, and setting out claymores takes time—but they are a part of the daily ritual in Vietnam. The monsoon season is beginning, and each day it rains for a little longer than the day before.

Quirin sends out 3rd Platoon to operate as an independent unit so we can cover more ground. Days turn into weeks, and I spend a lot of time thinking about Quirin—about what motivates him, about why he does what he does. I use him as a role model and copy his behavior. One morning before moving out, I hold a surprise inspection checking weapons. As an independent platoon, we are on point every day. We have been lucky; we have broken three ambushes in the last three weeks by ambushing the ambushers. But the platoon is dependent on the point man; his alertness saves or kills. Most days I have Ebert on point. He is dependable, but I am being unfair, just as Quirin was when he put 3rd Platoon on point for months. So today is Ebert's day off. I will be the slack (the soldier behind the point). It is Pvt. Moron's day on point. Most of our platoon cannot stand him, and rightly so. Whenever he is on duty someone else has to do his work. Five days in the brig haven't seemed to help him much.

I walk down the line of squads in formation, checking each man. Moron, as usual, is last in line in 2nd Squad. Everyone in the platoon has cleaned his weapon before moving out. Moron's weapon is corroded shut, the same way it was at the stand-down. It is not functional. A point man with a nonfunctional weapon is a death sentence for the platoon. Moron deserves a death sentence, and it would be my pleasure to carry it out. I would like to shoot him. He obviously wants out of the field. He does not care about the man on his right or his left, and does not care about himself. I call battalion on the radio. I give Moron an Article 15 and ask that he be confined to military jail for six months. Some men die in military jail. If anyone finds out what caused Moron to be sent there, he will consider death a pleasant outcome. We lose the morning waiting for a helicopter to extract Moron, but the platoon is safer for it. I keep the men around me as the basket is dropped from the helicopter. I hope no one in the platoon will take a shot at Moron.

We are working the hills when Father Murphy arrives in a helicopter on our resupply day. Normally, I am skeptical of Catholic priests. After all, they probably have caused half the wars in the last 1,700 years in the name of God. But Irish Catholic priests are a breed apart. Most Catholics will offer communion only to other Catholics. Irish priests offer communion to all. One leg of an Irish cleric rests upon humanity; the other rests upon God.

Father Murphy is such a man and it is through Father Murphy that I make God's acquaintance. Father Murphy does not stay in a chapel on a firebase. He brings God to the firefight. He is about 5 feet 8 inches tall, a rock of muscle, and he is humor personified. He carries an ancient Thompson submachine gun, probably because it was his family's preferred weapon in one of the innumerable Irish rebellions. The Irish never win; they just rebel. The Thompson weighs about three times as much as an M-16, but somehow Father Murphy carries it as easily as a chalice. The Tommy must be at least 40 years old.

One day after resupply when Father Murphy was with us, we were ambushed and 1st Platoon had a soldier seriously wounded in action (WIA). Murphy ran to the firefight. He found the WIA and the next thing we heard over the sound of the AKs and M-16s was his Tommy laying down a base of fire. 1st Platoon started to withdraw. Father Murphy helped carry the WIA to the rear, all the while laying down fire to keep Charlie in his place. He was impervious to bullets. Priests aren't supposed to be armed in combat but thank God that Father Murphy was. Catholics, Jews and Episcopalians decide after that firefight to visit Father Murphy more often. Whenever we stop he listens to sad stories, a wife's infidelities, a friend's death, and lots of guilt over spilt blood. Father Murphy takes D Company's sins upon his own shoulders, and everyone who receives his blessing enjoys a moment of peace.

That night Father Murphy and I sit together at Platoon CP. Father Murphy reaches into his rucksack and pulls out an immaculate 20-year-old bottle of scotch. He pours two heavy drinks, almost half of the bottle, into our canteen cups. The next thing I know I am telling him about the A Shau. Why didn't I tell the men before moving out to cross that field to hit the ground during an artillery barrage? Why was Blevins' death necessary? Why do incompetent officers get off scot-free? Murphy listens and says little, but he says one thing I will remember forever. He says, "God never said this world is just." He reaches into his pocket and hands me a small medal. He calls it a "Jumping Mary." Mary is floating to Earth with a parachute, her hands spread in a benediction. The text reads, "Our Queen of Angels Protect Us in Combat." Murphy says, "When you feel like this, just talk it over with her. She will help you. It is her job." The scotch settles in on me, but the next morning I am absolved of guilt for the men I sent to their deaths, for the men I have killed, and for the fact that I am alive while they are dead.

Father Murphy leaves two days later. As the helicopter rises he gives us his blessing, then a salute. He sits forward, starring out the Huey's windshield, gripping his Tommy. I still carry my Jumping Mary and look to her for advice. Later, when we returned to Camp Eagle, I tried to find Father Murphy, but no one there had ever heard of him. To this day, I do not know if Father Murphy was a man, or an angel with a Thompson submachine gun. Most people forget that angels were warriors first, and angels second.

I have been in country for three months. It seems several lifetimes have been squeezed into that time. I remember what an old NCO told me when I was going through the 101st orientation course: "No matter what you are when you get here, you will leave a man." Enemy artillery has shown me arbitrary death. On the Dong So, I saw a hero die and I escaped death three times. I walked away from what might be called a defeat, but it was not a defeat to me because I fought alongside two professional soldiers. One is an NCO, Top, whom I instantly liked. The other is a young captain who carries the weight of command like he was born to it. Together they have led our company through ambushes to teach us how to conduct our own ambushes, in which we kill the enemy and avoid casualties.

Nights are beautiful in Vietnam. On clear nights the stars seem to be suspended among the jungle trees like so many Christmas lights. I am content to be alive. Never have I been so alive. Death makes life real and moments of beauty supreme. To live my life in this moment would be perfection. Like many other nights, there is a gentle wind. Our platoon is miles from any other American troops, miles from artillery, and 50 miles from air support. In a land that belongs to the enemy, I always look for wind. It carries with it the very scent of the land—or the people who walk across it.

I remember a story told to me by one of Lt. Dickenson's platoon members two days before he left for home. Dickenson and I overlapped in Vietnam one month. He was handsome in a rough way, the kind of guy who must have been president of his fraternity, a good athlete and successful with the ladies. He had seen a lot of action at Pleiku. He was the ideal officer, and his men respected him. He would live the rest of his life with a memento of Pleiku, a nasty purple scar across his throat courtesy of an NVA sniper. He hated writing letters to the families of soldiers killed in battle. He had lost a good friend, a sergeant, in a firefight at Pleiku. He wrote a letter to his family. The friend's sister, Linda, wrote back wanting to know the manner of his death. They struck up a correspondence. She came to Vietnam to Camp Eagle to meet her brother's platoon. She was a beautiful brunette who fell in love with Dickenson. He proposed to her in Vietnam and they were married when he returned to the United States.

I will never forget the story of Dickenson's sergeant's death. It happened on a cool night just like this. There was a gentle breeze. Dickenson had made his camp for the night. He was, like me, miles from other troops and artillery support. When Dickenson smelled garlic, he knew he was in trouble. The scent of garlic, which the NVA use to season their food, does not belong in the jungle. The machine guns covered the major approaches to his camp. Trip flares and claymores were set around the perimeter. He set the coordinates for artillery and gunship support in case he encountered surprise visitors. In 30 seconds, his circular perimeter would become a ring of fire for 400 meters. All he knew was the smell of garlic and sweat. There was no sound.

The sergeant commanded 3rd Squad and he made Dickenson's job easy—well, not easy, but when the bell rings and the shooting starts he was there for Dickenson, pushing the men to fight and die well. The sergeant was from San Mateo—so many of our men were from California—and his men obeyed him. If he said, "Frag the machine gun and charge," six or eight grenades were thrown and his squad charged into a hail of bullets. The charge would have made Pickett proud, except the sergeant took his ground without casualties. For Dickenson, he was more than a squad leader; he was a sounding board in a sea of uncertainty. They shared a lifetime of experiences. They had graduated from the same California university. They had dated the same girls. That evening when Dickenson smelled garlic, the sergeant joined him at the platoon CP before returning to his squad. In the CP they watched the night turn from gray to black; they whispered about what it was like to be in San Mateo in 1966 when they watched the Temptations, the Supremes and Marvin Gaye perform live. The sergeant, the son of a bitch, boasted that he had a date for those concerts while Dickenson did not.

The darkness crept over them. They were on a minor jungle hill perhaps 200 meters high on a broad trail that saw a lot of traffic. As usual at night, there was a mist. It was not enough of a mist to totally obscure the view but it was enough to restrict night vision to about 10 feet. Night fell at 1800 and they were one hour into the second watch before it happened.

A trip flare ignited on the trail and 20 AK-47s opened up, firing way over their heads. Dickenson's platoon popped their claymores around the perimeter and Dickenson called in an artillery fire mission. Rounds were on the way in 45 seconds and gunships were 15 minutes out. The sergeant's squad was in the line of direct fire from the trail. The NVA were still firing high. Dickenson moved to join his sergeant and his squad, bringing another machine gun from 2nd Squad with him. God knows the size of the NVA unit that stumbled into Dickenson's platoon. It was an accident and should not have happened, since jungle nights were usually safe. No one attacked at night unless they wandered into each other, or intentionally planned an attack on a base camp. Dickenson's platoon must have been in the way of a major NVA troop deployment, but the NVA vanished as quickly as they arrived, fading into the jungle night as Dickenson's artillery created a circle of death around him.

They found mangled body parts the next day and 20 to 30 severe blood trails. The NVA took their bodies with them.

The sergeant was beside Dickenson, and Dickenson reached over to touch him—they had been through another moment that made brothers. But this time Dickenson's arm touched his sergeant's shoulder and he smelled the scent of blood and brains, so familiar to him. The sergeant had been shot in the forehead. Dickenson's arm was awash in blood, the essence of his friend, his partner fighting in hell. Dickenson brought his arm back and put the sergeant's head upon his shoulder and wept for his friend. What would the sergeant have done or been if he had not been killed? Dickenson lay close beside his sergeant. Dickenson drifted to sleep but soon awakened to see if the platoon was OK, sleeping with eyes wide open beside the corpse of a friend.

In the morning, the sun cast filtered light around him and his arm was still under his friend's head. His body was numb, the odor of the dead brought back the memory of other deaths, and his body could not respond to his mind's command. Dickenson moved his arm and the sergeant's head fell to the ground. He tried to pick up the corpse and move it to a position where it could be viewed with respect: defiant and not submitting to the bullet. Dickenson had heard of dead weight, but when he picked up the dead body it seemed to have no weight. The sergeant weighed 180 pounds when he was alive, but now his corpse seemed to be nothing more than a bag of salt. The sergeant's death made him believe that all of us have souls. How much did a soul weigh? Evidently, a lot. He carried his friend's body, so light without the weight of his soul, to the medevac helicopter.

Oddly, in the end, the sergeant's death led him to love.

13

The Way of the Sword

"Cannon to right of them,
Cannon to left of them,
Cannon in front of them
Volley'd and thunder'd;
Storm'd at with shot and shell,
Boldly they rode and well,
Into the jaws of Death,
Into the mouth of Hell
Rode the six hundred."

— Alfred Lord Tennyson, "Charge of the Light Brigade"

Months continue to pass and 3rd Platoon gets better and better. I try not to think of Dickenson and his dead sergeant. The NVA no longer ambush us; we ambush them. We feign a river crossing, the NVA give away their position and we wipe them out with machine guns and M-79 grenade launchers. Quirin has us put claymore mines out 30 feet in front of our defensive perimeter as a listening post (LP). If we see someone or hear an AK safety being released, we detonate the claymores and open up with two machine guns and the M-16s. We foil at least three attacks, kill 20 NVA, and suffer no casualties.

Perhaps the high point of these months is breaking up a close-in ambush. Every day our platoon walks point for the company, and as usual the point man is first, the slack man is second and I am third in line. Spc. 4 Murphy, the point man, raises his hand to signal a halt. He advances about 30 feet forward, and a squad of NVA with AK-47s open up. I hear an M-16 on semiautomatic fire amid the AK-47 bursts. All is quiet. Murphy walks back with an enormous smile on his face. He has killed four men with four shots. The rest of the NVA squad has fled. Semiautomatic fire with a good shot is deadly. If you fire on automatic, the weapon rises. Automatic rifle fire is often more useful to scare but not to hit someone.

In an artillery barrage you know fear. In a firefight, I do not know fear. In a firefight, the enemy fires at me. If they miss the ball is now in my court. I feel I am immortal. My body seems as graceful as a ballet dancer's. After I am fired upon I raise my rifle, release the safety and start to swing my weapon toward the enemy. I fire and hit a moving man running toward cover. He drops. I have shot my enemy in the head. It all occurs in slow motion. I can almost see my rounds hitting the head, blowing a large hole out the back of the skull. Hopefully I carved an X on my bullet, making it into a dumdum. A dumdum explodes within the body, making its exit 10 times larger than its entrance. Good bullet—next target. I feel like Superman, like I can grab a piece of coal and by focusing my strength on that black mass of carbon, the flotsam and jetsam of some prehistoric jungle, I can squeeze and transform it into a flawless diamond. To achieve this focus I must block out all sensory inputs except those that are essential to my task—to kill. I am immersed in the moment.

In the jungle the NVA are usually 20 to 80 feet away. I shoot with both eyes wide open. As I sight a man, I am aware of all that is going on around me. My feet are close together, left in front of right. I combine balance with flexibility. I can move the left foot six inches to the right or left and have a 280-degree field of fire, or I can turn about in a circle and shoot directly behind me. The trick is to keep the rifle moving at the same speed as the enemy you are trying to kill. I sight the weapon and swing past the man. I pull the trigger when the sight passes the NVA soldier. It is not aim in a conventional sense. Immediately, I identify another man and start my swing again. I am always moving my rifle in a swing, left to right, trying to kill an enemy before he kills me.

There is no time to think—only to dance. I am young; I have the power of life and death like a god. Those in front of me deserve to die. There is no time for fear. My rifle is an extension of my body, my being. I pull the trigger again and again. Then it is over.

Around November, Quirin again separates 3rd Platoon from the rest of the company, again giving me an independent combat command. It is a compliment, since commanding an independent platoon is similar to commanding a company in combat. By this time, I weigh 123 pounds, down from 165. We work alone for five days, coming together with the rest of the company on resupply day. The ARVN division we work with is called the Black Panthers. We both encounter an NVA company with a .50-caliber machine gun. It is a difficult afternoon, but we send them running.

I have gotten a tropical fever and my temperature is 104 degrees. I stop for a moment to relieve myself and discover that my stool is lime green, the color of the fer-de-lance.

My time walking the ridgelines is nowhere as intense as my time in the A Shau. But it had its moments.

We are running a joint operation with an ARVN unit, chasing a North Vietnamese battalion somewhere west of Firebase Bastogne. We have stopped for a lunch break and as usual we put out our claymores in case we are surprised. I am sitting in our platoon CP eating a can of peaches when a claymore explodes. There's a sharp exchange of gunfire—M-16s and AK-47s. I grab my rifle and rush toward the fire. Three NVA have wandered into our platoon and we have surprised them. Two are down and a third is firing at us. Ebert and I fire at the third and he goes down. Ebert goes to check the other two and I go to check the one we just shot. I am alone and no one is near me. I leave my rifle on the ground to check his pockets. My knife, which is always at my waist, is loose in its scabbard as I bend over my enemy.

Yes, I have killed many times but it was by rifle, directed artillery or directed air strikes. But that is not the way to kill if you are a real warrior. To be a real warrior you should be face to face with the enemy like a Roman legionnaire or one of King Arthur's knights. You should feel the rush as you put your blade through your enemy's heart. Suddenly, my enemy starts to move, raising his AK-47. I knock the rifle away with my left arm. My commando knife with its curved blade like an eagle's beak is in my hand. I plunge the blade into his throat. He makes a croaking sound and shakes violently. He stinks of sweat and garlic and I have to hold his thrashing body down until he is still. The dead man has bled on my hand, but it's not enough for me. I wash my hands in his blood. I raise my knife with my bloody hand over my head, a salute for the dead. I have killed my enemy the way a real warrior does. Eventually I wash the blood off my hand, or at least I think I do. I am elated but I will suffer many sleepless nights—the price of my elation. The knife will be stolen far in the future by thieves in Colombia, South America, but it is still in my hand. I look at my hand today and still see the blood.

Most of the days are spent in the boredom of continual patrolling. We climb up a mountain and we climb down a mountain, and we climb another mountain. My rucksack weighs 10 pounds more than I do, and I often slip on the mud. By the end of the day my skinned knees are infected by jungle rot.

There are moments of peace and of sublime beauty, and I have come to know and love the jungle. There are always orchids that hang over streams that rush down slopes to a valley floor. The rock formations covered with lichens jut upward, their tops covered by moss. A shot rings out. Our slack man is hit splattering me with blood. I am back in the A Shau Valley again.

One of our replacements is a Big Ten football star. He stands about 6 feet 3 inches and looks like a body builder. He thinks he is an easy target and fear overcomes him. He has a big body but a weak mind. He shoots himself in the foot to get a trip back to the United States and we have to medevac him out while we are trying to knock out a .50-caliber machine gun. It would be easier to shoot the coward rather than run the risk of letting the NVA know our position. I call for a basket extraction and hope some NVA soldier will do the job for me. I spin his basket hard as he rises above me. I tell him that he is a coward, and I raise my rifle and aim at him as he is lifted up. I hope the bastard shits his pants.

Two days later we are resupplied and someone sends us some hot sodas. My share is a can of Dr Pepper. We are moving up a ridgeline and there is a rock outcropping, which overlooks a river in a narrow valley. Other ridgelines twist and turn with rugged outcroppings standing in stark contrast to the jungle. It has just rained and a swirling mist obscures part of the view from time to time. What is before me is a perfect Chinese cup garden depicted in a Ming Dynasty scholar artist's painting. How many times did I visit the University of Pennsylvania's museum and look at similar scroll paintings? I sip my warm Dr Pepper, and it has all the subtle nuances of a glass of 1961 Petrus.

I am fighting in the Garden of Eden, for Vietnam is a beautiful country. I remember the haiku of Matsuo Basho, the haiku master, and compose my own poem:

> Hello Mr. Toad. Please
> Join me on the patio,
> It is lonely here.

I stay on my rock outcropping. The only thing that matters is that there is another hill and others behind this one. I remember what Crazy Horse shouted as he led the charge to Little Big Horn: "It is a good day to die." On those hills I will continue to dance with death.

I know Vietnam is a seminal experience in my life. It is because of the breathtaking beauty of the A Shau, the cry of the Indian elephant and the roar of the tiger, and the knowledge that I am only the distance of God's breath from death. It is the incredible feeling that I am leading a band of brothers, and that we are mutually dependent on each other for our lives. I know the man on my right and left, and we will die for each other if necessary. It is a compact between us, sworn in blood. Never again will life be this simple, this exciting, or this fulfilling. Whoever has lived the life of a warrior can love no other; war becomes the incomparable mistress of your heart, an addiction of unimaginable intensity.

So Vietnam, the land of sunsets, you are a panoply of adventure, beauty, and I live in the company of heroes. I have fallen in love with your women who glide across a floor in silk without effort, they beckon, they say explore me, but I cannot. They might have loved me with that mystical fusion of yin and yang. But they glide off into the nothingness of night. I will never kiss their lips nor touch their hands. I will love them, shed blood for them, but I will never know them. Their scent remains with me to this day, creating an almost physical union. I wish I could hold them and make love. But this is a deception created by the novels of D.H. Lawrence in the stillness of night and my imagination on a forgotten hill in Vietnam.

Thinking of women always leads me to Marsi, the women I love, and the women I could have loved. Will I ever know better physical love than from my dreams of passionate lovemaking while sitting on a rock ledge in a tropical jungle? Why is physical love a fixation for warriors? The act of sex is an affirmation of life. Abstain from physical love, and you know something of death.

I leave my ledge and return to the platoon. The night wraps around me like a blanket of forgetfulness.

14

Scrounger

Do not weep, maiden, for war is kind,
Because your lover threw wild hands toward the sky
And the affrighted steed ran on alone,
Do not weep.
War is kind.

— Stephen Crane, "War Is Kind"

29 Nov 1968
West of Firebase Bastogne
1000 hours

Our battalion rotates out of the mountains and assumes a mission of interdicting NVA resupply from the villages along Highway 1, the route the French called "La Rue Sans Joie," "The Street Without Joy." Quirin calls Top and me to his command post. The battalion has an upcoming annual government inspection and we will have to explain the 15 M-16s we had to bury in the A Shau, and document all government property lost or damaged. We have two weeks to create the records that document what the company has done over the past year. Quirin tells Top he wants him to focus on the inspection and he wants me to become a scrounger, flying around Vietnam trying to get better food for the company. The 1/327 will now be on duty conducting ambushes and guarding Highway 1.

After six months in the field, my new job will be to go all over Vietnam on the division's choppers and establish a network to circumvent regular supply channels. I am to raise money from the men and go to the Da Nang PX and buy sodas, beer, snacks and hot sauce. I am to find Seabee units and trade the weapons we have captured from the NVA for steaks, ribs, ham, etc. All the food I find is to be stockpiled at battalion and company HQ.

At Camp Eagle, Top quickly immerses himself in recreating the unit's supply history over the past year. He has lost all his excess weight, probably 80 pounds. He weighs 200 and can press two times his weight.

It is fantastic to have a shower once a day, wear clean uniforms, and in time cure my jungle rot. With $500 and a clean uniform, I go to the division LZ to hitch a ride to Da Nang. The Da Nang PX seems to be the largest supermarket in the world, and the captain who runs the PX is more than willing to give me a special deal on sodas and beer. The Seabee mess hall has food that rivals the incredible hamburger my father bought me at The 21 Club when I graduated from Penn. The senior NCOs are delighted to trade hundreds of pounds of steaks for a duffle bag of AKs. Traveling up and down the north coast of Vietnam from Huc and Da Nang, I soon create a new supply line for D Company and the 1/327.

It is also an opportunity for me to see the many faces of this war. The Marines fight their own way around Khe San and Hue; the 1st Division in the south conducts ambushes to trap Victcong in the muddy Mekong Delta; the 101st faces fully supported North Vietnamese regulars in valleys forgotten for 100 years. Division headquarters, the Navy and the Air Force all fight different wars.

The Air Force officers' clubs are the strangest places. There is the atmosphere of The Lafayette Escadrille about them. The Lafayette Escadrille was a famous American air squadron that volunteered to help the French fight the Germans in World War I, before the U.S. joined the war. I remember seeing aviators in old movies who looked like Errol Flynn, clad in elegant scarves and irregular uniforms, toasting with champagne at night only to die in a dogfight the next day. Today's aviators live well; they all have their own versions of a uniform, their way of retaining their personal identity. But each day someone does not return from a mission, and a new man takes his place. Their war is made all the more hideous because it is fought in what seems to a foot soldier like an elegant setting. Fighter pilots may live in elegance but they suffer arbitrary, horrible deaths. Facing anti-aircraft fire is more like experiencing artillery than a firefight.

I am back from two days of scrounging and worn out, but 500 pounds of beef and two cases of Tabasco sauce are on the way to D Company. I have loved my break from the field. Some of the best moments of my life are spent in Vietnam. The company's tents are empty since its men are in the field. Only one tent has lights, where five men are on their way to R&R. I stop by the CP to check on Top, who is trying to make sense of a bunch of records for the annual inspection. He is not happy, since he hates paperwork. I leave the lion in his cage and go to the tent where a party is in progress.

Sgt. Sizemore and four others are on their way to Australia. They are already on their second case of beer. They've been drinking 7 and 7 boilermakers. Sizemore asks me to join them and I grab a beer. One member of 3rd Platoon, sitting quietly in a corner, is a Hispanic corporal I'll call Rodriguez. Cpl. Rodriguez leads the 2nd Squad. He is a brave man, but he never says anything, he just does what he is told. Sizemore is telling me what he is going to do in the world when he gets back from Nam, telling me he wants to go to college on the GI Bill, when a bottle smashes against the back of my head. Glass shatters everywhere and blood covers my face, and Sizemore yells to look out. I turn around and dodge a broken bottle that Rodriguez is trying to shove into my face.

The tent is still, and it seems everybody is moving in slow motion. Rodriguez is circling me and shouting, "You son of a bitch, Lieutenant. I'm a fucking lifer. You gonna leave the Army but I'm gonna stay. You fucked me. I've missed my second chance to get my sergeant stripes. You like boys, Lieutenant Asshole? You got your favorites. You promoted Ebert, and Ebert is a cocksucker. He suck your cock, Lieutenant?" At that moment, Sizemore and the other three men grab Rodriguez's arm that is holding the bottle. A scuffle begins.

Where did this come from? Rodriguez is a good man, a good soldier. I could have him court-martialed, and his Army life could be over for this stupid tantrum. Rodriguez's body rises straight off the floor. Top lifts this 160-pound block of muscle by his shirt. Rodriguez is cursing in Spanish, kicking and punching, but Top chokes him with his other hand until Rodriguez calms down. Then he starts to cry. Top is yelling, "You stupid little sack of shit. Don't you know how the Army works? Thompson, your platoon sergeant, recommends you for promotion to me; I take his recommendation to the lieutenant. You fuck, you should be dead." Top coldcocks Rodriguez and throws him out of the tent. He yells to Sizemore to dump him head first in the shitter.

Top and I are alone. He hands me a towel and a beer, and I wipe the blood off. Top looks at me and says, "Rodriguez is a good man but he has a bad temper." For me, the problem is that Rodriguez is not really angry with me, he is angry with someone who humiliated his father or grandfather. Rodriguez's life is literally now in my hands. Top looks me straight in the eye. When Top was Rodriguez's age he probably would have made the same mistake. I reply, "Top, in college I was a cheap date— one drink and I start bumping into things and breaking glass bottles. Thanks for the towel." A smile briefly crosses Top's face. "Goodnight, Top." I try to walk to my tent with as much dignity as possible. Two months later, Top recommends that Rodriguez be promoted to sergeant. I hand Rodriguez his stripes; he salutes but never speaks to me.

While Top and I are dealing with the problems of a government inspection, Quirin pulls off a miracle. D Company is in the midst of walking out of the mountains to Highway 1. En route, the company walks into an NVA battalion HQ and hospital. Quirin withdraws the company without alerting the enemy and calls in an air strike, artillery and gunships. The result is the elimination of an NVA company that guarded the HQ. D Company assaults the NVA base to survey the damage and count bodies. That type of an operation would never have occurred under Career or Flattop. When Quirin commanded D Company, it had a vacation from death.

It is a beautiful evening in Camp Eagle. A full moon rises and it is a cool night without rain in the monsoon season. Top is handling the paperwork and suggests I go to the officers' club for the evening. When the sergeants major come around, a young lieutenant is an embarrassment. Our officers' club is made out of plywood, but it is stained like mahogany with knotholes. We have a bar with a mirror and tables and chairs, and there are plaid tablecloths. You can have potato chips and other snacks with your drinks; it is an island of civilization. A major is sitting at a table alone. I join him. No one else except a bartender is in the BOQ tonight. The major is tan and has the 101st patch on his left arm and a Special Forces patch on his right shoulder. He cannot weigh more than 160 wiry pounds. He has a fierce scowl and the sad eyes of someone haunted by his past.

He is drinking bourbon—glass after glass. I am drinking beer slowly. He becomes another person; in minutes, he transforms from melancholy to furious. He is shouting at me as if I had been the cause of all his anguish. His anger surprises me but I remain silent.

Slowly the story emerges. He was captain at the Special Forces base at Ta Bat when they were overrun. He is the only survivor, and this is an embarrassment for the commanding officer of all the U.S. advisers. He has a job in division but he wants to know what the A Shau is like now. What did we do on the Dong So? What remains of Ta Bat? I try to tell him but he is incoherent, trying to belittle me. He orders me to take a company and lead it back into the A Shau. I tell him about Company D's experience, and he ridicules me for a lack of courage. The bartender calls someone at division and a jeep arrives. We load the 10-year major in a seat and he is taken back to his quarters in a cloud of dust. I smell urine and notice he has pissed in his pants. He is medicating his depression with alcohol, and the outcome for him will be worse than the deaths of his soldiers. The Special Forces major is what the Army calls the walking wounded. A person's dependence on something external can lead to tragedy. The odds of overcoming life's trials are low enough: cancer, death of a child, parental abuse, a spouse's infidelity, a car crash. If you try to face such a crisis burdened with a severe dependency, your survival odds drop sharply.

I will learn this costly lesson myself. In the future traumas of my life, I, like the major, will use alcohol to escape the ghosts of the A Shau, the kisses of death. But unlike the major, I will hide it from others.

15

Christmas, 1968

"Being deeply loved by someone gives you strength,
while loving someone deeply gives you courage."

— Lao Tzu

22 Dec 1968
1/327 HQ south of Camp Eagle
1000 hours

I t is almost Christmas and Top is back in the field. My
scrounging adventure is over and we pass the government
inspection. It is hard to have the spirit of Christmas when
you are in the jungle and death is at your back door. I have been
temporarily assigned to battalion HQ and am learning to be an
S-2 (battalion intelligence officer). In that capacity, I visit other
platoons of our battalion that have recently had contact with the
enemy. On Dec. 22, one of our platoons carries out a successful
ambush in the hills north of Phu Bai. As usual, the claymores
do their job. I visit the site and we grab the heads of the NVA,
decapitated by the claymores, and set up a bowling alley on the
jungle trail.

Why do I permit it? Is it a way to show myself that I am not
afraid of my enemy? Is it a show of defiance, an act of vengeance
for all the men who have been shot and wounded before, or is it
the scream of a warrior in the heat of battle that confirms that

he can laugh at any death including his own? The horrific can be something that creates bravado. It is why some of my men secretly eat the flesh of NVA dead with their long-range patrol rations. I pick up a head and grab the hair. It is matted with blood and has the scent of burned brains. I touch pieces of skull that are sharp as glass as I concentrate on our bowling pins, the half dozen stakes placed haphazardly in the mud 10 feet in front of me. Mechanically, I swing my arm back and roll the head forward on the ground. About half way it hits a rut and bounces to the left, missing all the stakes. I would have done better to throw it like a grenade. The only way to excuse this behavior is to make a joke, for humor can take some of the pain out of war.

I feel something snap. It is the remembered scent of my machine gunner dead in the A Shau, of Stanchfield, who may have died in my arms, or my other friends whom I will never see again. I am panicked and short of breath. I admit the enemy dead have souls; they are warriors just like me. The man whose head I just bowled probably has a family. I do not feel guilty, but I salute the enemy dead. They fought well. My enemy is more like me than all those American soldiers who support us in the field, the ones we call REMFs, rear echelon motherfuckers. He is more like me than someone who dodged the draft back home. If the NVA succeed in killing me, they are welcome to bowl with my head. My eagle will fly above that game and scream our defiance. I pick my weapon up and check to see if the security is out and claymores are in place. I only feel secure looking down the barrel of my M-16 as it dances a cobra's dance in front of a jungle. It is an inauspicious way to begin a reunion with my child bride.

It is our resupply day and I am going on R&R to meet Marsi in Hong Kong. Quirin has given me money and a mission. We will split the cost but I must buy a gold Dunhill lighter that we will give to Top. Quirin will rotate out of country by the time I return. The helicopter lands in a clearing, and I hop on after the supplies are unloaded. The helicopter rises. Quirin is on the LZ, dressed the same way I first saw him, fatigue pants and a green T-shirt—no rank. Some people do not need to wear insignia. I give him a salute but he is too busy directing the resupply to notice. Goodbye, my captain.

I'm a skinny 126 pounds, down from my pre-Vietnam 165. My arms and legs have the open sores of jungle rot. What will Marsi, my 20-year-old wife, think? We have not seen each other for six months, and I have aged 20 years. What will she think of a man who spends the afternoon bowling with the heads of men just killed and tells jokes, and likes it? It is a hurried trip to Saigon since the Army does not waste its soldiers' time when there is a war.

At the 101st base camp near Saigon, I call Lt. Stein, a quartermaster officer who was part of our Vietnam orientation training. He has put on 15 pounds since I last saw him six months ago and must be 40 pounds over his ideal weight. He is going to show me what I have been missing—the real Saigon. I hope we are going to a fancy hotel for a meal on the rooftop where we can watch the ambushes around the city at night. But this is not to happen. Stein has a jeep and a driver, and he is a connoisseur of Saigon's whorehouses. His entire tour of duty has been a vacation interspersed with hours of dull paperwork. His most important problem is that artillery keeps him awake at night. I tell him I do not want to screw a whore. I am meeting my wife tomorrow. He looks at me as if I have two heads. All night he says, "It's two days since I got laid and I am horny as hell. It will only take me a minute. Get some practice before you see your wife." We go to a bar. The Temptations are the soundtrack and there are beautiful girls in ao dais dancing, their arms rising and falling in time with "My Girl." Most of them cannot be older than 16. Stein makes his arrangements quickly and disappears upstairs. Three young girls come and sit with me and I order beers for everyone. They want to know what I do. I look at them and I see heads of the same shape that I bowled with yesterday. They ask me if I like boys. Why not have a quick boom boom? Fortunately, Stein returns with a flushed face.

We get into the jeep and drive to a riverside restaurant. I order a bottle of Batard-Montrachet. It is a beautiful place beside the water with white tablecloths, crystal and silver. The moon rises and reflects on the water, and the scent of French Vietnamese cooking is everywhere. The women around me seem like goddesses in silk ao dais and each table has arrangements of tropical flowers. The food is fantastic—a garlic crab dish. I listen

as Stein extols the excitement of Saigon. The moon, the scent of
women, the flowers and the alcohol have their effect. We drive
back to the base camp in silence. How can a world of violent
death and an evening as beautiful as this exist side by side?

The flight to Hong Kong takes forever. We land in the evening
on a runway that seems to jump out of the harbor, surrounded
by a sea of lights. I leave the plane with 150 GIs on R&R. Most
of them will be drunk for five days. There is a dark-green Rolls
Royce waiting for me with the sign "Lieutenant Newhall." The
car has glass vases with orchids suspended near the windows. A
uniformed driver stands by the car with a silver bucket, a bottle
of Dom Perignon champagne. He hands me a glass.

Marsi sits in the car dressed in a yellow ao dai. Her dark
brown hair like a crow's wings brushes against her cheek. She
has the scent of youth, beauty and total innocence combined
with a perfume that is almost as exotic as our surroundings. She
is chattering constantly about her parents, our dogs, and her
college classes at Goucher. I inhale the champagne's aroma, lean
back against the leather seats of the Rolls and enjoy the moment
in full. I realize then that Marsi and I will live in separate worlds,
and we must find a way to bridge them if we are to make our
marriage work.

Jason Meyer, the new husband of Marsi's godmother,
has arranged our five days in Hong Kong. He owns hotels
throughout the southern United States, has met hotel owners
around the world and knows the owner of The Peninsula. He
flew with Gen. Claire Chennault and the Flying Tigers early in
World War II, flying across the hump from Burma to bomb
Hong Kong, which was still occupied by the Japanese. He later
flew for Pappy Boyington as part of the Black Sheep Squadron.
It was a squadron of insane, highly decorated killers.

Jason told me the story of how he ended up with Pappy.
Chennault had given him leave. Jason was a wild man. He put
on his dress whites, rented a speedboat and bought an iced
chest of Dom Perignon. He decided to water ski up the Ganges
in his dress whites. He gulped champagne and threw half-empty
bottles over his head, creating arcs of champagne. Ultimately, he
saw a formal party of senior officers in whites. He threw away his
rope and slid through the party, knocking over tables, and ended

up in the pool with a partially consumed bottle of champagne in his hand. Gen. Joseph "Vinegar Joe" Stilwell had been giving the party for Chennault. Stilwell and Chennault walked over to Jason, who had started talking with some pretty young lady. Chennault said, "With all your animal spirits, Lieutenant, I am sending you up to fly with Pappy Boyington and the Black Sheep. Perhaps that will calm you down." The Black Sheep were the most decorated warriors in the Pacific. They were also the craziest.

The lobby of The Peninsula is all polished marble, sparkling chandeliers and gleaming gold. We are given a suite overlooking Hong Kong Harbor, and when we get off the elevator a young boy in a bellman's uniform runs ahead to open the door to our suite. Hong Kong Harbor stretches before us, an ever-changing display of lights. We undress and fumble our way through clumsy lovemaking that lasts no more than 15 minutes. Our desperate haste springs from the knowledge that this is only a momentary intermission in the war. Living to enjoy R&R does not mean you go home and each of us is aware of this, although it is unspoken between us. About eight days from now I will be in another firefight where I again will wash my hands with blood, but the memory of Marsi in Hong Kong will give me the courage and strength to survive.

Each day in Hong Kong is a new experience. The Tiger Balm Garden, created by a Chinese entrepreneur, is an Asian Disneyland. We call to each other over brightly painted concrete dragons and tower over the Chinese around us. The sun is out and the weather is cool, and we are in love and cannot stop touching each other. We wander through the streets of Hong Kong. Marsi asks why I am frowning, and I make a joke about the dogs for sale in the food market. She loves dogs and cannot stand that they are being sold as food. She thinks my joke is in poor taste and punches my arm and hits the shrapnel. I swear. My hands are cold. She does not realize that she hurt me.

For lunch we go to one of Hong Kong's floating restaurants where the fish are kept in pens beside the restaurant. The meal is delicious and we share a bottle of Meursault. We are both having clothes made. Marsi picks out a brocaded silk for an evening dress, and I am having several suits made. It is my hope to go to business school after Vietnam, and we both hope I will have the chance to wear my business suits at Harvard.

To be young and in love in the exotic surroundings of Hong Kong is a feast for the heart and a joy forever. To this day when I am facing a crisis I look back on those few days, for they were some of the happiest of my life with Marsi. Love can transform hell into a Garden of Eden. My young wife has stolen my soul and I am naive enough to believe that I can keep her from harm by letting her feed upon my heart. She has truly given me a kiss that I can build a dream on. But it will not be enough and she will disappear like ashes on the wind. Was I selfish to take her as my wife, the anchor that will pull me back from war? I know that if love is not a soft place to land, it is not love. Yes, Marsi has given me a soft place to land. What I do not know is that it will destroy her. Years later I will discover her frustration in being a young bride, how she wished she could go to parties, and make love to young men who were untouched by the ghosts of war. In Vietnam I do not know what the future will bring, and all I seek is the touch of a woman's hand across my forehead that will shield me from my sins and give me peace.

We shop for Marsi's engagement ring. We delayed buying a stone for it until we could go to Hong Kong. Jason helped us since he knows the man who used to buy for Gump's in Hong Kong. Our jeweler is a courtly white-haired man, perhaps 60 years old. He has graceful hands. With a flick of his long, slender fingers, he makes a felt pad seem to unroll by itself on his desk. The stones materialize out of a rosewood tray that a beautiful Chinese girl brings him. We select an emerald because this is the stone that Marsi loves, although it is as fragile as she is.

That night we dine on Peking duck and 10 other courses. Tropical flowers add an erotic scent to our evening. We return to the hotel suite to watch the ships move across Hong Kong Harbor and drink champagne. We make love looking at the stars. After our lovemaking, there is a moment when there is no time. We fall asleep in each other's arms. Hong Kong is a kaleidoscope of color and excitement and a soft bed for lovers.

On the evening of the third day we are invited to a cocktail party at the owner's suite on the top floor. It is a Hong Kong party—expatriates from everywhere. We meet a sveltely groomed old gentleman with a white mustache. His expensive clothing is threadbare, for he is a white Russian who fled to Hong Kong with his parents after the Russian Revolution to an everlasting winter of lost dreams. British officers are in dress uniforms. They sport muttonchop sideburns straight out of Rudyard Kipling. They live in the illusion that their empire will last forever. The most beautiful Asian women are there in their silks, moving across the room effortlessly. An overweight Chinese is pawing a beautiful Caucasian blond girl who looks like a Texas cheerleader. There is even a gentleman in a Red Army uniform who spends most of his time at the bar looking disdainfully at the capitalist pigs. Marsi is bored, but we meet a young Australian couple and make a date for dinner the next night.

On our last night we have dinner at the new Mandarin Hotel across the harbor with Peter and Margo Natress. Peter is a young gynecologist from Perth. He and his new bride are vacationing in Hong Kong. Marsi is wearing her beautiful yellow ao dai. Peter orders a bottle of Chateau Yquem with dessert. Peter knows several Australians serving in Vietnam and we drink a toast to them. Marsi spills some sauterne on the ao dai, staining it. My flight is at 0600 the next morning.

That last night, we talk about the time we made love in the woods when she was still in college. There were people 50 feet away from us but they did not see us hidden behind the bushes. Marsi contained her cries of passion. We were totally absorbed in our lovemaking, oblivious to the world. Now, despite our hunger and desire, we are impotent knowing this may be the last time we touch each other. My mind is already back in the A Shau Valley. We do not speak. We turn away from each other and face the walls. I think I hear Marsi crying. I lean over to touch her but she is asleep—or feigning sleep. I do not sleep, frustrated by my inability to express my physical love for her.

The morning arrives in what seems like seconds and we rush to the airport. Marsi must say goodbye in the lobby since civilians cannot go to the gate. We both show a stiff upper lip. It is as if time stands still as we look at each other for a last time, then I pass through the doors to the gate that leads to Vietnam.

It is to be one of the most difficult goodbyes of my life. Within 15 minutes, we are airborne, en route to Vietnam. Young love is a feeling of floating. Your senses are confused and at times it can be hard to breathe. Does it make sense to have a glimpse of this while you are fighting a war, or is it a joke played on you by one of the mad gods?

Those nights we spent together, the touching, the sense of our bodies, maybe they were real. But perhaps they were not.

16

Curly and The Reporter

What place do "courage," "comrades," "loyalty" and,
above all, "sacrifice" have in the world? ... Selfishness had
replaced sacrifice, profit had been placed before patriotism,
loneliness before companionship. ... They realized in their
bones, which we know with our minds, that the war had
a turning point, at which civilization reached a high water
mark,and then receded towards barbarism.

— Nigel Jones, "The War Walk"

25 Jan 1969
Village south of Camp Eagle
1200 hours

The descent into Saigon does not seem as exciting as when I first arrived in country. The plane banks and descends quickly to the runway. The pilot does not want to run the risk of a shoulder-launched missile from a house near the runway. I wait at the airport to catch a flight back to Da Nang in order to avoid another one of Lt. Stein's Saigon tours.

A lot can happen in a week. Maj. John Hubbard, the son of friends in Baltimore, has requested me for division intelligence. Hubbard is a career Army officer and a West Point graduate. He is a direct descendant of Thomas Jefferson and looks like Jefferson with a flattop. Unlike their famous ancestor, Hubbard's family has served in the military for generations. The MacArthurs, the Pattons, the Pershings, the Stilwells, the Lees and the Hubbards are part of a vanishing breed of gentlemen military career officers. I have been privileged to meet several representatives of these families. Pershing's grandson was killed a few months earlier when he was serving as a platoon leader with the 101st. I often wonder who will guard our country when this breed of warriors becomes extinct.

Hubbard's request prompts our new battalion commanding officer, Col. Smith (call sign: Big Daddy), to give me a job in battalion headquarters. Smith is over 6 feet tall with jet black hair. He is extremely fit and a good war leader. He will eventually award me a Bronze Star for valor and a Purple Heart, both earned in the A Shau Valley. He encourages all his officers to excel and tries his best to help their careers. He accepts failure, but God help you if you do something that violates an officer's code of conduct. He is a man I would follow anywhere.

Unlike World War II, where you stayed for the duration, it is a common practice in Vietnam to rotate off-line after six months. It's the Army's way of preserving enough officers with combat experience so that there are enough captains to command companies who have some idea of what they are doing. The odds of surviving 12 months walking third in line are poor. Short combat tours also reduce civilian complaints about the war.

Quirin has left me a note: "Chuck, I talked Col. Smith into giving you a permanent job as battalion S-2. It's a captain's job. At division you will be carrying coffee and running errands but at the battalion level it will be your show. You will learn more if you work at it, and in case you make the Army a career, this job will help you. If the Army is not your career, this will help you. Best of luck, Peter."

It is nice to be wanted at division headquarters but the choice is not hard. At the battalion level I can stay in touch with my platoon, perhaps work with them again, and Top is still here. The only unpleasant surprise is that I find my old friend Sgt. Curly is serving as the acting S-2. I watch him deliver a briefing. All he cares about is sucking up to the colonel. The battalion sergeant major, one of Top's friends, is there as well, and it seems to me that he is not pleased with Curly's performance.

After Smith and his executive officer (XO) leave to get some sleep, I am left as the officer on duty to monitor company radio activity. The sergeant major asks if I knew Curly in the A Shau. Curly smirks and gives me a look of utter disrespect, and says to the sergeant major, "Yes, our young lieutenant was one of the heroes of that cakewalk in the A Shau, ducked a few artillery shells. No one was killed and he will probably get a medal."

I am monitoring the radios, but within a fraction of a second I'm in midair aiming to kill that chicken-shit Curly. The two RTOs pin me to the wall. The sergeant major, red faced, shouts expletives at Curly. The sergeant major has Curly in a half-Nelson. The sergeant major whispers something in Curly's ear and he deflates like a balloon and leaves the bunker. The sergeant major is mad and tells me, "Officers do not fight with enlisted men." He seems to think for a moment and says, "But you did do a good job on the hill." The next morning the sergeant major has a smile on his face. Smith has transferred Curly to another battalion, and he left ours at 0500. I never see Curly again. It is obvious that the senior NCOs have struck again, sending Curly someplace in the rear where he will tell war stories at the NCO club, harass recruits and disgrace his uniform. I think back on Capt. Flattop, Capt. Career and Sgt. Curly; sometimes the greatest threat to a band of brothers comes from within. It is a lesson I will see repeated again and again before it sinks in. The enemy within can be far more dangerous than the enemy without.

One day I am being driven to a neighboring village. It is warm and sunny, a beautiful day on Highway 1, the street without joy. Women, men and water buffaloes are working in the rice paddies beside the road. We are driving behind a 2½-ton Vietnamese truck carrying supplies from some point to another. It is about 100 meters in front of us. There is a great explosion and a huge cloud of dust. Wheels are blown off the truck, gasoline is ignited, flames are everywhere. I hear the screams of men trapped inside the truck as I rush to help them.

The A Shau Valley has stalked me and caught me unaware because I have been careless. My hands shake as I start to swing my rifle, looking for snipers. The truck has run over a landmine that was meant for me. Another 30 seconds and I, not some poor Vietnamese civilian, would have been burned alive. I try to breathe. That night I do not sleep. In my mind, I stand sentry duty in the A Shau, as I will do many nights for the rest of my life.

One of my first experiences as S-2 occurs at the battalion HQ in a small village on Highway 1 on the road to Phu Bai. Our job is to prevent the NVA from getting to the village and confiscating rice, raping women and stealing whatever they want. I learn the cost to civilians who oppose the North. A beautiful young villager, the wife of an ARVN soldier, is eight months pregnant. One morning we find her; she has been raped by NVA soldiers. After they are finished with her they strip her, nail her to a tree, then they use a knife to rip out the fetus and nail it between her split legs. Bound and gagged with her entrails hanging out, she bleeds to death. We find her in the morning covered with flies. I write a note to her husband in the field. The NVA kill and torture civilians in our area of operation virtually every week.

Our approach is to encircle the village at night and set ambushes. Our ambushes have contact once or twice a week. We leave the dead NVA naked on a berm along Highway 1. Many of the villagers take their own form of vengeance. At one point we have 10 to 15 bodies in various levels of decomposition. The raids on the village decline and the village women are safe. The one problem is that there are too many villages and too few American soldiers. We receive orders to move to a new location and our village must manage on its own. It returns to a ritual of robbery and rape. To know this certainty is more than I can stand.

Our new battalion HQ is outside Phu Bai. It is the middle of monsoon season. It rains every day, and our sandbag walls collapse. Everyone is drafted to fill new sandbags and repair defenses. It is a quiet time. We patrol and patrol. We set ambushes, but the NVA have departed. Undoubtedly they have left for a base camp in Laos or Cambodia. Why fight if the weather is unpleasant, when you are fighting for the newspapers?

Occasionally, we are fortunate in intelligence. We find a Chu Hoi (North Vietnamese defector) who willingly leads us to an infiltration route. I ask Col. Smith, Big Daddy, if I can take Sgt. Dillon and my old 3rd Platoon to see if we can make use of this information. Smith gives me permission.

We leave around dusk from Loc Tri and travel across rice paddies to an outlying cluster of houses with a village street. We believe the NVA come into the village around midnight or just after. I am in the middle of the village street at 1900 trying to set the machine guns so that there can be no harm to the village. It is curfew, but three Vietnamese men are hurrying past our platoon. An AK-47 reflects in the fading light. I fire and the platoon opens up. There is a blood trail but the NVA are well away in seconds. A search of the village after curfew would be a disaster, stumbling around in the dark. I am so out of practice that I blow the ambush and Dillon laughs, as do the men.

We speak in hushed voices and catch up with each other's lives. We do not sleep that night. The colonel is waiting for me at the battalion CP the next morning. I salute and he shakes his head, winking at me as he does. "Not as good as you used to be." We are putting up sandbags around the officer's tent and Smith asks me to help. If not on a combat mission, officers fill and install their own sandbags just as they go last in line for food. It feels good to fill sandbags and build a wall—a bit of physical punishment is justified.

Gregory Peck visits our battalion one afternoon. He is dressed in jungle fatigues like the rest of us. He looks just like he did as a lawyer in "To Kill a Mockingbird." He talks to soldiers throughout the battalion. We feel as if we just had a visit from a much-respected father. We feel as if we are loved, and somehow all will be right with the world.

When Gregory Peck leaves another civilian arrives. He is a reporter for the New York Times. It is clear to me that the young man I meet at the LZ is a cowboy. He is wearing camouflage jungle fatigues, the uniform of the long-range reconnaissance patrols that cross the border into Laos on a regular basis. He also has a Special Forces beret that looks ludicrous on top of hair that comes down to his shoulders. A soldier would never wear a uniform that he has not earned. That's like wearing medals that he did not earn. The colonel gives me the job of escorting this white-faced dude. The subject of his article is black soldiers in Vietnam. At the battalion CP we have the battalion staff, headquarters company and an artillery company that provides fire support for the battalion. We have plenty of black soldiers. Our reporter conducts interviews during the day and drinks in the bachelor officer quarters at night. He is unhappy; he has interviewed some 50 soldiers over the week and has not found the right black soldier.

I am receiving battalion intelligence reports from the whole division, and another unit of the 101st operating west of Hue has uncovered slit trenches filled with women and children. I am told that during the Tet Offensive the NVA rounded up the females who had husbands sympathetic to the South Vietnamese government. They copied Hitler's SS techniques during the Holocaust in which women and children were told they were being moved to another area. They arrived at their destination to find an empty field with a slit trench 12 feet across and 12 feet deep. A bulldozer stood nearby. The soldiers told all but the youngest to stand in line by the trench to await transportation to yet another location. The young women were taken aside. It was then that the machine guns opened from the wood line, killing the women lined up by the trench. The sound of the guns and the cries of the victims must have blended together in a cry to heaven. The bodies fell and then there was silence except for the cries of the wounded. The bulldozer pushed the wounded and the dead into the trench, leaving a 30-foot gap as soldiers bayoneted children. Now it was the young girls' turn to cry as they were raped and then shot by their rapists. Their bodies joined their children and their mothers in the grave. The executioners then left to join the defense of Hue against the Marines and the 101st. That battle will be depicted years later in the movie "Full Metal Jacket."

It is now 2100 and our New York Times reporter after two glasses of scotch is telling us about justice. This is an unjust war and the United States is trying to establish colonies around the world. We are interfering in a civil war. We are the war criminals. We murder, rape and steal. I ask him about the slit trenches west of Hue, how many trenches there are and how many thousands, or tens of thousands, of women and children fill them. After the war, 2 million Vietnamese will die at the hands of the North, another fact to be ignored. Our reporter replies that the trenches do not exist and if they did they are irrelevant, since Vietnam is an Asian civil war and Asians do not have the same regard for human life as Americans. He is typical of some other reporters I will meet in later life. He will not alter his opinions when they are contradicted by facts; when he writes a "factual story," it is really propaganda. The fact is that the trenches do exist and they are the real answer about the morality of the Vietnam War.

17

Medal of Honor

Ah, but a man's reach should exceed his grasp,
or what's a heaven for?

— Robert Browning, "Andrea del Sarto"

4 March 1969
Camp Eagle
1100 hours

Lural Blevins' fate still bothers me. Three times up the hill, he was wounded, and his last time up was the day after he was supposed to leave Nam. Every man who came down that hill owed his life to Blevins for each day he called the gunships and fighter support. On the last day, the day after Sgt. Herman was seriously wounded, he walked ahead of 1st Platoon so he could walk the damn bombs into the bunkers himself. He ended up covering the withdrawal of what was left of Lt. Copeland's platoon and he climbed up on one of the rocks with an M-16 to try to stop the NVA from getting to the mortars. He was shot in the head and seconds later an NVA platoon came through the staircase. His body was left behind, a violation of the 101st's first rule of war—no bodies abandoned.

He died exemplifying what is the best in mankind.

Someone has to do more than return his personal effects. Capt. Career wrote only, "I regret to inform you that your son, Sp.4 Blevins, has been killed while conducting operations in the A Shau Valley. His death upheld the highest traditions of the U.S. Army." I research how to write a recommendation for the Medal of Honor. I have to do a lot of work before sending it to a board of inquiry, and I write and rewrite and finally submit it.

Sgt. Miller, who before he was wounded served with Lt. Dave Meiggs in Charlie Company, is in charge of awards and decorations for the battalion. He calls me on the field telephone to say Blevins' award has come through. He is upset and when I arrive at his tent, he is crying. He had just received a call; Meiggs is dead. He was two months short but he refused to leave his platoon for a staff job like I did. He had a safe job, road guard duty. At night he set up ambushes and tried to catch the NVA moving into the villages around Phu Bai to steal rice. Meiggs was walking back from such an ambush on a dusty road when he tripped off a Bouncing Betty mine. The mine popped up and blew off his head. Meiggs was one of the infantry lieutenants who arrived in country with me, bound for the 101st. He was a great officer. Most of those who went to the field are now dead or wounded and evacuated to the United States. I forget about Blevins for a second. Miller has beer hidden in an ice chest so together at 1600 on a hot afternoon at Camp Eagle, we drink a toast to David Meiggs.

I stand up and am about to leave. "I forgot," Miller said, and he hands me an award sheet. It is my description of what Blevins had done on that hill in the A Shau, but the board of inquiry had downgraded Blevins' Medal of Honor to a Distinguished Service Cross. Miller takes his seat and is looking blankly at his desk. "Why?" I asked. He looks up. "It seems Blevins had a record. Men with records are not awarded the Medal of Honor." So that was the price of stealing a hubcap; your blood is not good enough for the USA. Well, perhaps that is a little hard. I hoped the DSC would give Blevins' mother something to remember Panther 1. I know I will never forget him. Much later I will learn that Blevins' family never got his DSC. That is something I will try to fix.

18

Smitty and Ted Kennedy

"The sign of a decadent civilization is to not know what is going on with a war your country is fighting."

—Francis Fukuyama, "America at the Crossroads: Democracy, Power, and the Neoconservative Legacy"

30 March 1969
Camp Eagle
1200 hours

We move to Firebase Roy, where the battalion operates beneath a mountain called Bach Ma. Bach Ma was an exclusive resort during Vietnam's tenure as a French colony. It rises 3,000 feet above sea level and on a clear day the view is spectacular. Most of the time it is shrouded in mist and 18 degrees cooler than sea level. The artillery is on a hillcrest behind us and during the day it fires continuously in support of our battalion and the ARVN units in the area.

Our battalion is on a hillock in front of the artillery. We are defended by an infantry company, and our defense line glistens with the barrels of four quad 50s—four .50-caliber machine guns that are mounted on a mobile turret and fire in unison. Four guns cover our entire forward perimeter with death. God help anyone who gets in the way. The view of the South China Sea behind us is breathtaking, as are the sunsets. The food is hot. What more can anyone want? There is a beach behind our CP. A pistol range is located in the corner of the beach and I practice every day. It is a pleasant way to spend a free hour: swim and then target practice.

In late February 1969, the 101st had returned to the A Shau. This time it is the 2nd Battalion, 501st Parachute Infantry Regiment, supported by an ARVN unit and the Marines. Several of my friends from Officers Basic Training School in Fort Benning are there and one of them is Smitty, an intelligence officer who volunteered to spend the second half of his tour as an infantry platoon leader. Smitty and I spent many a night talking about life, love and the future of mankind. He was a tall, lanky Southerner with a flattop and freckles. He was great fun to be around but he also had a strict honor code. Together we may not have solved all of life's problems, but we solved a few. I try to talk Smitty out of volunteering to lead an infantry platoon in the A Shau, but he cannot be dissuaded. He is not a career officer, but he wants to see what it is like to be a warrior. We all know that the 502nd will find the same welcome in the A Shau that the 1/327th found.

In the evening, we hear the radio transmissions in which the day's action is discussed. It is a bloody mess and Smitty dies on the third assault of that hill—Hamburger Hill. Twenty years later there will be a movie of the same name. John Del Vecchio, a Vietnam vet, will write "The 13th Valley," an account of the 101st in the A Shau, a memoir of our hills. Toy soldier sets will be made depicting the 101st assaulting Hamburger Hill; all of the soldiers will be depicted looking forward and upward, for they are trying to pick their way to the summit.

Smitty is shot in the head on the third day of the fight. I remember his smile. The 101st newspaper reports: "At Dong Ap Bia, 539 NVA are killed, individual and crew service weapons are captured, and 200 tons of bombs were dropped." But Smitty is dead, and for me another light in life goes out. About that time Sen. Edward Kennedy calls Hamburger Hill a disgrace and a humiliation. He says it was a conspiracy by officers: Enlisted men were sent up a mountain to die so officers could get medals.

The mountain has no value whatsoever for the war, a quote our press uses as the title of the article about Kennedy's speech. His speech gets lots of press attention. But I know the meaning of that hill. The A Shau was the launching ground for Tet. Own the A Shau, and there cannot be another Tet. I write a letter to Time magazine in response to Kennedy. Kennedy is on the Senate Armed Forces Intelligence Committee, and is briefed on the reason for military actions. He is speaking to those who oppose the war, but he defiles the death of my friend.

19

The Bach Ma and Drugs

But ranged as infantry,
And staring face to face,
I shot at him as he at me,
And killed him in his place.

— Thomas Hardy, "The Man He Killed"

20 June 1969
Fire Support Base Roy
1400 hours

The mountain in front of Firebase Roy, Bach Ma, continues to interest me. Every morning I get up and look at it. I cannot help but feel that the mountain is a strategic point for the NVA infiltrating the plains around Phu Bai. It connects several other valleys to the A Shau. The sensors we use on the trails soon establish a pattern of use. There are numerous instances of helicopters receiving fire from shoulder-fired missiles, and we talk to village chiefs who claim that the NVA raiding their villages come from the valley behind the Bach Ma.

Col. Paulson, our new battalion CO, gives me the OK to use a light observation helicopter (LOH) to see what we can find. The LOH is a three-seater that floats like a butterfly and stings like a bee. It carries an M-60 machine gunner in the back seat, a pilot and one passenger. As the passenger on a reconnaissance mission, my job is to know where we are all the time and have the eight-digit coordinates to call in artillery if we are fired upon. When we see movement and draw fire, I can have artillery on the way in 45 to 60 seconds. During my reconnaissance missions, we rack up kills. All of this occurs in what are called free fire zones. If we are in a free fire zone, anything that moves is the enemy.

After about three months of work we have put together a considerable amount of data. Paulson suggests I take it to division intelligence. Maj. Gen. Melvin Zais, the division commander, makes a surprise visit to the firebase when the battalion staff is out in the field. I give him a 45-minute intelligence briefing. He takes a copy of the data with him. Eventually, I drop the data at division intelligence. After I leave Vietnam, the 1/327th goes after the NVA bases behind the Bach Ma.

There is good news and bad news. Bach Ma is a successful operation. Several base camps are found and the NVA lose a valuable source of supply. But several friends I knew toward the end of my year in Vietnam, and several friends a year behind me at Penn who were assigned to the 101st, end up dead or in a veterans hospital in Valley Forge, Pa. More deaths on my conscience.

While guarding villages along Highway 1, drugs are a continual problem for us. In the A Shau, we did not have a problem with sentries. Cigarettes were in short supply, and you couldn't smoke at night and give away your company's position. You were also far from civilization so there were no children selling opium or the milder stuff.

One day we receive some good information about an infiltration route from a Chu Hoi. Second Platoon of the Cutthroats (the name of Company C) sets up an ambush. At the battalion CP we dial into the platoon leader's radio frequency. Shortly after dark the platoon leader radios that an enemy platoon is approaching. We hear the platoon open up and illumination rounds are called.

We contact the platoon leader and he is furious. One of the men in his 3rd Squad managed to buy opium and inject it with a syringe. When the NVA approach down the trail, this berserker charges them naked with a canteen cup. The NVA open up with AK-47s and the platoon returns fire, but the NVA are far from the kill zone. The private with a drug problem is nowhere to be found, but later he is discovered in a ditch, asleep and unhurt.

Perhaps the greatest problem with road guard duty is that you get careless. It is about this time that the 501st returns from the A Shau Valley. After leaving Hamburger Hill, they are given a job guarding artillery at FSB Tomahawk along Highway 1. They have taken Dong Ap Bia —Hamburger Hill—and like the 1/327 they are given a five-day stand-down, then road guard duty.

The 1/327 had an advantage. We had walked out of the A Shau but we had stayed in the hills. We managed to decompress gradually. The 501st does not have this luxury. They go from a mountain that is hard to climb because you slip on mud and blood, to a hill that overlooks a balmy ocean. Women live in the villages by the ocean so there are women to love for a few dollars, and it's easy to feel as if you are on vacation.

Just after midnight, June 19, Fire Support Base Tomahawk erupts in explosions. The firebase is receiving heavy mortar fire, the command post is hit, almost all officers are killed, and casualties are heavy. It is chaos. In the morning we drive to FSB Tomahawk. It is desolate: Bunkers are collapsed, body bags line the road, but there are no mortar craters.

We tour the perimeter and find the problem. One bunker in the line is manned by four people. Their throats are cut. There are marijuana cigarettes in their hands. A stoned guard is useless. My only lesson from this is that when you feel the safest, you are at the greatest risk. Time and time again this is a lesson that must be repeated before it sinks in. This is as true for business as it is for war.

After Tomahawk, I flip out. After weeks of peace, I am back in the A Shau Valley—sweating and suffocating, forever short of breath. It does not make sense to sleep. I cannot sleep. I walk the line at night checking on sentries, although this is not my place as battalion S-2. My rifle is with me at all times. I tell the men on sentry duty if they are not awake and alert, there will be consequences. If there is pot, the consequences will be dire. But they do not believe me. They do not know me.

Our firebase is ringed by bunkers, each manned by four men. Each man has a two-hour watch and each night the watch is the same, two hours staring into nothing. But nothing is deceiving, for who knows what lurks there. There could be an NVA battalion creeping toward you with AKs ready. They are always there, with AKs pointed at you, the sound of the shot, and the muzzle flash. I make the rounds inspecting sentries for a week. The men are awake, but tonight I approach a bunker and smell pot. My spine almost jumps out of my body. I move quietly toward the bunker. I am not aware that I am breathing. It is black night, all is quiet, and the stars are bright overhead. The still blackness of the night permeates my soul, for my heart is black. The men in front of me are asleep; they are my enemies.

I round the corner of the bunker and three men are asleep. Joints litter the ground and the man on guard duty is sprawled on his back. His mouth is open and his eyes are shut and he has a joint between his fingers. I creep forward. The sounds of the night are so loud they almost deafen me.

He is lying in front of me. He is a pig. If I had caught someone like this in the field when I was alone with my platoon, I might have killed him. His actions endanger everyone; most of all they endanger the honor of the 101st. Sentries of the 101st do not sleep. Many die when sentries sleep. I am in the valley. My rifle swings gently like the head of a snake preparing to strike. I shove the barrel of my rifle down the asshole's throat, through his gaping mouth, and hope to break his teeth. The fucking asshole cherry deserves to die for this and end up in hell. Simultaneously I drive the heel of my boot into his stomach. The bastard awakens, eyes white, as I shove the barrel deep into his throat and chamber a round. My safety is off; at least this bastard knows he has only the twitch of my finger standing between him and oblivion. He is sweating and he smells like he has shit his pants. I say nothing, trying to decide whether or not to kill him. We stare into each other's eyes as I lean on the cocked rifle and he starts to cry. He is only 18. I withdraw my rifle barrel from his throat. He rolls over on his side, sobbing. I kneel beside him. Somehow my knife is in my hand. The words come out as a whisper: "Why shouldn't I kill you, douche bag? You were trying to kill me." I draw my knife across his throat. The knife is over his eyes. He stares at the blade. It curves like an eagle's beak. I can feel the presence of the eagle over me. Again I whisper, "You are my huckleberry, Sweetie pie. If you ever do this again you are a dead man." I draw my knife over his testicles. "Do this again, Sweetie pie, and I will kill you and then eat them. Each night I will be there behind you and if you pull this shit again, you are mine." I back slowly away and fade into the dark stillness knowing that he was too scared to recognize me. I sit and watch. The sentry picks up his rifle, spits blood, and sobs to himself. His head twitches when I put my rifle back on safety. I back away from the bunker, swinging my rifle from right to left looking for muzzle flashes. A thought crosses my mind: Have I been in this country too long?

The sentry never speaks of our encounter. I stop my midnight walks checking sentries. I hear the headquarters company platoon leaders say that no one sleeps on sentry duty anymore. The next night I pull my own sentry duty hugging my rifle, and wondering whether this was an overreaction. There can be no overreaction in the valley of the shadow of death. The valley is a part of me, ready to grab me.

If drugs and alcohol are the enemies of a soldier or anyone under unusual or continual stress, so is boredom. Sgt. Jung, my Vietnamese interpreter, and I are on our morning rounds, visiting village chiefs. We stop by to see Capt. Chris Shore, a West Pointer and A Company, Assassin Company, commander. In my opinion, Shore is almost as good as Quirin. West Point does a good job controlling quality. A Company and a company of 1st Division Marines are assigned to one village. The units act like two male dogs, eyeing each other and waiting to prove who owns the territory. We share a cup of coffee with the Marine company commander and Shore when machine gun fire erupts, followed by M-16s. A major firefight is underway.

We follow Shore and the Marine company commander to a village street that is now a war zone. Marines and paratroopers are firing at each other. In the center of the street is a 101st machine gunner laying down a base of fire against the Marines. A Marine machine gunner lies 25 feet in front of him, face down in the dust, his body almost torn in half. Shore, the Marine commander and I, following at a distance, wave our arms and walk in between their men, and the shooting stops. A Marine and a 101st machine gunner had an argument about who was the quickest draw. The way to settle it is a shootout at the O.K. Corral, the two best machine gunners in each unit facing each other. Machine gun blasts mark the start of the contest, and the Marines lose. We later hear that A Company's best machine gunner is broken in rank and must spend 12 months in a stockade and another 12 months in Vietnam.

When warriors get bored, stupid things happen.

A week later I receive a letter notifying me that I have been accepted by the Harvard Business School for the Fall MBA program, Class of 1971. I am relieved and overjoyed. The letter is from Fred Foulkes, an HBS admissions director my father had introduced to me. Fred was following my military career and knew that, despite terrible board and math scores, I had a 4.0 average at the University of Pennsylvania in my major and could accomplish miracles when properly motivated.

I promise Fred that I will make him proud.

20

Two Days and a Wake Up

When Johnny comes marching home again,
Hurrah! Hurrah!
We'll give him a hearty welcome then
Hurrah! Hurrah!
The men will cheer and the boys will shout
The ladies they will all turn out
And we'll all feel gay when Johnny comes marching home.

— Patrick Gilmore

2 Aug 1969
Camp Eagle
1900 hours

Each sunset on the South China Sea is more beautiful than the last. As Nasty, my first RTO, used to say, happiness is being short. You are short when you are 30 days and counting. I am five days and counting. Someone has told me that Capt. Quirin volunteered for another tour in Vietnam, this time with the 173rd Airborne. Quirin has not returned from a long-range reconnaissance patrol he had been leading. The sunset has lost its beauty—five days and counting.

I have had three captains in life whom I have respected: Rose at Penn, Holt in basic training, and Quirin. There is no way to thank them for the wisdom they imparted to me.

Quirin is missing in action—I cannot get this out of my mind. Quirin is probably dead, and he will have no homecoming. I think of Walt Whitman's poem:

O CAPTAIN! my Captain! ...
But O heart! heart! heart!
O the bleeding drops of red,
Where on the deck my Captain lies,
Fallen cold and dead.

If there was anyone who knew what it was to be a leader, it was Peter Quirin. He believed leadership to be the art of getting men to accomplish what they believe is impossible. We used to talk about the war, and I was angry that we did not enter Laos with a surprise attack rather than act as bait. We could have landed behind them, attacked them from the front, and crushed them between us. Quirin would always say, "What you have no hope of changing, don't worry about." He did not care for medals, and promotions would take care of themselves. He always put the men's welfare before his own, but he drove them to accomplish the mission. He loved being an Army officer. He used to say that the secret of life is a mirror. When you look at it every morning, be proud of what you see, what you do, and forget the rest. His advice has done much to simplify my life. Many thanks, Peter.

Many years later, I learn that Quirin is alive and well. He made colonel and retired with two Silver Stars and a host of other decorations. He is a beloved police captain in Wisconsin. I bet he is still teaching his young cherry officers how to survive in their jungle.

It is the last time I see Top. He is sitting at a big first sergeant's desk in the company HQ in Camp Eagle. He has his beer belly back and he is flicking that gold Dunhill lighter that Quirin and I gave him. He stands at attention when I enter the room, and I nod and he stands at ease. We shake hands. He looks me in the eyes and says, "Good luck, Lieutenant," and salutes. Upon reflection, he has always called me lieutenant. He calls other officers Lt. Smith or Lt. Jones. I guess it is a compliment from the man on my right. I salute him, turn and leave the tent for my trip back to the world. He saunters to the tent's door and lights a cigarette. The gold lighter sparkles in the sunlight and he watches as we drive off. The bright sun is hidden by dust; I never see Top again. Yet when I face a life-and-death problem I

will always ask Top and Quirin: "What the hell would you do?"
Somehow, they will always be with me to answer my questions
about how to be.

The trip to Bien Hoa is uneventful. I am no longer a part of
the 1/327. I am an orphan and my identity is gone. I will never
see this family again and it hurts. My shoulder and left side hurt
from shrapnel that is still working its way out, but I am going
home. But where is home? There is a part of me that thinks home
is a cliff overlooking a jungle stream that looks like a Chinese
scholar's painting. But it is a home to which I can never return
for it is in a country haunted by the shades of friends.

Sleep is good in a bunk as sunlight streams into a BOQ beside
Bien Hoa Airport. My last moments in Vietnam are scenes in
a war movie. I remember the sergeant in Vietnam orientation
saying, "No matter what you are when you get here, you leave
a man." There is no doubt that this garden of death has burned
the fat off my soul. My last night in Vietnam, the NVA mortar
our base. It is only two rounds but I wake up sweating. This is
the A Shau telling me that there are no goodbyes; we will have
many visits on our road to the ultimate reunion. The A Shau, the
A Shau, thou art my bride. Goodbye my country Vietnam, for
which I have shed blood.

The plane's engines burn my ears and they take me away
from the A Shau, from Vietnam. How I wish I had re-enlisted. I
knew it would be this way—the yearning to stay, the yearning to
know life as it can be known only in war.

My knife is in my duffle bag. I feel naked without it; its
carefully bent blade fits the contour of my hip. Every day I have
sharpened my knife as I have cleaned my rifle. They are part of
my body, but now I have had an amputation. My rifle is in an
armory at Camp Eagle; its much-loved stock is destined for the
hands of another.

I have worn a uniform off and on from the age of 8. I have
trained, and one year I have fought. Half my life has been spent
in the company of warriors. The battles of my imagination are
as real as the battles of life but it is time to give it up, to leave
my friends, and to leave the Army that is my only family. The
military is ripe with symbolism and I am bidding goodbye to
all of that. I wanted to make the military my career but was

interested only in running special operations in the field. They don't let you do that after age 35.

One of the mysteries of life is that the rules change. The peacetime Army, the wartime Army, they have different rules. Youth, adolescence, marriage, manhood and old age have different rules. The rules of the next game are not like the rules of today's game. The continual change of the rules on every level is what makes the challenge of life. The rules of World War II expire, and then we have the Cold War, the Berlin Wall falls, the Cold War ends, and now we have wars with rogue states, terrorism and an arsenal of nuclear weapons that can be bought. When we landed at Iwo Jima, the strategy was to take the island and the rules of engagement were to shoot anyone not in an American uniform. When we invaded Iraq, the strategy was to establish a Jeffersonian democracy and the rules of engagement were don't shoot unless it is an enemy. But who is the enemy? War has changed from certainty to ambiguity.

War from the time of the Greeks consisted of armies confronting each other on the field of battle, conquering cities, and winning victories or suffering defeats, all within fixed time parameters. During the Middle Ages, Europe added the code of chivalry to war—don't kill civilians intentionally, treat prisoners well, etc. It was more honored in the breach than in the observance. The Geneva Conventions resulted. Courage is honored and the defeated are respected and helped to recover.

But there has always been another style of war, co-existing with the Greco-European gentlemen's war tradition. It is the war of the barbarians. It is a style of war that avoids violence unless odds are overwhelmingly in your favor. It is a protracted war of attrition. It is a war of deceit, cunning and expediency. It is a war in which the victors own the defeated and they are expected to rape, torture and kill them at will.

One Greek general defeated the barbarian for a while and absorbed Afghanistan willingly into his empire—Alexander the Great. The warriors of Afghanistan voluntarily fought with him in India. Alexander turned the barbarian's tactic against him. If the barbarian attacked him and killed 100, he attacked the barbarian and killed 10,000. If one of his units was attacked near a village, he burned the village, killed all of the animals and people, and then salted the earth to make the land useless. At the same time he made allies among the barbarians; rewarded, educated them, and combined them into his own forces as equals. He married a barbarian princess. The barbarian allies led Alexander to where his enemy was hiding. But his victory did not last after his death. Such a tactic cannot be followed by Western countries, unless a lot of innocent American lives disappear in a mushroom cloud.

If you fight the barbarian following the rules of the Geneva Conventions, ignoring Von Clausewitz, you will forever fight a clever, hard, deadly and dedicated foe with one arm tied behind your back. We fought this war in Vietnam. Now it is the war in Iraq and Afghanistan, and it is the war our children's children will know.

The plane taxis to the end of the runway and noise fills the cabin. I think of Jason Meyer. Here is a man I do not know well, but he has changed my life. Before leaving for Vietnam, he gave the use of his quail plantation, which was my introduction to a gilded world. It was a world of drama, because Jason was always in the midst of some crisis—a bank is in trouble, a hotel is opening. It was also a world of sensuous beauty—the plantation house surrounded by the Spanish moss hanging from live oak trees so alive and mysterious. My memories are the scent of the leather on a quail wagon and the rush of a covey of quail as they explode into the air; you blink as you look into the sun. The art, the furniture and the flowers throughout the plantation house make each moment in their midst magical. It is a world so different from the world in which I was raised. It is not that one world is better than the other; it's just that Jason's world is so alive, stimulating and deadly. In that world I live every second, as opposed to just waiting for dinner. Jason knows more than most that death is an arbitrary everyday occurrence. Jason opened the doors to Hong Kong, where I could talk with White Russians, pick my fish from a tank for dinner, or make love under the stars above Hong Kong Harbor. How can you thank someone for showing you such things exist?

Jason taught me a lesson. He flew with Pappy Boyington and Chennault, two combat legends. He survived being shot down and avoided Japanese patrols in the jungle. He walked through the valley of the shadow of death. When I saw him last he said, "Never let the bad guys get behind you." I know the bad guys now—they are the stuff of nightmares. I fight them forever.

Jason and I are the lucky ones; we think, we love, we live with more intensity than others. Our existence is arbitrary. In a way, it is our duty to live, because so many of our brothers, the real heroes, have not been so lucky. We cannot let a day pass without grasping hold of whatever there is to be done. Jason and I loved the story of Leonidas at Thermopylae. For us it was the story of the warrior's creed. We would stay up late drinking and quote the memorial the Spartan women left on the battlefield:

> Tell the Spartans, stranger passing by,
> Here according to their laws we lie.

About five years after my return from Vietnam, Jason will die from a bee sting.

Many times on the flight back to the U.S., I look out our plane's window and see reflections in it. Can they be Blevins, Noldner or Herman? The bodies of men I have killed with a knife, with a rifle, or with bombs and artillery float behind them. Why am I alive on this plane listening to the hum of engines when everyone else is dead? Perhaps when I feel up to it, and have perspective, I will bear witness to how they lived, fought and died. But forever I will feel guilty because I am alive and they are dead. I too should be dead, for it is a lieutenant's job to lead and die first.

I vacillate to this day. In the A Shau we had 20 killed and 80 wounded. We counted 500 NVA dead. A 25-to-1 ratio is not bad. In blood heat I think that no, I want 100 to 1, or 1,000 to 1, or best 1 million to 1, any bomber's dream.

But then when the heat subsides, I think of our 80 men without arms, legs or stomachs. I think of the 500 NVA dead and pray for the families who no longer have fathers, and the fate of the mothers and children. I feel as if I should take on the burden of the dead I have killed or those who died by bombs and artillery I directed.

In some way I have killed my brother warrior in an angry rage. Vietnam was not a crusade. For me it was a conscious effort to stamp out an evil that should not be. It was not a time to dance for victory; it was a time for sadness, for although my actions were justified, I will pay the price for the rest of my life. Killing marks you forever. It is a brand upon your heart. It may heal but it can never be removed. The best you can hope for is that it becomes a scar. For 30 years I will see a psychiatrist to combat post-traumatic stress disorder, as I will see other doctors to alleviate the pain that results from a back that was destroyed by a rucksack that weighed more than I did. Alcoholism, a defense against depression, will shadow me throughout my life. I will be lucky because I can pay the mid-six-figure sums of these doctor bills, but most veterans cannot, and their suffering is forgotten.

Still I cannot cry. In my ensuing life, I will encounter more traumas. Each one will bring me back to Vietnam. I will learn to cry. On some clear summer's day when something triggers a memory, Vietnam and my future traumas will all combine to leave me crying uncontrollably, as if I were seeing Marsi's death. Those around me will never understand my moments of grief.

In the future, I will vacillate between sorrow and blood lust anger. What makes it difficult today is when I see injustice—a slime ball lawyer who lets a crook go free, a CEO, a partner who betrays for greed, or a pedophile in Texas—my blood lust grows. As I age, my ability to control it diminishes. For these were the things I sought to eliminate from this earth in Vietnam. I did not succeed and could not have succeeded. I fear that someday the dam of my anger will burst, destroying the innocent and those whom I love.

On the flight back from Vietnam, I do not sleep. We stop for an hour in Tokyo but we cannot get off the plane. What have I learned in the past 12 months? The Army always talks about leadership. I do not believe leadership is complicated. At the end of the day, you must be able to look yourself in the mirror and know you have done your best. If men value you, they follow you into harm's way. They tell you everything, the doubts and passion of their soul, their hopes, their dreams, and most of all their fears. If they cease to bring you their problems, then you are no longer leading them. Leadership is eating the same food they do, wearing the same clothes, encouraging them, and always being willing to take greater risks than your men face.

Always be the last to bed and the first to rise. The mission and my men's welfare are my honor. I am privileged because I have led the best of men. Almost all of us would give up our lives to save those around us.

It is anticipating defeat that makes a man a good leader of warriors. Such a leader anticipates defeat at every corner of the road and plans a strategy to turn defeat into victory. But the skill that makes a leader of warriors survive in combat can destroy love and family in peacetime.

We fly into an Air Force base in Alaska. A great mountain covered with snow looms before us. We are allowed to stretch our legs as the plane refuels, but it is cold after Vietnam. The air is clear and crisp, the clouds are white, and it is a different world. From there we fly to San Francisco, my favorite American city, and end up at the Oakland Overseas Replacement Depot. Much of this seems unreal; these are my last hours on active duty. I am offered an instant promotion to captain if I remain in the service. I turn it down. We enter the building soldiers and leave civilians. We wear our uniforms but we must put them in storage when we get home. I leave the Army that had raised me since I was a child.

Behind me there is a shout: "Newhall." It is Capt. John McElfresh, an intelligence captain. We went through Fort Benning Basic Officer Training together. He has just returned from a tour in Vietnam. Most of his time was spent in Da Nang. He is a UVA grad and a good friend from those long, hot training days in Georgia. Many a night we would sit under a bug zapper with a glass of beer and see who could predict the next bug to be zapped. "How about a beer to celebrate?" McElfresh asks. The flight to Baltimore will leave in two hours; it is 1800. We go to the nearest bar. My uniform has three rows of ribbons, a CIB (combat infantry badge), jump wings, two presidential unit citations. John's uniform had two rows of ribbons, meritorious noncombat awards. We both have served our country with honor.

The bar we visit is crowded with college students who part to let us approach. The bartender is a fat man with a ponytail wearing an aloha shirt with a stenciled "Ban the bomb" sign. He looks at us and laughs, saying, "We don't serve your kind here." He spits on the bar. Two college students grab our arms and start to move us away from the bar. The 101st usually would rip a urinal like this out of the wall. McElfresh is alarmed; he figures my 130 pounds are no match for our football player escorts. He does not understand that I would have hurt them quickly but for his interference. Kneecaps are a good target when your opponent is big and strong. Break a kneecap and even a big guy falls to the ground. Then use the heel of your fist to drive your enemy's nose into his brain. McElfresh is a good guy, but there is no honor in allowing the bartender to get away with this.

Perhaps the point is that there are no more triumphal marches for warriors. Two thousand years ago, victorious Roman generals rode a chariot in triumph through Rome. Slaves were positioned behind the generals and it was the slaves' job to say, "Sic transit gloria mundi." The glory of the world passes quickly. For most American warriors, Vietnam is the parade's end. Today the only reason to do something is because it is right, for you receive no thanks from your country nor from most of your friends.

The Baltimore airport is empty on the morning in August when my United flight arrives. Marsi oversleeps and is 45 minutes late to meet me. I sit on my duffle bag on the sidewalk and watch the sunrise over America. It is good to be home and, as Nasty would say, "in the world again." Little do I know that I will face more wars of equal intensity. I will survive and keep my honor, but will I be alive? Such thoughts do not plague me now; they are for another day.

Tomorrow I will see my grandmother and report to her that I have returned from war with my honor intact.

Evangeline Abbott Newhall
What is honor?

Gladys Brantley Newhall
One of the most beautiful women I have ever seen.

Charles Watson Newhall Jr.
My father became a struggling
entrepreneur and a venture capitalist.

Captain Asa T. Abbott—The Fighting Cock

Abbott rode into their camp with two Army colts blazing and a sheathed saber.

First Uniforms – Father and Son

I wore a uniform on and off from the age of eight.

Shattuck 1930

I faced the Lords of Discipline at 13 and lost any fear of them.

Shattuck Dormitory

A young impressionable boy, raised in Ivanhoe's castle.

The list of those who died in the war was in the entrance hall flanked by suits of armor.

Shattuck

As cadet officers, we took our responsibilities seriously.

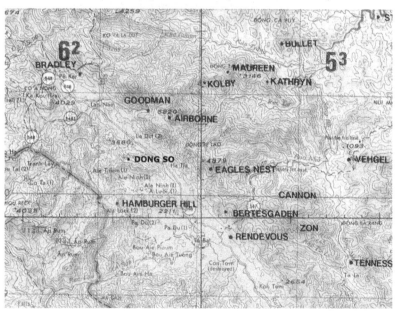

A Shau Valley

The valley borders Cambodia and Laos, and
connects Hanoi to its army in the south.

Combat Assualt

I will bear witness
to how they lived,
fought and died.

Author in Light Observation Helicopter (LOH)

The LOH is a 3–seater helicopter that floats
like a butterfly and stings like a bee.

3rd Platoon - The Heroes of the A Shau

My company is like a minnow on the end of a fishook. Minnows are expendable.

Peter Quirin

Peter believed leadership to be the art of getting men
to accomplish what they believe is impossible.

Nasty and the Author

Nasty Naylor, a corporal and RTO, is the unofficial platoon leader.

Fearful Odds

They've got to get the bird airborne as soon as possible. A sitting chopper is an easy target for a rocket propelled grenade (RPG).

Stephenson, Noldner, Nasty and Sizemore
The band of brothers is a culture of we.

On Patrol
We were pack mules in the world's largest sauna.

Head Wound

The rear of the company was ambushed while we were crossing the ravine.
Carelessly, the men took off their helmets when we stopped.
The result is devastating.

Sergeant Northcut

The last sinews attached
to his foot break. The foot
falls to the ground.

Lt. Charles W. Newhall, III
Come back with your shield or upon it.

Hue 1969

It is well that war is so
terrible, or we should
become too fond of it.

–Robert E.Lee

Hue

For many American warriors, Vietnam is the parade's end.
There are no more triumphal marches.

Hamburger Hill: Round 2

Sir: All this nonsense by Ted Kennedy about Hamburger Hill [May 30] makes me furious. I cannot see how he can make such a statement after what has been happening in the A Shau Valley during the preceding weeks. In early May, the 1/501st Infantry, 101st Airborne Division found one of the largest enemy caches in the history of the war about seven miles from Hamburger Hill. Two weeks later, the 3/187th Infantry, 101st Airborne Division found another cache almost as large three miles from Hamburger Hill. The A Shau Valley is the logistical center that keeps the rockets and mortars coming into Hue and our firebases. Shortly before Hamburger Hill, Firebase Airborne was attacked. Twenty-five men were killed and 60 were wounded by enemy sappers. The firebase was about six miles from Hamburger Hill. Last August, the artillery pieces that wiped out 40% of my platoon and plagued every step of our movement fired from that hill region.

My only regret is that I cannot put Mr. Kennedy, with all his armchair strategy, in the middle of the A Shau Valley and watch him stew as the enemy artillery rounds are landing around his head.

CHARLES W. NEWHALL III
1st Lieutenant, U.S.A.
A.P.O. San Francisco

Time Magazine, June 13, 1969

Kennedy was speaking to those who oppose the war,
but he defiled the death of my friends.

Marsi

To be young and in love in the exotic surroundings of Hong Kong is a feast for the heart and a memory forever.

Somehow, Marsi picked me out from among all those swirling young men. For her it was romantic to think of knights in armor on a battlefield of honor.

GIVE UP

You win
if you ever care

Life is its own
reward or
demise

The pain
is more real

Marsi's Diary

I, like Karenina's husband,
found the diaries.

than it should be.
Chuck is powerful in
his fineness, in his
steadfastness. He IS
LOVE + COMMITMENT

Why, just because I love
+ appreciate + need my.
+ am giving him up —
letting him go — because my
demands + aspirations are too
great on him

oh my God, my god why have
you forsaken me

Relating to other people from
one's vantage pt., from one's
insular, 1 sided sensitive
perspective viewpt. is DIFFICULT. I hate

not getting thru to M.

I'm too hard on him because I need + values his own esp-brand of understanding + uniqueness + oddballness.

Marsi, LET GO.

for the love of God

June 29, 1981
God I need you. I love you. Sustain me. Only you know what I FEEL, what I'm going thru.

As God is my witness, let Michael's soul hang in abeyance until he learns who his friends really are + DAMN HIS DIFFIDENCE.

Chuck, I need you. I need the depth of your caring. Sometimes I wonder why you put up w/ me —

An exerpt from Marsi's Diary

With Amy and the boys in the summer of 1983

Amy saved our lives.

Chuck Newhall

2013

The A Shau Garden

"Tell the Spartans, stranger passing by,
Here according to their laws we lie."

21

The Paths of Glory

The paths of glory lead but to the grave.

— Thomas Gray, "Elegy Written in a Country Churchyard"

10 July 1969
Owings Mills, Md.
6:30 p.m.

Marsi and my parents plan a party for me. They send out engraved invitations like they use for debutante parties. They read, "Mrs. Mary Washington Newhall and Mrs. & Mrs. Charles W. Newhall Jr. invite you to a small party in honor of 1st Lt. Charles W. Newhall III home from the wars." Marsi gives me a white tin pencil holder for my desk. The dark green invitation is embossed on its side.

It is a beautiful cool summer evening. The clouds are fluffy white and the sky a bright blue. Mother's garden is in full bloom and the view of Caves Valley from our hillside is breathtaking. They have invited 80 people for cocktails and hors d'oeuvres—mostly friends of my parents.

Before the party, my father asks me to put out my Vietnam souvenirs. On the display table I lay out an SKS Chinese rifle. I killed the previous owner. I also have an NVA helmet, bandoliers, claymore bags, a war picture scrapbook and a host of other things.

My father has copies of an article on Vietnam that I had written for the Baltimore Sun. My medals are on display, too: A Silver Star, a Bronze Star for valor with an oak leaf cluster, an Air Medal, an Army Commendation Medal, a Purple Heart, three campaign medals, my jump wings and, most important, a Combat Infantry Badge. I had been told I was to receive a Vietnamese Cross for Gallantry, but the paperwork never arrived.

Our guests arrive slowly. The women wear bright Lilly Pulitzer summer dresses. The men are every bit as colorful in blue blazers and white linen pants. The conversation is hushed compared with that of other parties we had given. I never see anyone so much as look at my display table. Few people talk to me and no one asks me a question about Vietnam. The guests leave quickly and the party is over in an hour and 20 minutes.

In retrospect, the party was inappropriate given feelings about the war. But to this day I keep Marsi's pencil holder. Whenever I look at it I think of the honor Marsi gave me. That kindness was all that mattered, even to this day.

In August, Marsi and I take a month-long vacation in Nantucket, before I start my first year at Harvard Business School and Marsi completes her last two years of undergraduate education at Simmons College. It is the one-year anniversary of my time on the Dong So ridgeline. Marsi's parents, the Millers, give us the use of a Nantucket cottage. We bring along our German shepherd, Sartoris.

We visit friends whose families have had houses in Nantucket since 1920. I admire scrimshaw and wander around the cobblestone streets, and Marsi falls in love with pink and purple dresses. We visit the cold beaches of Nantucket and lean into the stiff ocean breeze; the water is too cold for swimming. After Vietnam it is like being on Fantasy Island.

I do not talk about the war, but Marsi tells me how difficult my absence was for her. She was taking classes at Goucher College. The students painted a "Ban the bomb" sign on the door of our Volkswagen. Her classmates often sat apart from her; only a few would talk to her. Living with her parents was awful. She had gotten to love her freedom at Bennett, her junior college. Living with Mom and Dad was like being in high school again except that she could not date on the weekends. Most of all, she missed the touch of a man who could put his arms around her.

Nantucket is a long college weekend for us. We eat well, drink well, and enjoy being in bed all morning. Long walks on the beach and spectacular sunsets. For the first time in months I feel as if I can breathe, rest and enjoy Marsi's company. She tries hard to please me in every way. We are happy together and do not want to be apart ever again.

At the end of our vacation, we pack everything in our car and begin the long drive back to Baltimore. Just before we leave, we take Sartoris for a walk. We don't notice him drinking salt water. On the drive home through New York, we are caught in an incredible traffic jam of hippies in psychedelic buses headed south from a concert/orgy/love-in at a farm near Woodstock. Sartoris is dehydrated, and we are afraid he is dying. We feel like fools. The hippies are preventing us from saving our dog. We are held up by cars filled with free love, by thousands of people who deny our existence because of Vietnam. Eventually, we stop at a gas station and force Sartoris to drink fresh water; somehow he survives. Once home, we immediately start preparations to move to Boston.

Marsi had visited Boston before I returned from Vietnam and found the perfect apartment at 33 Chestnut. The building, which once belonged to Henry Cabot Lodge's grandfather, is made of gray granite with a three-story bow front. We have the second floor. We have a porch and a garden below us that's perfect for Sartoris. The rest of that summer in Boston is an idyll. We fill our days and nights with symphony concerts beside the Charles River, quiet walks through Beacon Hill's cobblestone streets, and countless other pleasures. I'll start at Harvard in a few weeks; it's the one MBA program in the country that accommodates English majors. Marsi is not worried about Simmons College. She is excited about learning.

My father is concerned about my preparedness for business school. Math is not my strong point. So, before school opens, I study statistics and accounting with a tutor. It is stressful because I have problems with both courses. Without tutoring, I would not have made it through the first year.

Boston and Baltimore are very different. Boston is a city of the mind, a city of entrepreneurship and federal townhouses. Baltimore is a city of comfortable living, a city of trust funds and horse farms.

Wealthy old Boston families of the day live off of the interest from their trusts. Many still tithe: 10 percent goes to charity, 50 percent goes to Uncle Sam, 30 percent is saved, and they live on 10 percent of their incomes. Capital is hardly ever drawn upon except in great emergencies. Baltimore, at least Protestant Baltimore, is the city of trust fund bums who freely spend their forebearers' last few cents. They marry rich women from out of town, wear pink coats to the Hunt Ball and perpetuate their lives as country squires. When we go to a Baltimore party, the conversation centers around which horse won which point-to-point race, who has committed the faux pas that will mean ostracism from the community (cheating at golf, getting caught sleeping with your best friend's wife, or getting unpleasant articles written about you in the newspapers).

In Boston, the conversation at parties varies greatly: How important are the Luminists of 19th-century America compared to the French Impressionists? How is the American style of painting unique? Should we believe museum curators who say that French Impressionism is the only thing that matters when it is a worldwide phenomenon? Are Pol Pot's executions in Cambodia as serious a crime against humanity as Hitler's concentration camps? What is the real plan to renew the Back Bay and is it founded on a sound promise of economic reality? The question that is most on everyone's mind always seems to be, what company will be Boston's next new thing?

Another thing differentiating Boston parties from Baltimore's is the mix of people. In Boston we have all ages. In the parties we attend given by the North Shore's grand dame Catherine Coolidge, there will be Nathan Pusey, the president of Harvard; a student poet who has just published a controversial book against the Vietnam War; several mutual-fund managers; a lawyer; an artist who is doing a show; and of course, beautiful women, Radcliffe graduates, who can comment knowledgeably on all of the subjects. This is the first lesson from Boston. There are three levels of conversation: the arts and sciences, business and geopolitical events, and entrepreneurship.

Baltimore's parties are homogenized milk. Partygoers tend to be graduates of a mixture of private schools in the area. Their idea of diversity is to mix members of the classes of '68 or '69, or pushing the envelope and including a few souls from the class of '70. There are no next new things in Baltimore.

Being dumped from Vietnam and Baltimore, into one of these rarified Boston parties is like encountering a hallucinogenic drug. I hear the repartee across a table that holds 20, set with flowers and 18th-century silver, and realize for the first time in my life that this is how some people spend their Sunday afternoons instead of watching football games. Art is an integral part of Boston life. Marsi and I thrive. We absorb Boston like a sponge absorbs water.

22

Boston Brahmins

My dear, dear girl ... we can't turn
back the days that have gone.
We can't turn life back to the hours
when our lungs were sound,
our blood hot, our bodies young.
We are a flash of fire – a brain, a heart, a spirit.
And we are three-cents-worth of lime and iron
– which we cannot get back.

— Thomas Wolfe, "Look Homeward, Angel"

19 Sept 1969
Boston, Mass.
6:30 p.m.

Something wonderful happens to Marsi after we move
to Boston. She is going to Simmons College to finish a
four-year degree in English literature, and her mind
opens like a flower. I am busy studying for Harvard, but when
I take a breath, Marsi comes to me with breathless questions.
What is the meaning of Rembrandt's "Polish Rider," an enigmatic
young soldier portrayed against a dark and threatening skyline?
Is he a Tartar fleeing Christian scouts, or is he a Polish rider
expecting a Tartar ambush? Then we change the subject and
discuss Tolstoy's "Anna Karenina." Anna is a young, beautiful
girl challenged by aspects of life such as faith, marriage, fidelity,

the role of family, and the role of women in society. The book takes place in mid-19th-century Russia, a world in which social values are rapidly changing. The concerns that the book raises—including those of deceit, carnal desire and jealousy—will become the leitmotifs of Marsi's life as all of our values are questioned and our world turns upside down. But in the beauty of a Boston fall, the quiet of winter snow, the rush of spring, and a summer by the cool ocean, we ignore the difficult aspect of these concerns because we have been adopted by a group of Boston Brahmins who will teach us far more than Harvard or Simmons.

Linzee Coolidge, Marsi's distant cousin through the Speer family of Pittsburgh, graciously invites us to his mother's oceanside estate on Coolidge Point north of Boston. He introduces us to the Brahmins, families who have created success over many generations and epitomize the value system of the men who won the Revolutionary War—duty, honor, country.

He takes us to a friend who collects American Luminist paintings. On the walls are the magnificent works of Fitz Hugh Lane. Beneath the paintings are the sharp lines in mahogany and satinwood of the best examples of New England federal cabinetmaking. The paintings are of the American sublime, forgotten by museums and curators who believe the only real art is modern and contemporary. I remember Top Hansen's advice to me in Vietnam: "Art is a refuge from an insane world. Don't let curators transform art into bigotry."

In 1970, anti-war sentiments are at their peak in Boston. I believe I am a patriot, but as I walk Boston's downtown streets I know that most of the people—had they known about my time in Vietnam—would regard me as a war criminal. I am the enemy. Many think the soldiers I killed were freedom fighters. But Boston is a city with two faces. The anti-war movement is in stark contrast to the spirit of the old Boston of proud patriots and daring entrepreneurs.

John Adams once said that a man must study the craft of making a nation and the art of war, that his children might build the city on the hill and create an engine of commerce, so that his grandchildren would have the freedom to study literature, science and art. The people who were Adams' grandchildren in spirit, if not descent, somehow seek out Marsi and me, open their homes to us, and give us the greatest of all gifts that I will spend the rest of my life opening. They represent the Boston that allows me to think whatever I want and be the person I am.

When I think of Boston, I think of a man we met but hardly knew, Linzee's uncle. His name was Bill Coolidge. His friends called him Cuckoo behind his back. Many considered him the wealthiest man in Massachusetts. He was the brother of Thomas Jefferson Coolidge, Catherine's deceased husband. The first time we meet Bill is at one of Catherine's Sunday luncheons. He arrives in an orange fishnet shirt and light gray pants. He is bald except for a monk's crown of hair that stretches from ear to ear. He has puffy pink cheeks, a deep voice, and his speech is witty and filled with irony. To me, he is John Adams' grandchild of spirit.

He invites Linzee, Marsi and me to luncheon on a Sunday one month off. We arrive at his Beverly estate, a Georgian Paladin mansion that will be left to Harvard. A small stream meanders across the back of the house and geese strut across the park-like setting, pulling up grass by the roots. We sit and watch this spectacle from his broad stone patio, but it is the house that draws our attention. I walk into the entrance hall and look over my shoulder. I know the artist instantly. It is a desert scene by Delacroix. A lion has jumped from a rock ledge onto the back of a wild stallion. His claws rake his prey's hide. The eyes of the stallion are wide open with panic and his body writhes to shake off his tormentor. We stare at the painting, open mouthed, while Bill conducts his tour. Each room is better than the last. I think that my life would be fulfilled if I could ever have such a house and live in the midst of such furniture and art.

The furniture is mid-18th-century Boston mahogany Queen Anne and Chippendale. The dark, deep, highly polished wood reflects the paintings on the walls. The surfaces appear to be three-dimensional. Highboys, lowboys, sofas, wing chairs—we see the best of New England colonial furniture. If the furniture is great, the art is priceless. There is a Christ, carrying a cross, by El Greco. I stare at El Greco's elongated figures and see the sorrow of the Passion. There are several Rembrandts of prosperous burghers that show incredible insights into the sitters' personalities. There is a wonderful Japanese screen from the Edo period that shows the beauty of Japan in the Tokugawa Shogunate palaces and the splendid costumes of the samurai. The paintings are hung close together on the walls, salon style. Marsi is enthralled.

Luncheon is served on a dark Queen Anne Jamaican mahogany circular table that would accommodate 12. It is made from a tree with a 12-foot trunk. Trees like that are now extinct. Its size makes it a rarity for its period; there are 12 matching Queen Anne chairs with trifold feet and old needlepoint seats. The leg of lamb is accompanied by a 1945 La Tache. The scent of the orchids on the table, the aroma of the wine, the art and the furniture are sensory overload.

Linzee introduces me to Dick Hall and Danny Pierce. Dick Hall is the son of the founder of Choate, Hall & Stewart, a leading Boston law firm. His partner is Danny Pierce, the heir of S.S. Pierce, the patriarch of Boston retailers. Danny works for Scudder, Stevens & Clark, a leading Boston investment management firm. They have formed an angel partnership to finance start-ups and have been successful. Soon after we meet, they invite me to work with them between my first and second years at Harvard, to help them make venture investments. It turns out to be a perfect summer job.

Harvard, Simmons and the Sunday luncheons at these houses will alter our lives permanently. Our only passions now are for entrepreneurs and the arts. We can feel the excitement that permeates the city. We can almost feel its pulse, and we want to understand more of the history of what is going on around us. In Taoism, there is the concept of yin and yang, the male and female, the two parts that make a whole. If Harvard teaches me the yin—how to succeed in the world of business, Manchester teaches me the yang—how to appreciate what is creative in life both in business and the arts. Marsi and I share the enchantment.

We are invited to Coolidge Point often. The house is a massive modern mansion. A Stanford white mansion was torn down to accommodate modern lifestyles where large household staffs are unavailable. Catherine Coolidge, the grand dame of Manchester, loves orchids. When Pierre DuPont of Longwood Gardens in Delaware was alive, she was his primary competitor.

Both of them searched the world to find the most exotic orchid species and conducted breeding experiments to create hybrids. She has four greenhouses filled with orchids. Every room in the house has sprays of orchids in continuous bloom. Her gardener, Bruno, has published many articles on the esoteric aspects of creating orchid varieties. When we are invited to the luncheon we are served drinks in a great drawing room with 12-foot ceilings and 10-foot windows with a 280-degree view of the Atlantic Ocean. On a point in the distance is a 10-foot Greek urn from 200 BC that provides a focal point amid beautiful perennial borders. The entrance to the drawing room is framed by two eight-foot Japanese urns of the Edo period that have three-foot bouquets of orchids. Together, Marsi and I discover our love of gardens. The elegant circular columned marble foyer contains portraits of the first six presidents, painted from life by Gilbert Stuart—Washington, Adams, Jefferson, Madison, Monroe and Adams—exuding vitality and elegance. All of this is the result of Catherine's husband, a direct descendant of a New England sailor and Thomas Jefferson's daughter. She had fled to Boston to escape Thomas Jefferson's bankruptcy. She carried with her some of the best art in Monticello. She chose her husband well; in time he would found United Fruit.

Boston teaches me this lesson: If you live your life amid violence and in harm's way, art and gardens are the defenses of the heart and soul.

This is Marsi's finest moment in our marriage. She is modeling regularly and taking great pride in her clothing and appearance. She is learning rapidly and stretching my intellect. We attend concerts and plays and spend long, happy hours in the Boston Museum, the Isabella Stewart Gardner Museum, and a host of historic houses and small museums around Boston. We host black-tie dinner parties for Henry Cabot Lodge and other Brahmins. Marsi greets our guests at the top of the stairs in a long, black-velvet evening dress. Mrs. Coolidge's chauffeur delivers armfuls of orchids. Marsi sleeps peacefully amid the scent of flowers.

When we went to Boston, I was a raw soul—a beast straight from war. I do not clearly remember a single person in the second half of my tour. The loss of Blevins, Northcut, Noldner and the others changed me, but I am strangely detached from the experience by day and haunted by dreams at night. I want to pace the floor but only restlessly change positions, hoping it will make a difference. I know that I must sleep but fear that I will. Why did I not know more about the soldiers who served with me? They died and disappeared in the mist. I cannot recall their names. Why are they not still here beside me? Why was I the one who lived only to be haunted by the memories, as fresh in my mind today as they were then? What I want is to return to the A Shau. To have a second chance, get into a LOH, draw fire and bomb the hell out of the NVA. I want to join my old platoon on ambushes. I want to stick the barrel of my M1 down a pothead's throat and just as I pull the trigger ... I wake up.

The dreams bother me. I am back in the A Shau and find my hands reaching toward Marsi's throat. But my hands are silk, and she sleeps deeply. I pull them away and lie sleepless through the night frightened by the beast within me. Over time, I learn from the Brahmins that you can control the inner beast with the beauty of gardens, art, classical music, stimulating conversation, beautiful interiors and extraordinary views.

Marsi is the face of beauty. She is long necked, like Napoleon's Josephine, with all her impeccable taste. Marsi's legs are two-thirds up her body, and she is mine among the scent of orchids. Lobster is 99 cents a pound and great white Bordeaux are cheap. Get thee away, inner beast, you have no place in our life.

Marsi and I spend hours collecting pictures from magazines and planning the beautiful and stimulating life we will build. The love of gardens, art and flowers will pull together two souls into a complete union. It is a time of joy in anticipation of our next adventure and mornings together with mind-bending sex. I think the beast has left me forever.

The A Shau taught me that enemies will return stronger unless their will to fight is destroyed. The beast is only momentarily at bay, waiting to reappear with greater fury when I go to war again.

23

T. Rowe Price

Diligentia Ditat
Hard work enriches life.
—Newhall Family Motto

10 Oct 1970
Boston, Mass.
11 a.m.

During my second year at Harvard Business School, I abandon some of the traditional curriculum. I find it hard to believe that you can build a statistical model of what it takes to create a successful start-up. Instead, I spend hours in the library reading about venture capital. My senior thesis is "Financing Change: The Role of the Venture Capitalist." With my father's contacts and those I have developed, I spend hundreds of hours interviewing well-known venture capitalists.

As the interview process begins, I realize there is too much competition in Boston because everyone in the Business School wants to live there. I notice that T. Rowe Price, a large investment firm headquartered in Baltimore, is interviewing. I know the firm was founded by T. Rowe Price, a former stockbroker at Legg Mason. Mr. Price believed it was possible to produce superior investment returns by identifying, investing in and holding well-managed growth companies, with unique competitive advantages, operating in growing markets. The two men interviewing me are not initially as impressive as the urbane Bostonians who have interviewed me before. There is Tommy Broadus, a somewhat overweight Harvard MBA, who grew up in Knoxville, Tenn., and knew Jason Meyer. The other, a white-haired professorial type, is Bob Hall. He is the type of man who is born old, but whose looks never change as he ages. You'd expect to see him sitting in a wing chair beside a fire in some ancient Oxford college, drinking port and giving a lecture on the merits of Suetonius' "Lives of the Twelve Caesars."

Tommy is an investment counselor with a great love of wine, and we immediately begin to compare vintages. He manages portfolios for large pension funds that invest in America's great growth companies of the time such as Xerox, IBM, Polaroid, Digital Equipment, Wal-Mart and Avon. He is hypomanic, very intense and occasionally biting his fingernails. Bob is another extreme, much calmer on the surface but equally intense. Bob's focus is a new interest of Mr. Price's—investing in companies with large holdings of commodities such as gold, oil and timber. Mr. Price believes these companies will appreciate in value more rapidly than the stock market indexes because the assets are becoming scarcer and inflation is a permanent part of our economic future.

The question comes around to what I want to do in my life. Both Bob and Tommy immediately understand my passion for creating and growing companies, even though it is a field far apart from their personal interests. They focus intently as I describe the companies that Dick Hall and Danny Pierce helped to start. They know many of them, such as Teradyne and Millapore. They both have an interest in my military record and ask me emotionally demanding questions. In retrospect, I think my Boston interviews are superficial. They would not hire a warrior. They all thought we burned babies in Vietnam.

T. Rowe Price has a mutual fund called New Horizons that focuses on emerging growth companies, the type financed by venture capitalists. What is more, T. Rowe Price is developing a plan to enter the venture capital business. Cub Harvey is the man at T. Rowe Price who has responsibility for both initiatives. They immediately offer me a job as an analyst for the New Horizons

Fund. I will help plan T. Rowe Price's entry into venture capital. This, of course, is subject to my meeting Cub, Neil Bond, Kirk Miller and a number of T. Rowe Price's senior managers. They tell me that T. Rowe Price is a research-driven firm. Despite my shock at actually being asked to join a firm, I say yes, and make plans to visit Baltimore within the next week.

T. Rowe Price's offices are at One Charles Street Center, the first of Baltimore's buildings designed by I.M. Pei and built at the beginning of the revitalization of Baltimore's Inner Harbor, a project helping to pull the city out of a long torpor. Baltimore's Inner Harbor is being developed by the Rouse Company. Skyscrapers are being built. Newly organized sports teams like the Colts and Orioles are winning world championships. Baltimore's museums are opening important new exhibits, challenging conventional wisdom in the art world.

To a young man whose life had been spent away at Shattuck, Penn, Fort Polk, Vietnam and Harvard, Baltimore seems like home. It is a city of dreams, full of possibilities and potential. I wonder what the future will hold. Baltimore is not San Francisco or Boston. I can change that. Why can't Baltimore be a home for new companies? Why can't we create a vibrant entrepreneurial center alive with new technology? A place that draws artists from all over the world? Baltimore can again become the city that it was in its heyday, after the Revolutionary War. I can make it happen.

It seems so simple. The mid-Atlantic has only three venture firms: Greater Washington Investors (DC), BroVentures (Baltimore) and Data Science Ventures (Princeton). T. Rowe Price's entry into the venture business will be a catalyst for a high technology revitalization of the region. Or so I think— the young Don Quixote riding out to battle the Knight of the Evil Countenance.

The interviews at T. Rowe Price go well and I'm welcomed aboard. Cub Harvey, president of the New Horizons Fund, is a man I would have chosen to be my father. He appears calm, but that calmness conceals a passion for small-company investing. Cub knows everybody in the venture business. I look forward to meeting the men whose names are as familiar to me as my own. Cub, I discover, started his career in the aerospace industry and for a time had worked for my father when he was president of Flight Refueling. He knows what it is like to have fought your way uphill in the A Shau with only fighter support.

The other senior people at T. Rowe Price also take interest in their new young analyst. Kirk Miller, chairman of T. Rowe Price, turns out to be a relative of Marsi's. He regales me with stories of the early days of Avon, Polaroid and Xerox, when he called upon those companies as an analyst. A.C. Hubbard, George Roche, Al Pacholder, Francis Rienhoff, Jeff Little and Bob Hall are members of the research department and will soon become Marsi's and my best friends. It turns out that T. Rowe Price is a self-contained universe. The people you're working with are the people you see at social events. Marsi and I share our new friends with the friends we made growing up in Baltimore. Marsi is invaluable to me. We entertain all the time and she makes close friends with the T. Rowe wives.

Marsi volunteers as a docent at the Baltimore Museum of Art. We both develop a passion for the furniture and art of Baltimore when it was the Athens of a new republic. We study the neoclassical values of that time and Marsi is soon teaching courses about Baltimore, its furniture and history in our newly rented home, which belongs to Dr. Johnson.

Our house, called Turkey Cock Hall, is the first house built on the Johnson property early in the late 17th century. It is built in the Huguenot style and has long, sloping porches. The house had numerous additions around 1800 before the family moved to their Robert Mills federal mansion on the hill. Turkey Cock Hall is a colonial masterpiece, with period floorboards given to the Johnsons by the Baltimore Museum. The kitchen, also a keeping room, is equipped with a massive colonial fireplace. It is the best house for Christmas. Decorated with evergreens, hollies and poinsettias with the crackle of pungent fires in the five downstairs fireplaces, it is truly magical. The windows were made in England. On their wedding nights, a hundred young brides have carved their signatures with their wedding rings on the window panes of Turkey Cock Hall. In the rooms of our rented home we place our federal Baltimore dining table, our Baltimore chest of drawers, our Pembroke table, our English sideboard and our English Country Regency sofa, which are the beginnings of what we hope will be a great collection. Every free cent we have, we spend on art and furniture, selecting everything together.

T. Rowe Price in those days is riding high. Growth stock investing is at the peak of favor. It is the day of "one-decision stocks" such as Xerox, Polaroid and IBM, stocks that are bought and held for 15 years, practically guaranteeing superior performance. In the first half of the '70s, growth companies are trading at stratospheric multiples, four times their brethren. T. Rowe Price has a hard time seeing the gathering clouds.

In 1973, my parents decide to move to Florida. We buy their house. After all the years of traveling, I feel that I finally have a real home. Marsi and I swear we will live there forever. Our children will live on the property, as well as their children, and in time it will become an ancestral estate. We create our first garden there.

Marsi is enchanted with Neoclassical Baltimore: furniture, art, glass and architecture. We study Thomas Jefferson's library to understand why he said: "I could not live without my books." Because Marsi is a Washington descendant, we are allowed to take picnic dinners to Mt. Vernon, where we can sit on the great porch overlooking the Potomac, read The Republican Court, and develop an intuitive understanding of the classical America that was formed during the Revolution. We always begin with a tour of Mt. Vernon's rooms, restored to their historic colors, bright hues of green, yellow and blue. From room to room we imagine ourselves with Hamilton, Jefferson, Madison and the heroes of the American Revolution. We quote Latin phrases to each other while basking in the sweet summer breeze.

The Millers, Marsi's parents, let us use their house, Gaymcrest, on the eastern shore of Maryland, near the tip of Benoni Point. It is a great white brick house surrounded by cornfields. Like most old eastern shore houses, it faces tributaries running from the Chesapeake Bay. In colonial times in the tidewater of the bay, planters grew tobacco. Their houses faced the water highways. Cargos of tobacco and other farm produce were sent to Annapolis and shipped to England. The tobacco factors built great houses, and lived off the debt provided by the English traders who marketed their raw materials. Together

Marsi and I fall in love with the 18th-century Tidewater, great houses and furniture designed by William Buckland, the English joiner and master of Rococo Chippendale design.

Marsi and I invite our T. Rowe Price friends down to Gaymcrest Farm. The Harveys visit and we catch fresh bluefish in September, when the gulls swarm over the blue waters of the Chesapeake Bay. We invite Francis Reinhoff and his wife Annie, along with A.C. Hubbard and his wife Penny, to experience some of the best Canada goose shooting on the eastern shore. We drink good bourbon, claret wines like Chateau Magdelaine '61 and Orme de Pez '67, and cook oysters Rockefeller. We gather oysters from an oyster bed off our house. During the midday when the goose shooting slows down, we get into a motor boat and wind our way down to Oxford, where the great colonial plantations lie nestled in their own bays, with sunlight-dappled verdant lawns flowing to the tributaries. Fall is always ablaze with colors. The air is cool, and there is no humidity. We are in constant motion. It is the best of times to be alive.

Neil Bond manages the T. Rowe Price Growth Fund, and Cub Harvey, my boss, manages the New Horizons Fund. They take Marsi and me under their wings. Neil takes us to his house at the shore. Visiting Neil's house is like a *Pilgrimage to the Isle of Cythera*, Jean-Antoine Watteau's great painting. You sail from Neil's dock directly into the bay. Neil and his wife Jody have a relationship that is like jousting knights in medieval times. But it is always interesting to be around them. T. Rowe Price is so close knit that you always know what is going on with others' marriages and children.

In 1972, the energy crisis occurs. It becomes evident almost overnight that world economies can be held hostage by a cartel of Middle Eastern oil countries. Cartels never last forever, but they can last for years. This causes a serious re-evaluation of the Nifty Fifty, the great growth stocks. It does not help that several of the most glamorous growth companies like Polaroid and Xerox encounter fundamental problems. Growth stocks' prices decline massively and the genius portfolio managers of T. Rowe Price are now considered fools.

One trouble never comes alone. Charlie Shaffer, the firm's CEO, decides to retire. All the company's free cash flow is used to buy back his stock. Charlie is a great salesman and an investment counselor. He appoints one of his star investment counselors, Don Bowman, to follow him. Investment counselors not only manage portfolios but they keep their clients, the large pension funds, happy. Most of the firm's senior employees come from the research department—holding jobs as fund managers, or senior investment counselors as they are promoted. There is always tension between sales and research. The counselors say they bring in the business; the research department says it produces the ideas that generate the results that attract the clients. It is an uneasy peace at best—but with scores of unhappy clients, and many lost accounts, tempers flare. Everyone blames themselves for not having foreseen the decline of growth stocks, except the few like Dave Testa and Bob Hall who did foresee it but could not change the firm's strategic direction. Growth stock valuations collapse and T. Rowe encounters hard times.

In war and business, fortune changes. One moment you are a victor; the next moment you are leaving the battlefield, defeated, trying to save whatever is left. It is T. Rowe Price's time to suffer defeat after long years of victory. One of my good friends, another analyst, George Roche, takes me out to lunch. The topic of conversation is always the same, it is the lesson my grandmother drilled into me as a young man—your defeats are only lessons that will enable you to win future victories. So what is the lesson of the growth stock collapse? It is conversations like these that I have with George, during the bleak times. We arrive early at work, and pass long lines at each gas station. When a gallon of gas is pumped into your gas tank, you realize you are supporting a cartel that is destroying our economy. Saudi Arabia professes to be our friend, while they rob our economy.

Life with Marsi is changing quickly as well. It is no longer a summer idyll, and she is busy renovating our house, made more complicated by our crooked builder's bankruptcy. It is during this time that we bring our first son, Charles Ashton, into the world—the child that Marsi has longed to have. She is overwhelmed at first, full of joy and fear. Her days are consumed with child care and she worries that she will never have the career she desires.

The stress of the business is great and the hours are very long. I travel most of the week. The pace of our life together changes dramatically from happiness to one of palpable tension. The world I love that we have built around us seems to dissolve in an instant.

Cub takes me aside one day and tells me that the plans for a T. Rowe Price venture fund are canceled. All of the firm's free cash flow is needed to buy out retirees. My dream is gone. I try not to let anyone see my disappointment but I know it's evident. We cannot launch a new product when our core business is in jeopardy. The people we loved at T. Rowe turn their backs on us now that I am an ordinary junior analyst. There are no more weekends away, private invitations or dinner parties. Cub is to be promoted, and Tom Barry will take over the New Horizons Fund. Tom had left T. Rowe Price to start his own investment management firm, but is returning to T. Rowe Price. He is a friend and, in retrospect, one of my greatest mentors.

Tom tells me, "Start your own firm."

24

NEA

In the room the women come and go
Talking of Michelangelo
... Do I dare
Disturb the universe?

—T.S. Eliot "The Love Song of J. Alfred Prufrock"

15 Jan 1977
Baltimore, Md.
10 a.m.

I decide to start my own venture capital firm. It is frightening to think of leaving a secure job, especially in Baltimore. There are virtually no local venture firms, other than BroVenture, the Brown family's fund. If I fail, I have to leave Baltimore with no place to go. One of my good friends, a young analyst recently hired by Alex Brown, is John Nehra. John covers the small medical device companies. We often work together. We analyze companies and I buy them for T. Rowe Price through him.

John has a client named Howie Wolfe, who manages the estate of three women who inherited a good part of the John Deere fortune. He suggests that we spend some time together at an upcoming medical conference of the Society of Artificial

Organs in Montreal. Over dinner in Montreal in the spring of 1976, John, Howie and I discuss opportunity in the venture business. I explain my frustration—I can put together an investment team, a plan, and have a partnership agreement that is already drafted. Howie says, "Pull it together and I could have an interest."

While at T. Rowe Price, I tried to recruit Loring Catlin, who is a partner in the famous venture capital firm of Payson & Trask. I ask him to join a T. Rowe-backed partnership. I ask him to be my partner and raise a fund ourselves. He says no. If T. Rowe Price were involved it might work, but with the two of us, no way. I am back to square one.

Frank Bonsal is one of the senior young partners at Alex Brown. He has largely been responsible for leading Alex Brown, a traditional Maryland underwriter of Maryland tax-free bonds, into the roller coaster business of high technology underwriting. He invests Alex Brown partners' capital in a few venture deals. Moving Alex Brown into small company banking is the best decision the firm will ever make. I have known Frank for many years, since he is one of Marsi's second cousins.

Over the next several months, Frank and I start to work together visiting small companies. Frank is no longer popular; the small companies Alex Brown has underwritten are casualties of the energy crisis. The stocks have collapsed and customers are unhappy.

Cub and Don both agree that this is the time to enter the venture business. T. Rowe Price cannot do this; the firm has too much going on. Also, many people in T. Rowe Price believe that it is not right for the people who manage one of the firm's products to have a direct economic interest in that product. All T. Rowe Price employees should have only one economic focus— how the total firm does. A system that allows three people to have profit interests in their product could create jealousies that could tear the firm apart.

Don, Cub and Neil know this works for an investment manager, but managers of venture funds share in the capital gains. The business does not control enough capital to justify large fees, so capital gains are the only reward that justifies the long lead time and difficulties encountered in creating great companies. They encourage us to go ahead and indicate they will try to get T. Rowe Price to make an investment. They offer us office and secretarial support when we leave our jobs. I write the prospectus that will be the model for NEA's culture. It is based on "*Band of Brothers*." I create NEA's culture—a culture of we.

Cub takes me aside—I have hardly seen him for six months—and he quietly says, "I will support you, but you will have to find a real venture capitalist as a partner. Why don't you give Dick Kramlich a call? I bet he must be tired of playing Arthur Rock's Bob Cratchit." T. Rowe Price commits $1 million, 17 percent of the firm's net worth; and Landmark (Howie Wolfe) commits $4.5 million. They each get 4.5 percent of NEA's 25 percent profits interest.

There is no need for him to make this recommendation to hire Dick. Dick is the California venture capitalist I respect the most. We have worked on numerous public companies together in which I had an interest. But for the moment, Dick is trying to sort out the financial impact of leaving Arthur, something that is difficult because Arthur can be draconian when he is in a good humor. God help you if you approach him on the wrong day, for he will be vindictive. Dick, Frank and I talk and meet often. Dick helps us in every way he can, and always holds out the possibility that he will join us. I write a prospectus for a venture firm outlining the firm's values and strategies.

Meanwhile, Frank and I need a third partner with substantial venture capital experience. We know we have Howie Wolfe and the Deere family's backing for $4.5 million, and Don Bowman and Cub Harvey have overridden substantial internal objections to have T. Rowe Price commit to a $1 million investment.

Frank and I both know Jim Morgan, one of the AR&D partners. AR&D is a famous Boston venture capital firm founded by Gen. George Doriot. He sees the writing on the wall for AR&D, yet desperately loves the venture business. We court him, spending weekends and giving him and his wife tours of Baltimore. Jim loves his home on Marblehead, outside Boston, and after a moment of flirting with us decides to stay in Boston. He tells us the day we publish the prospectus with his name in it. It must have piqued the General that an English major was poaching one of his own. In an amazing stroke of good fortune, Dick Testa, AR&D's counsel, who is seen as the best venture capital lawyer in the business, says he is willing to represent us at no cost until we raise our funds. Dick is Gen. Doriot's counsel and friend. If we do not succeed, he will eat the cost. It is obvious that Gen. Doriot holds no grudges, and whispered to Dick to support the two fools with liberal arts degrees. Very kindly, Dick delivers to me a letter from the General: "Best wishes, Chuck. I admire your determination. I welcome you to the *Band of Brothers* who seek to build companies that change our destinies. By the way, I am giving to you the name "New Enterprise Associates." It is the first name I selected for American Research and Development Corporation. In retrospect, it is a better name for what we do. Take it if you want and bon chance." That letter astounds me; we have the General's blessing despite our liberal arts backgrounds. He adds one more line—"half the VC's I know don't have technical backgrounds."

Frank and I stall in our fundraising. About that time, we receive a call from Dick. He will join us. It is the best day of my life. By December 1977, NEA is now real because Dick has joined us.

Don Bowman was the CEO who pushed the approval of NEA through the T. Rowe board; he is a marketing-oriented manager. With the crash of growth stocks, the conflict between the sales-driven investment counselors and the research department breaks out in the open. Don is terminated and Cub Harvey is made CEO. The whole issue of the NEA investment is up for discussion again. Several senior managers have doubts, and I almost panic. Cub sees me several days later and says the board has reconfirmed its commitment to make the NEA investment.

In December, Dick negotiates a separation agreement with Arthur, in which he can join us but must give 50 percent of his time to Arthur for two and a half years. About this time he is approached by Tom Perkins and Eugene Kleiner, two of San Francisco's great venture capitalists. They ask him to be the third partner in their new fund. They say they are Dick's friends and are known quantities. Chuck Newhall is a young analyst with no technology background, an amateur. Frank Bonsal is an investment banker who pretends to be a venture capitalist. Dick says no—he has given his word. When asked why, he responds, "I believe we share the same values, and besides, I just like them." Dick believes his word is his bond. He is no Arthur Rock. Kliner Perkins becomes a legend, but NEA continues to give them a run for their money. Kliner Perkins and NEA will be as different as night and day. Frank, like Dick, has a safety net. He is still being paid as a broker by Alex Brown.

I will be without salary for what will approach 18 months. Fundraising is terrible in this environment. The cover of Newsweek asks: "Are Equities Dead?" I have close to $400,000 in capital, mostly made from venture investments as well as public investments. The entire sum is invested in NEA. It is a step onto a bridge—perhaps to nowhere. We travel close to seven days a week trying to interest someone to invest in our dream. When Marsi gives birth to our second son, Adair Brantley, I am unable to drive her to the hospital because of a business meeting. I arrive late at the hospital and Marsi is furious. I try to explain the critical importance, but Marsi is inconsolable, hurt and shaken.

Frank and I try to interest all potential investors. Despite spending one-third of our fundraising time in Baltimore, we cannot find an investor other than T. Rowe Price. We call on probably 1,000 investors all over the U.S. and are turned down by 99.9 percent of them. My life and family are in jeopardy. Marsi supports me, but she is scared and has trouble sleeping. I cannot blame her.

In June 1978, we close our first fund. It is $16.5 million. Months pass as if they are seconds; years pass as if they are minutes. The years of 1978, 1979, 1980 and 1981 go by in a blur. We do not see our T. Rowe Price friends. We spend our social hours with entrepreneurs, with other venture capitalists, and the parents of our children's friends. I am in California 40 percent of the time, and Dick is often on the East Coast. I travel 6.5 days a week. Everything is NEA; not Marsi, not the children, just companies in crisis, or doing well, or just getting by. Everyone says we are nuts to have an office on both coasts. We travel together, live together and make it work. Marsi is deeply unhappy with my schedule and sorry for the loss of her T. Rowe Price friendships.

As I tiptoe through the minefields of venture capital, Marsi, my beloved wife, disappears, and another woman lies beside me in bed. She is a counterculture hippy. She wears Russian peasant blouses, not Courreges Couture dresses. Throughout our relationship, I have given her anything she wants that I can afford. Now she ridicules my gifts even when I acquire from a distant relative a Baltimore painted table that has been in her family for 200 years. Eventually the table will be worth hundreds of thousands of dollars. Five years ago she would have fainted with joy. She no longer cares about the house. She expects me to take care of it over the weekends: clean, vacuum and polish. She does not love warriors, she hates them. NEA can go to hell. She knows that I have made a significant amount of money on paper, but we cannot spend it. She wants to enjoy herself, not change the world. She tells me she does not love me. I hope she will change back to the person she was and soldier on alone.

In 1981, Lynne Kramlich goes into the hospital for a routine heart valve replacement. Dick calls me, frantic. Something has gone terribly wrong. The beautiful wife he loves—who knows if she will live or die? NEA is one of the best performing funds, but without Dick we would not have that record. Lynne is on life support one, two, three months. Dick takes care of a family of four: Mary Donna, Lynne's child by a previous marriage; Rix and Peter, his children from a prior marriage; and an adorable young blonde, Christina—his child with Lynne. We visit him constantly. He never misses a board meeting or fails to follow up on new investments. He stands vigil over Lynne each night. He does not sleep. He takes board calls while he holds Lynne's hand.

Dick calls me at the end of six months. He is in the hospital room and has instructed the doctors to turn off Lynne's life support system. He is told that Lynne is dead. Dick starts to cry; it is the most terrible cry of pain I have ever heard. I cry with him.

Marsi and I, Frank and his wife Helen, and Nancy, our chief administrative officer, fly to San Francisco. It is March 1982; the grapes in the Bordeaux Region will this year produce one of the wines of the century. NEA's internal rate of return exceeds 60 percent. But there is nothing at all to be happy about. We sit quietly, absorbed in our own thoughts. Marsi tells me that if I continue this crazy business, she will end up like Lynne. She has no intention of doing that.

The service is at a small Episcopal Church in Pacific Heights on a crisp, cool, sunny day in San Francisco. Dick sits in the front of the church with his children clustered around him. In the middle of the service, I am haunted by thoughts of what might happen to NEA.

We hire Neil Bond from T. Rowe Price as a partner. He moves to California as a general partner. Neil's wife, Jody, is diagnosed with breast cancer. Her doctors are skeptical. Her odds of survival are low. They believe that Jody has only a few years to live. Despite the diagnosis, Neil and Jody will enjoy the happiest time of their lives, 3,000 miles from provincial Baltimore, their home for 30 years. Dick turns full attention to NEA and at last he has a partner. Marsi and I are delighted that this might mean I will not have to spend so much time in California.

Many years later, when Jody's courageous will is exhausted, she dies watching a sunset over San Francisco Bay. All the NEA partners will join Neil for her funeral. This time the flights will be east. She wishes to have her ashes scattered across the Chesapeake Bay. As with Lynne's funeral, the day is sunny and crisp as only Maryland's October can be. The church is beside the bay and during the service we listen to the murmur of the waters. Great flocks of Canada geese fly over with their mournful honking. NEA's performance is fantastic, the companies we have created are internationally known, but again we are sad, and have little but pleasantries and condolences to say to each other.

After all of our struggles, NEA is back in business—surely there will be calm waters ahead.

I can now fix my life with Marsi, for I am a warrior and a venture capitalist.

6 March 1982
Owings Mills, Md.
7 p.m.

We are waiting for our minister, Bill Baxter, and his wife, Susan. They are coming for dinner and we will celebrate my victories in the venture capital wars. It will be the victory party I never got when I returned from Vietnam.

NEA is now making history. When we go to parties, everyone wants to talk to us. There are frequent news articles written about the firm. Our friends want to hear about the next new thing. I am successful, full of myself—and a complete fool.

Since Vietnam, my life's dream has been to be a venture capitalist. When I was young I thought I wanted to be a writer so I could influence mankind. But on the Dong So ridgeline I discovered my purpose in life. As a child I grew up among entrepreneurs like my father. I understood romantics who seek to change the world. As a venture capitalist I can finance entrepreneurs and to the best of my abilities help them accomplish their mission to achieve the impossible. The money will be good, but that is not my reason for entering the business. If we are successful at creating great companies, the money will follow. I did not start a career. I began a quest for the Holy Grail, to change the way the world is.

Now, after five years, my quest is close to reality. NEA is a series of partnerships with 12-year lives. When we wind up NEA I, the partnership will have a 3.5x multiple on invested capital. We will have turned $16.5 million into $58.8 million. The partnership has a 37 percent compound annual rate of return. But if you hold all the stocks and do not sell, over the next 30 years NEA I will be a 28x partnership. We will have turned $16.5 million into $462 million.

I started my career at T. Rowe Price, a Baltimore investment firm. My experience there provided me with the ethical framework that will be transformed into NEA's culture. But at T. Rowe Price, I was a junior analyst interviewing the entrepreneurial CEOs of great companies. During these interviews I would make suggestions on how they could improve their companies. They were amused by my suggestions. A few actually implemented them.

But now I'm not an analyst. I am a venture capitalist who sits on boards and can influence events. One of my companies is Chomerics. Chomerics makes conductive composite materials for touch panel screen boards. NEA funded the company in 1978. Now I am a board member of Chomerics, along with Dick

Kramlich. I am the bad cop and Dick is the good cop. Bob Jasse, Chomerics' CEO, kicked me off the board three times but he always invited me back. I routinely attended all-night strategic planning meetings. I am involved with the significant decisions at the age of 38. My comments are only suggestions, not orders. Gradually my influence increases. I am no longer a junior analyst. I am a card-carrying venture capitalist. There are no limits to my horizons. My father, with the company he financed that later became Thiokol, helped put man on the moon. My ambitions are far greater. We are building companies that will change the future of the world: the ethernet—the Internet's predecessor – balloon angioplasty and the Chomerics touch panels that will be used on all electronic devices of the future.

Life away from work had also been wonderful. Marsi and I have two fine boys, Ashton and Adair. Yes, they both have severe learning disabilities, but Marsi and I overcame similar afflictions. If you retain self-confidence into adulthood, learning disabilities give you a competitive advantage. You can do five things well at one time while your competitors can manage only one. I hope my sons' accomplishments will far surpass mine.

I think often of "Candide," where Dr. Pangloss says: "This is the best of all possible worlds." Marsi and I recently have had troubles but we will overcome them as we have overcome other troubles to build our perfect life together.

That evening I cook dinner for Marsi and the Baxters. I grill wild teal duck breasts with brandy, a touch of flour and freshly squeezed Florida orange juice that was a gift from my parents. The ducks I killed on a recent Mexican hunting trip with Jasse. It is a perfect duck a l'orange service with wild rice and haricots verts. I ask everyone to join me in a toast: "To our marriage and the best of all possible worlds." At that moment I am so full of myself I can hardly keep from bursting.

A week later I will be with my minister again, but under very grim circumstances.

25

The Ides of March

"It is not only soldiers who are the casualties of war."

— Ruth Ellen Patton, 1950, commenting on her sister's suffering

13 March 1982
Owings Mills, Md.
7 a.m.

March is always a cruel month in Baltimore. March is winter's last chance to wreak havoc with a surprise snow. In March, Maryland trees are gray, the sky is gray, even the leaves in the woodland seem gray, at last released by dirty melted snow. It is the month, for those confined in Baltimore over the winter, that is the bleakest.

It is Saturday morning. For me it will be the Ides of March. Last night, I was watching "The Big Red One," a movie about the 1st Division in World War II. I was in the A Shau Valley in mind and body. I could not leave the movie because my platoon depended on me to save their lives. This mood was encouraged by three glasses of bourbon. Marsi shouted to me to come to bed but I did not hear the urgency of her cries. She was asleep when I went to bed. This is where guilt comes from.

Ashton and Adair, our sons, are my responsibility on Saturday. It is part of our new regimen. Because I travel during the weekdays and work long hours trying to establish a venture capital firm, the weekends are Marsi's to do with what she wants. Today, she tells me she will go skating in Towson and then study for exams in the Towson library. A friend is picking her up so she will not need our car. She is months away from completing her master's degree. Today, she'd left before I woke up.

The bleak March skies are my morning's first view. I catch the scent of the A Shau Valley and I shudder. Our marriage is now an uneasy truce. I don't understand what went wrong over the last five years, but we have drifted apart.

The first decade of married life had been an idyll. We had no money, then a little money, and comparatively little responsibility but I had long hours of work while Marsi rode horses. Together at Fort Polk in Louisiana we explored the antebellum South: New Orleans, Natchez, the River Road, Charleston and Savannah. We felt we were Scarlet O'Hara and Rhett Butler. She was so excited whenever I tried to jump over the moon. She never undermined my foolish dreams. She was a constant cheerleader who gave me the courage to take the next step.

Later in Boston and in Baltimore, Marsi's intellect came alive. She went from attending a junior college, to earning a B.A. from Simmons College in Boston, to almost completing her master's degree. She read and studied all the time and we spent hours working on projects together. Our interest in collecting became a passion for both of us. She fought hard to have children and we were successful, although it took us eight years. She was self-confident and optimistic about our future.

But Marsi had a sudden, radical transformation. She went to counterculture meditation centers. She lost her interest in cooking and wanted to eat alfalfa sprouts. She found a new set of friends with strange ideas about how life should be lived. Instead of wanting to buy couture dresses, she took to wearing blue jeans and a T-shirt without a bra. Life became one continual emotional challenge—in business, socially, and in our personal lives. She started to swear. I never heard her swear before. Marsi even had an affair that led to a brief but very painful separation. This dreary Saturday morning I'm relieved that we're back together, although we seem to be a long way from recapturing anything resembling our earlier life together.

She had stopped encouraging me and ridiculed everything I tried to do, especially at times of crisis. Several times before I left on a business trip she hit me in the face, drawing blood. She ridiculed my clothes, my conversations with other people, the way I walked. We no longer had sex. She was a beautiful woman who walked around the house nude, flaunting the object of my desire. Everything she did destroyed my confidence and faith in the future or of any future of us being happy together again. I deliberately shut out these feelings and keep plodding ahead. But our conversations became vapid. She would ask me, "How is my aura today?" No matter what my response was, it was wrong. We used to have intellectual jousting matches that we both loved. We no longer discussed things that had any meaning to us.

The night before, I had walked out on our newly completed stone patio and garden. Dark clouds scudded across the sky. It had been raining. My garden, ravaged by snow, will take weeks to put together. How many times have I stood upon this spot and consumed a last glass of wine alone.

When I awake on the 13th, the rain is over. The day is overcast. Ashton, 6, and Adair, 3, will want breakfast. Adair is just recently out of diapers and is not above making a mistake. Ashton is a piece of work and is always on the move. Both boys are learning disabled and hyperactive, a genetic trait that Marsi and I share.

My jobs for the morning are to do laundry, vacuum the house, make beds and polish some furniture. Polishing furniture is my idea of relaxation. It is my game of golf, a moment to indulge my fantasies. Too soon, the children interrupt my reverie. Ashton wants to watch cartoons. Both boys are soon occupied in front of the television. Adair is playing with his toy cars. A short while later I prepare lunch for the boys: sandwiches and applesauce. At least the days of baby food are behind us.

A fog creeps up the Caves Valley toward our kitchen. The pasture behind the house, empty of animals, stretches for 250 feet. I cannot see what remains of the fence posts at the end. Both boys take a nap after lunch. I continue my work around the house. It is such a change from office routine; it is pleasant to not think about anything but shining silver. Marsi is not home by 3:00 pm. The boys are up and want me to entertain them. This is not my strong suit—amusing little children. I am great with young men, but not until they can ask a reasonable question. Where is Marsi? Something inside says I should be worried. She has been so quiet over the last two weeks.

I call Marsi's parents around 4:00 pm. They have not seen or heard from her all day. I start to put away the laundry in the chest of drawers off the bedroom. I notice the top left-hand drawer of the chest is open and the .22-caliber pistol my grandmother had given me is missing.

I call her parents again to tell them about the pistol. Dr. Miller's father, Ernest, committed suicide by shooting himself in the head several years ago. He did it in the bathtub because he did not want to get blood on the floor. I will later learn that there have been at least four other suicides in the extended Miller family during the past 20 years.

The Millers arrive soon after our call. I am close to them, and that bothers Marsi. They have always treated me better than I was treated by my parents. But Marsi is happier when I keep my distance. It is difficult to keep distance when my in-laws' property adjoins our own. Fortunately, Mrs. Miller has made it plain that she will not be a babysitter. Our interactions thus are tied to invitations, most of which we initiate.

Mrs. Miller suggests that I check our property. We own close to 18 acres of woodland. Marsi may have wandered off and been hurt. The Millers take the children. It is almost 5:00 pm and getting dark. I take Pippin, our German shepherd, and start walking through the woods on either side of our long driveway. Something seems to pull me toward the pasture.

I come around the right corner of the house and Pippin starts sniffing the ground. I walk diagonally across the pasture. There is a heavily wooded ravine on the left. I stop and look across the valley. The fog has lifted somewhat. Pippin has disappeared. I start making my way down the ravine, climbing over fallen trees. If I ever have enough money I will clear out the fallen trees.

About 50 feet in front of me is a flash of blue. It is a light blue. I know what it is. It is the quilted blue satin of Marsi's dressing gown. Pippin, our dog, is sitting silently beside her, staring straight ahead. Pippin was Marsi's dog and he followed her everywhere. The .22-caliber pistol is in her right hand. When she died the pistol fell to the ground, and it is pointing directly at me as I approach her body. A deafening buzz fills my ears, although the woods are silent. I feel as if my finger is plugged into an electrical socket. The world whirls around me, as if I am caught in a tornado. I am no longer the same man I was a second ago. I will never be the same man again. I fall and hurt my knee. I cannot hear. I start to cry, not just cry, to sob. I cannot stop sobbing. Marsi's suicide has taught me to cry so grief will not burst my soul—her last gift to me. In an instant I shut out all sound, smell, and the very sense of being alive so I can deal with the situation in front of me.

In a different way the same thing happened in Vietnam. When the light switch flipped in Vietnam, when I was in danger, everything happened in slow motion. I could smell everything with acute intensity, the organic fecundity of the soil, the scent of flowers, the odor of men's sweat when they encounter terror. I could hear an insect walk across a leaf. I am short of breath and start gulping in oxygen.

I sit down beside Marsi's body as if a punch has knocked the air out of my stomach. Pippin and I stare ahead. After one sorrowful howl, he is whining softly. Gradually, I focus my eyes.

She has been out here like this since before I woke up. It is almost 12 hours. I wish I could take her into my arms and make everything right. There is a small hole in her right temple. I have seen it before. In the A Shau. Her brains have oozed out and discolored the hair over her ear. I want to scream again.

For many minutes I do not touch her. Finally, with my left hand I brush my fingers through her hair. We have been married 15 years. How many times have I done this? She thought she was losing her hair. I was unsympathetic. How could she be losing her hair? It is so full and so beautiful. In my mind it is an ocean filled with pearls; the highlights still sparkle in brightness that fades with death. Even in death, she is so beautiful. I am alone again and I cry uncontrollably.

During the first 10 years of our marriage, when Marsi still found me attractive, we would make love often and I found it overwhelming. We would lie together naked with my arms around her shoulder and as the morning came, I would silently hum a stanza from a John Denver song:

You fill up my senses like a night in the forest,
Like the mountains in springtime,
Like a walk in the rain, like a storm in the desert,
Like a sleepy blue ocean.
You fill up my senses, come fill me again.

Will I ever be able to say again, "You fill up my senses, come fill me again"? Will I ever again be able to fall asleep just before sunrise with a tranquil smile on my face?

I sit bolt upright, my hands shaking violently. Mechanically, I stand and run back to the house. I tell the Miller's their daughter is dead. I do not tell the children. I do not even know where they are. I call the police.

Dr. Miller walks with me out to Marsi. I know Marsi is his favorite child. Mrs. Miller is closest to the boys.

Dr. Miller approaches the body. He is a tall man, but he seems to visibly shrink. The noise in my mind is unbearable but the forest is silent. I sit with him and something about him seems to change as I watch. Together we make our way back to the house. Two squad cars careen down our driveway, sirens blaring. It is dark outside, night has fallen. The bright car lights and rotating red domes make hearing impossible.

The house lights are incredibly bright. The police ask questions. I am not even aware of my answers. I take the boys into the family room overlooking the pasture. I tell them their mother is dead. Ashton seems to understand. Adair is just too young. He hardly talks. What will their mother's death do to them? Will they remember her? Will they still be able to love her?

Minutes or hours pass. The police take a stretcher into the woods. They return with Marsi's body. I ask to see her. I sink to my knees sobbing. There is nothing in my universe except her inert body. She is as light as a feather, for her soul is gone.

Can I raise these boys on my own? How do you survive the deconstruction of your life? How do you move forward?

The next thing I know I am walking down our driveway with Bill Baxter, who is the best minister I have ever known. I do not understand his words, but his voice soothes me. He is talking to me about life and death. The tall gray oak trees on either side of the road are silhouetted against the clouds. It is windy. The moon appears and disappears. The trees gyrate, seeming to have a life of their own. They seem to be trying to grab us. I know God will never take the place of the person I have lost.

It serves me right. I am too full of myself. I think I have seen everything, done everything, because of Vietnam and the founding of NEA. I believe I am invulnerable, a superman. There is this hard inner core in my body into which I can retreat and survive anything. It is total conceit. Death I have seen. Death I have dealt. But this is not death. It is annihilation. It is as if someone has dropped an atomic bomb on our house and all that remains is ashes. Radioactive ashes—I stand knee deep in them. Nothing remains.

I have failed the most important thing—my family. My grandmother said to me, "Your father has left our ancestral land. Our lives were entwined with Shattuck School for over 100 years. Promise me that you will find a place that can be our family's home for a long time, a place we can put down roots." I made that promise to my grandmother. My grandmother said the head of the household is first of all responsible for his family. The household is the core value of our democracy. It is the way we equalize the aristocrat with his large land holdings and the peasant with his modest plot: Each household has equal voting rights. But the head of the household has a sacred duty to protect it. The wife I nurtured and loved and introduced to the world of literature lies dead at my feet. The wife who introduced me to color, passion and the love of art is dead. Our marriage was a failure; it wilted before it could blossom into its full beauty. My two sons are at risk for their lives. NEA, our third son, is also at risk because Dick Kramlich, an NEA co-founder, and I face similar overwhelming challenges: ashes, ashes, ashes. Dick lost his second wife, Lynn Schamburger, a year earlier when she died after her heart valve was replaced. I have brought shame to my family. "All right," my grandmother would have said, "get on with life, fix it, and behave with honor."

I do not remember going to bed that night. I remember seeing the boys to bed. But the next thing I remember is morning. Well, it is not exactly morning. It is 0400. But I have enough sense to realize that this is now what will be my morning for the foreseeable future. There will be no more "You fill up my senses, come fill me again."

I am luckier than most. Sleep, for me, has been an inconvenience throughout my life. The night is the time of the stars, the union of the mind and creation, a time of passion. At least I can deal with the nightmares, since they have been my companion since the A Shau. Sleep, who needs it? But nights without Marsi are different. I am alone. My passion is spent remembering the past. Over the past few years our lovemaking has been a wasteland. I now face a life of celibacy.

My military training goes into gear. Marsi hated this aspect of my personality. I prepare three game plans: one if the enemy comes from the front, one if they come from the flanks, and one if they come from behind. As always, I become obsessed with completing these plans. How many times did Marsi try to talk to me when I was oblivious to anything but planning my battles? I should have been more sensitive to her needs—more guilt. Yes, I traveled sometimes six days a week and worked hard. But all my friends did the same thing. Without anticipating all alternatives, I never would have lived through Vietnam, founding NEA or Marsi's suicide.

I get up several hours before the boys awake. There is a funeral to plan. I will serve the food she loved. Her favorite flowers will be everywhere. I choose her favorite wines, and lay out the tables and chairs to be used as well as help to clean up after the party. Marsi died Saturday. We will bury her Monday. Sunday is spent on the phone notifying friends and family. The Millers have a family plot. At least that is no problem. At the time I thought it was a blessing. Now I think it's a curse. In death, Marsi will lie in her family plot away from her husband and her children. I will lie in our new family plot. Was it a conscious decision by the Millers to keep us apart, even in death? I tell my parents not to fly up from Florida—my father is ill with Parkinson's. It is just as well. Taking care of them would drain my energy. I tell friends not to cancel vacations. It is spring break. My partners are both on vacation with their children. Dick Kramlich and Frank Bonsal, my partners, are already in the air flying to Baltimore. The NEA family stands by its own. They heard what happened and they went to the airport. How many people will attend the funeral? Food arrives constantly.

I pull out the family silver and china. Everything must be perfect for the reception. Making them perfect keeps my mind off of reality. Two of the platters have the Lurman crest on them. The Lurmans were among Marsi's ancestors. The china was used in a fleet of their clipper ships that sailed from Baltimore to Hong Kong. I found those platters and gave them to Marsi one Christmas past. The Lurmans owned one of America's first merchant banks. They were thus among Maryland's first venture capitalists. The Lurman clipper ships were renowned—most returned to their home ports. Our family, which I thought of as a home port, no longer exists. Marsi will not return to her home port—ever.

The funeral is held at St. Thomas Church. It is an Anglican Church built in 1769. The ceremony amazes Dick, my California partner, who thinks it is more like a wedding than a funeral. At the end of the ceremony, the ushers release the rows of pews in the same manner they release the rows of pews in a wedding. It is eerie because a year ago Dick buried his wife, and Marsi and I attended the funeral. The day is cold and damp; sunlight between clouds highlights the gravestones with narrow shafts of light. Many of the gravestones are body-sized marble slabs on brick mounts, a grave form unique to Maryland and Virginia.

Marsi's casket is covered with white rubrium lilies. Our family always buries its dead with the scent of lilies. The fragrance overwhelms the church. The boys stand beside me, having no comprehension of why we stand before the altar. The church is filled. The overflow people stand in the graveyard. People arrive from everywhere. More sunlight peeps through the clouds. It is cold. I cannot show my grief to anyone. When everyone is gone I will cry.

Marsi's coffin is lowered into the ground. I throw a red rose on top of it. Mrs. Miller surprises me by throwing another red rose on the coffin. The red rose is the flower of true love. I feel as if my whole body is static electricity.

I am driven to our house, where we set up a receiving line. Food and drinks are available for 200 to 300 people. The line is endless. I do not remember what anyone says, but I act as if I am hosting a cocktail party—trying to be charming and more concerned for my guests than I am for myself. It is over as quickly as it begins. The staff and a few friends clean up the mess. The children are put in bed. When everyone leaves, I am agitated and restless.

Wandering aimlessly around the house, I wonder what to do next. I have had no appetite for days and decide to drink myself to sleep. When I finally collapse that night, my dreams take me back again to the A Shau. I become keenly alert, a killing machine, ready for the next wave of the enemy assault. I am shouting orders to "Take cover!" and no one hears me. The incoming explosions consume my senses and in the dim haze of the attack, I see Noldner and Blevins looking up at me, their faces coiled in fear and pain. As I reach out to them, they are vaporized in another blinding flash of incoming fire. There is no sound, only the piercing pain of hot shrapnel ripping through my body. I scream out "Medic!" but this time, Marsi appears out of the shadows. As I move toward her for comfort, she raises an AK-47 and pulls the trigger.

I wake up drenched in sweat. I am already in motion and reaching for my loaded Uzi in bed beside me. I move quickly through the house, room to room, checking each locked door. All my umbrella stands are filled with canes, shillelaghs and sabers with eagle handles—101st Airborne! All the way!

Outside, I check the perimeter and calculate if my imaginary machine guns have good fields of fire. I scope the rooftops and trees for snipers because I know that they are coming back for me, and I want to kill them all. Hours pass on the patio watching and waiting in the darkness for the attack. In the garden at sunrise, I dance with a Kamakura samurai sword, practicing moves and cutting the wings off butterflies in flight.

I stay awake fearing that this will become my daily routine: sleepless nights rolling into restless days that end in an alcoholic stupor. My world is turned upside down. I try to take charge, stabilize the boys' daily routine and continue to press on with business, but I quickly lose any capacity to focus and be productive. What was important last week, our year-to-date sales, earnings and other facets of my companies that were second nature to me are now a frustrating puzzle.

Mrs. Miller arrives the morning after to recover Marsi's jewelry and other "family" objects. She tells me she will give them to the boys. She also takes what she wants of things she has given us during our 15 years of marriage, including the picture of Marsi that was taken by a professional photographer during my first year at Harvard. That black-and-white photograph of my beautiful Marsi was to sit in our entrance and look forever at our house, her beautiful creation. Mrs. Miller can take the things she has given us, but what right does she have to take my precious possession, the image of my wife as I would remember her? She has stolen the last piece of my heart.

I try to hide my feelings from the boys, staff, business associates and friends who call, but I have little to say to anyone. They want me to join them, to get out. But I defer all invitations, assuring them that I am fine by myself, that I am seeking professional help. But no appointments have been made—only arguments within my disillusioned mind, weighing the pros and cons of a situation and never finding a resolution. Since there is no agreement, no action is taken. I become dormant, lost and alone.

I know that the only course I have is to seek professional help for the boys and in dealing with the crisis in my life. A friend refers me to Dr. Theodore Kaiser, a well-known child psychiatrist who has experience dealing with suicide and I make an appointment. Almost immediately, the questions I will ask begin rolling around endlessly in my mind as I try to control my feelings of anxiety. How do I comfort two boys who have lost their mother, who are learning disabled, and who now will surely suffer from post-traumatic stress disorder? What do I do at a board meeting when the room dissolves around me and I am in the middle of a firefight? What do I do after my child does something wrong and I lash out at him as if he were a prisoner of war? How do I deal with the compounded guilt of my wife's suicide and the loss of the men under my command in Vietnam?

The day after Marsi's funeral, in the parking lot outside Dr. Kaiser's office, I start to shake and sweat. I close my eyes and grip the steering wheel until my hands are locked in place, pressing both feet to the floor and arching my head back against the seat, stiff and rigid. I open my eyes and stare straight ahead into the empty lot, inhaling slowly until the rage finally passes.

Dr. Kaiser will have his hands full.

26

Guilt, Grief, and Anger

The sickness rolled through me in great waves. After
each wave it would fade away and leave me limp as a
wet leaf and shivering all over and then I would feel it
rising up in me again, and the glittering white torture
chamber tiles under my feet and over my head and all
four sides closed in and squeezed me to pieces.
— Sylvia Plath, "The Bell Jar"

15 March 1982
Pikesville, Md.
2 p.m.

On my first visit, Dr. Kaiser tells me that when there is a suicide, each family member must articulate guilt, grief and anger at the person who is gone. For 3-year-old and 6-year-old boys, grief and anger are immediate. He admits that it will take time for the boys to reveal their true feelings, but that there are techniques to help them to move forward. Art is a means of expression and reflection and can be used to open a dialogue. He asks me to have the boys draw their parents and over the next several weeks we have art sessions. Mothers without arms are a sign of anger. At least I, the surviving father, retain my arms.

Ashton finally says to me late one night that he thinks he was awakened by a loud explosion on the day Mommy Marsi died. He says if he had only run out to see where the explosion was, he might have saved his mother. I explain that there is no return from a gunshot wound to the head, and I feel agonizingly powerless to assuage Ashton's feelings of guilt.

On another day, Adair and I are standing by an open window. It has a screen that is shut and Adair is looking at dead flies at the bottom of the sill. He has a hard time understanding the concept of death. I ask him if he will see his mother again. He nods yes. I say no and point to a fly. Mommy Marsi is dead just like the fly. He cries—it is his grief. We bury the fly outside and cry together.

Several weeks later, Adair is back at that window looking at the flies. He kills one with a spoon. He asks me, "Did I kill Mommy?" Now it is my turn to cry as I try to assure him that he had nothing to do with her death. Mommy was sick. She killed herself. It was not her fault. Mommy was very sick. This is his guilt.

Does this dialogue help? I do not know. It seems to me that quite often what happens in our childhood gets buried deep within us. It can creep to the surface when we are adults, causing us to act in unproductive ways. We often react to adult situations with our childhood conditioning. Will this time spent with the boys, and with a psychiatrist's constant attention, keep the demons at bay? I can only pray that it will.

Around the house, I revert to military style management. I tell the boys on Friday night: "You will report for duty at 0700 hours. There will be an inspection. And then we will drill."

I show no emotion to them, but at night I break down sobbing. My tears turn my pillow into a swamp.

The NEA annual meeting is this week. Our limited partners arrive. It is a whirlwind. Kirk Miller, a cousin of Marsi's, and Bill Scriba, both friends from T. Rowe Price who have experienced suicide in their own families, contact me to try to help. NEA's administrative partner Nancy Dorman takes over my checkbook and keeps my life from falling into disorder.

Later at NEA's annual meeting, presenting in front of 60 people is daunting, but our limited partners are sympathetic and the firm's performance is good. On the way to dinner I sit next to Branco Weiss. He is a Swiss entrepreneur from Zurich. He tells me he has lived through what I face now. It will be better. The night of our limited partners' dinner, a tree falls on my newly constructed addition, breaking windows and walls. I built the addition with Marsi. To both of us it symbolized the transforming of my parents' house into our house. Now a windstorm has taken that away from me. I do not care, I feel nothing.

Seven months after Marsi's suicide, the dreams continue and my nightly recon missions are intensifying.

In Dr. Kaiser's office, it is now my turn.

29 Oct 1982
Owings Mills, Md.
1400 hours

> I love you honey.
> It's your presence I miss.
> And I terribly long
> For that one last kiss.
>
> — Marty Pijanowski, "One Last Kiss"

Dr. Theodore Kaiser: Well Mr. Newhall, we've talked a lot about guilt, grief and anger with your children. How are you dealing with these emotions?

Newhall: The anger has passed, but there is plenty of guilt and grief. For the rest of my life I will wonder: Could I have stayed closer to Marsi, should I have traveled less, could I have been a better husband? Guilt for Marsi's death is my shadow for life. The very violence of my guilt and sorrow frightens me.

Dr. Kaiser: No anger? That is unusual. Was Marsi perfect?

Newhall: Well, no sir. She wasn't perfect at all.

Dr. Kaiser: What do you mean?

Newhall: It started to happen several years before her suicide. She just started changing. She was always so self-assured about everything she did. It just seemed natural.

When we were married, she wanted to be a model. She liked to entertain. She was fascinated by art, history and literature.

Maybe I was too absorbed in work to notice the extent of the changes but one Sunday when I was taking care of the children, she started joking with the house painter. She sprayed his pants with the hose, making it obvious that he was not wearing underwear. He had an erection. Then she sprayed herself. She was wearing white linen shorts, a skimpy blouse, no underwear, and her nipples were erect. After she sprayed herself she started dancing around in a provocative way.

Dr. Kaiser: What did you do?

Newhall: Well, I put the children down for a nap. The painter left and I asked her to put some clothes on. She was furious with me but she obliged. After she returned she reluctantly admitted that Michael, the house painter, was her best friend. She had taken to asking him over for dinner when I was out of town. This shocked me; the last person on the earth who would ask men over for dinner when I was out of town was Marsi. I told her that I loved her and that she was my wife. I wouldn't try to spy on her, she was my wife.

Dr. Kaiser: What happened?

Newhall: She started hitting me. She started hitting me as if she really meant to hurt me. She even started throwing things and drew blood. I tried to calm her but she spat at me and said I was too selfish. It was only my business that mattered. Maybe she wanted me to get mad at her for having a lover. Maybe she wanted me to show outrage and emotion. She wanted us to go to a marriage counselor.

Dr. Kaiser: What did you do?

Newhall: We went to a marriage counselor. Well, it wasn't a marriage counselor, it was a faith healer. She was a disaster. She did not believe in the institution of marriage and it was always the man's fault.

Dr. Kaiser: If Marsi was under so much stress, why didn't her parents help?

Newhall: They told us right from the start they were not babysitters. Her father was a doctor and he believed his daughter had no problems.

Dr. Kaiser: What did you do?

Newhall: I found a psychologist priest who was acceptable to Marsi, and suggested we visit him.

Dr. Kaiser: Was he an M.D.?

Newhall: No, but he did seem to help Marsi. He was much better than the faith healer. I feel so guilty. How could I have prevented the suicide?

Dr. Kaiser: Take that word "guilt" out of your vocabulary. No, you could not have prevented her suicide. Ninety-five percent of manic-depressives who commit suicide are not diagnosed until they are dead. There are 500,000-plus suicides a year worldwide. My guess is that the real number is two or three times that. Think of the alcohol or drug overdoses that are suicides, the number of car crashes that are suicides and the number of falls that are really jumps to death. These are never recorded. This number is increasing rapidly. The aging population that has the largest number of suicides is growing geometrically as baby boomers age. The number of youthful suicides has increased from 5 percent to 20 percent of suicides over the past 10 years. For you, going forward, your children have four times the risk of suicide because of their family history. Of course, for everyone close to a suicide it is natural to feel guilty.

Newhall: How do I get rid of guilt? Where do I start?

Dr. Kaiser: You look into your heart.

Newhall: I am afraid.

Dr. Kaiser: But you must look.

Newhall: Well, how do you begin? To me it is obvious in the last five years of our marriage that Marsi was unhappy. My mere presence inspired anger in her. I made the bed, took care of the children, cooked the dinner and cleaned up. I gave her everything she wanted: dresses, jewelry, trips and parties, but it wasn't enough. She blamed me for everything that went wrong in our lives. She hated me for every aspect of our life together.

To me this was not rational behavior. I started reading the Harvard psychology textbook; the symptoms of depression were there: 1) lack of sleep; 2) moments of deep, dark rage alternating with manic highs; 3) discussion of death; 4) infidelity; 5) low self-esteem; 6) weight loss; 7) lack of interest in her children and violent anger at their slightest transgressions. You know this list better than I do.

Dr. Kaiser: What did you do?

Newhall: I went to her father, a doctor, and expressed my

concerns. He said that Marsi was not sick. Problems are just part of life. That door was closed. I showed Marsi articles on depression and suggested she get help. She laughed at me and said I was trying to pack her off to the funny farm. She had tried seeking help and it did not work. She degraded everything from my masculinity to my intelligence. Her anger shook my conviction. Marsi most of all, the woman I love, who bore my children, despised the core of what I am. It hurt—no, it is like the very marrow in my bones was on fire. So the guilt is there. I must compartmentalize the guilt—put it in a box and throw it into a river. To be saddled with guilt will castrate me—eliminate my ability to deal with the children, NEA, and the future.

27

Marsi's Diary

There's something demoralizing about watching two people
get more and more crazy about each other, especially
when you are the extra person in the room.

— Sylvia Plath, "The Bell Jar"

19 March 1983
Owings Mills, Md.
1400 hours

Newhall: Dr. Kaiser, I reread "Anna Karenina." It was Marsi's favorite book. It was a message in a bottle for me. I, like Karenina's husband, found the diaries.

March 31, 1980:

The temptation to do exactly what I want physically engulfs me. The tension of desiring what I have never had courses through my body. To enjoy one's body fully with another adds a provocative dimension to this whole crazy mad experience called life. To give freedom to my desires that have been sublimated and repressed ever since I was born is not frightening to me. I will feel relief and anticipate eagerly all it will release. I finally have allowed myself to experience and savor forbidden sex — the unfaithful wife — and I relish this joy that is my entitlement.

I am letting the purely feminine physical side of me find its voice. It is the voice of an ocean of passion. I cannot give up what has been awakened by my Michael even though it may hurt the lives of others close to me. Didn't Chuck always assume that I'd always be there — that I'd always care and support him? But I felt ignored and restless and was ripe for the picking.

Michael said that going to bed would ruin our friendship. When sex comes to the forefront of an affair the possibility of friendship is lost, and eventually it becomes a no win situation. But Michael has come to my emotional rescue and has given me some of the most magical moments of my life. The excitement of falling for him, his terrific smile, his looks, his height and his animal quiet will always lie beside me when I go to bed. The casualty is Chuck for my relationship with Michael will distract me from giving my intimacy to Chuck, which is after all a husband's right.

Chuck thinks I'm beautiful and sexy but he does not send chills up and down my spine or spasms coursing up and down my body. Just having Michael grunt when he has an orgasm makes me ecstatic. The grunt tells me exactly how strongly he feels his arousal. We are united in the same emotional energy field. The grunt means so much more to me than all of Chuck's poetry, generosity, caring, and heartfelt love. Without physical love there is no union of the souls. Chuck wants that union with me but I do not want him. We are after all both products of the egg and the environment.

Little things anger me so much. Ashton drops a jar of currant jelly. I yell and hit him. It is so easy to lose control around my children. It is only in passion that I escape my anger. I have discovered my body and it is good. Men hunger for it. I am a life force ripe to make love – to violate and be violated. I want this before I float down the river of life, inexorable as it is.

Michael when will you tire of me? I love your body, your strength. I could never do what I do for you for Chuck. I want you to own every part of my body. I love you to explode in me – hallelujah.

Oh yes, I love my husband and children but they are not enough. I want more, so much more. The conventional life I despise. I need to change therefore I act. I have two children. What if I was divorced, I would have to find someone to support me but I do not care.

What is important is to be oneself, to have inner peace—my aura shines—a manifestation of God—God is love—natural beauty—nature speaks to me. The validity of life is the experience. Michael—what do you mean to me? The impact of Michael in my life is immense in many ways—especially when we make love. I have no desire for our relationship to grow to a different level, I just want his passion.

Chuck is an emotional and physical turn-off and his life is so stressful, so demanding. It bores me. Michael fills me with rapture and I cannot get enough of him. I initiate our lovemaking in the morning, the afternoon, and at night. We put the children to bed and it is our time. My needs are so consuming, so pervasive—caught up in the freedom of encountering him and I will do anything to please him. I will separate from Chuck and give Michael his chance. If Michael does not want me, I will go to California with the children and start a new life.

Michael keeps saying he does not know what I want of him. He says he cares. I know I have touched his life as he has touched mine. I am no longer living to please anyone but myself.

Michael, I know you are having other women than me. I want you to be totally mine. I am afraid I'll be just another woman you have screwed, and I want more.

My Michael is a painter – he paints my house

Loyalty instead of passion can linger longer than beauty failed

I fell in a dream – sipping my coffee looking at gutter wrapped in a rainbow

Sing my free spirit, you light up my life

August 1981:

I'll be 32 tomorrow and I am very restless. I've come to grips with myself and laid a deeper and finer foundation for my life these last four years. But what am I searching for? I love my husband and my two sons and have worked hard on my marriage and worked to have children. Why am I welling up with discontent and unleashed vitality? There is a persistent and vague yearning for more. I no longer make the mistake of belittling what I have achieved but I certainly feel the need to push on—to go beyond my established routine, beyond the conventional life I appear to be leading. There is an impulse to act without being sure exactly what one wants or how to go about it. One thing seems certain. The need for a change is very real, the need comes from within me and is based on a desire to perform where I have not achieved before. For me it's never having earned my own money to the point I could support myself, and now I have two children and we live in inflationary times. What if I was divorced? How would I get on with the business of living without succumbing to a 2nd marriage for financial security? It is a very relevant question. What could I do?

* * * *

What are the chances of a child bride?

I am a slow blooming woman come of age. I do appreciate where I was, who I am. But it was necessary to release the pain of the past and in so doing unleash the positive—I embrace the whole experience in its entirety for better and for worse.

A limiting childhood causes a child bride to be unprepared. She may have raw talent, potential was there, instinct sound and true grit, and a terrific lack of experience except a veneer of sophistication—lack of understanding of the complexities of living—a feeling of being tossed out to sea—of being put upon—of treading water—no ability to take responsibility for my actions—for many years as I had a sense of being manipulated—a need to be free—my one "out" equaled marriage. But now being around my husband overwhelms me. He is like an elemental force of nature.

The irony is that I am unprepared for the only thing I had been raised to do—marry—a woman's traditional outlet. I went through an apprenticeship as wife and student. I had a yearning to become a mother and expand my mind by being a volunteer docent at the museum. The problem was reconciling motherhood with an awakening individual—with powerful forces that won't be stilled.

Oh how I want a room of my own—a space to work. Women need an area of competence outside of the home to prove their capabilities, test their talents, use their capabilities. To be truly creative in the home is necessary but it is also necessary to prove oneself beyond the home. I need to test and prove myself outside of the home as women have never been allowed to until now—being denied intellectual stimulation or monetary reward in a man's world and forced to stay home can be stifling. Individuals want to create—they need experience—they need expression. I want to be a woman but I need to stand on my own and prove myself which my life has never allowed me to do. Chuck's departure to Vietnam left me neither a wife or a widow, a divorcee or a date—total no man's land.

I suppose much of the pressure I feel comes from within. The trivia of living is there, unavoidable but the tenseness is mine alone. What a pity I have to waste myself physically and emotionally worrying. I worry that I'm cracking, that I'm not holding up, handling my responsibilities as flexibly as I might. I wonder what people think when I can't come to the phone, when I take it off the hook for long stretches to get some semi-interrupted peace. I wonder what the delivery man, that nice red head, thinks of Mrs. Newhall, who's become the lady in the blue wrapper, who is never dressed at 11:00 a.m. and whose hair is somewhat disheveled and whose white shepherd definitely strikes fear into his heart. It's fantastic how much time I spend worrying, or feeling driven, or feeling the need to explain to some imaginary person what I'm doing, when every moment is so crammed with other activity.

In August of 1967 I became 19. Two months later I was married. I recognized I was very young to be getting married but my mother was delighted at such a wonderful prospect for

*her daughter. Besides what are daughters for but to get married
in style? I had many conflicting thoughts and emotions
around my pending marriage which are as vivid to me today
as they were then. I knew I wasn't ready for marriage but I
saw no other option open to me and I was instinctively drawn
to my husband. I knew then what I still know now. I'd never
meet anyone finer than Chuck and a second thought followed
very fast behind, jabbing my consciousness. Probably no one
else would ask to marry me if they knew I lacked a sense of
self-worth. Today I know differently. Today I value myself but
that has taken 13 years. The vulnerable and unsure girl of 19
who embarked on a life journey with a man she respected and
loved to the best of her ability at that tender age has become a
woman. I was fearful of my femininity, of my very womanhood.
I was too embarrassed to look my brother or parents straight
in the eye after our honeymoon. I cast my eyes down and felt a
very real discomfort at being referred to as a woman. I didn't
understand my discomfort. I didn't realize I was still very
much a child, albeit a sophisticated and intuitive one.*

    *I didn't realize how much my mother intimidated me then.
I thought she was a role model to be emulated and at all costs
to be pleased. For my unspoken code of conduct had always
hinged on trying to gratify my mother in an effort to maintain
my own sense of well-being. One often tried from early age
and hence almost unwittingly to please the parent, for on that
rests emotional and physical security. Some children have
an especially strong need to please their parents and others.
They'll sacrifice themselves long before they realize they are in
a vicious circle. It will not be broken until they are happy in
their own skin.*

    *One is usually one's worst critic and I am no exception.
I sit in judgment upon myself. Tolerance of myself or others
is simply not allowed. This leads to an unspoken conviction I
cannot measure up personally or academically. So I began the
arduous campaign to always try to go the extra mile to please
those around me, in a bid for approval (approbation). There
was only one person I never sought approval from—myself.
It never even occurred to me to seek sustenance strength
from within. Much later, when I was 28, I knew I couldn't*

go another day looking to the outside for validation. I had to find that in myself. Chuck and I went to a minister that was a counselor.

That was the beginning of a very profound awakening of the soul and spirit deep within me which had long cried out to be set free, but at a high price. Regeneration took 4 years and nothing about it was easy, though always challenging and often gratifying.

Dr. Kaiser: What do you think when you read Marsi's description of her affair with Michael?

Newhall: I did not feel anger. I did not throw up. All I felt was sorrow mingled with forgiveness.

Dr. Kaiser: Did Marsi ever write you?

Newhall: It is such a coincidence you should ask. Here it is. Marsi wrote me a letter. I constantly reread it, but it makes me cry. I cannot control my grief. I have always controlled it so well before.

You will think I did this because I don't love you or the children or my parents but that is not it. I've done it because I can't stand to live with myself. This is the height of selfishness in one way. God forgive me.

How can I explain this? Mom's feelings towards me are disastrous. Mom's father abandoned her as a young girl after her mother died. He embezzled the trust fund that was left to her. He left mom with her grandmother—did not see her or talk with her. He still does not talk to her. Maybe she hates men after that? She emasculates my father and my brothers. She pits my brothers, Corbin and Stewart, against each other. She uses her money, their love for her, and anger to manipulate them. Corbin actually tried to kill Stewart by pounding his skull with a large rock. Mother says boys will be boys.

Everyone is afraid of Mother's tirades because we don't understand what causes them. So in my relations with Chuck, I imitate my mother. I become an actress on a stage of emotion. Those closest to me fear this violence, but it is a way to get attention I desperately need.

Why do people hurt and destroy those they cherish deeply—enough to leave scars that will never be erased. Within a family there are levels of dependency and coercion. If continued long enough, more often than not unintentionally, they can destroy your ability to cope with life. I know this because I will deal with the scars of Vietnam forever even though I was not there: constant worries about Chuck, my classmates painting our car with a ban the bomb sign, and my desires to be free of any responsibility. Chuck and his dreams are walking scars that will never heal, and through him they haunt me.

It is so ironic to have grown up like this. Our family is so intelligent. We enjoy verbal volleyball. My best memories of home life were being encouraged to speak and never let the conversation lag. But it left me insensitive to the beauty of silence.

Yes, I have been given material comfort, a good education, wonderful camps, the excitement and stimulation of travel. I appreciate the advantages and recognize my good fortune on one level of being. But I intuitively feel there are other levels of being. So I tested my parents to discover what I was missing. The result was really ugly scenes. My testing created a torrent of unpleasantness that was dumped on a soul that was too sensitive and too passive. My temperament caused me to internalize the pain. My tolerance for frustration in any relationship is low. Anything sets me off. I stand apart, sensitive, unsure how to put the parts of a paradoxical puzzle together, if indeed they ever can fit. What I do now is because the parts of the puzzle do not fit.

I want a family; a place to find myself; but it is hard to live through the present. Outwardly I conform. On the inside I fester. The day will come when restraints will be abandoned. Will I be able to live with the consequences?

Chuck, that is where you enter the drama. My marriage to you is not a merger of souls for a future life. We are two people fleeing an unhappy past. I came to live the false life that my parents bred me to live. Now my rebellion against those standards, has brought down our house upon your head. Forgive me.

You challenge me. You force me to seek education, to have the courage to love art, to begin to value myself. But at the same time I am out of control, unfocused, and continually searching for roots that have rotted and no longer exist. Now I am exhausted, too tired to continue the search. I am finished with life. Out of sight is out of mind; I remove myself from your sight. It will take time but it is for your best and for the children. In some way this is an act of love and my finest hour. I am a damned soul that goes to meet her destiny in hell. It is a just fate for what I have wrought during my life.

Do not feel anger at my mother for what she will do to you. She is no more than a puppet on a stage, manipulated by the strings to her past. She is not strong although she seems to be a tower of strength. Her life as a child was precarious. Her bravado and bluster is no more than whistling when you walk beside a graveyard. Forgive, but beware of her.

When you walk by my grave wherever it will be, do not whistle. Stop by once in a while, but not often, and talk to a woman who wished she could give you the love you sought. Yes, for you too my friend, did not marry me to find a soul mate. You too my friend, were running away from the past. So now you hold our future, the children, in the hollow of your hands. Be strong. Find new love. Raise our boys, the result of whatever it was we shared.

Let me give you one last bit of advice. Make sure that when you contemplate another relationship, that you are running to someone, not from something. Do not run from your childhood. Do not run from an empty bed. Do not run from fear that you cannot manage life by yourself. Run to someone. Know the life which I, Marsi, sought but never found.

Goodbye.

Newhall: Whenever I read Marsi's diaries, I try to touch her hair and calm her. But she no longer lies next to me. She lies in a coffin six feet underground.

28

Dr. Kaiser

There ought, I thought, to be a ritual for being born twice—
patched, retreaded, and approved for the road.

— Sylvia Plath, "The Bell Jar"

25 March 1983
Owings Mills, Md.
1400 hours

Dr. Kaiser: I cannot believe how painful that was to discover that after her death. But you must express your grief and then bury it. You discovered the details of her affair after you found the diary. You have mentioned these diaries several times. Tell me about your feelings for them.

Newhall: The Marsi I knew was the rope I used to climb out of the heart of darkness into the light. Without her calling me back I would have volunteered for two more combat tours in Vietnam. The diaries introduced me to a new Marsi, one I never knew existed. There was the Marsi I knew, loved and lived with for 15 years. Then there is the Marsi in her diaries, the Marsi I never met until after her death. I do understand the Marsi of the diaries but I wish she could have been my uninhibited lover rather than Michael's. My life is unfulfilled passion.

Dr. Kaiser: What did Marsi do in March 1980?

Newhall: She asked me for separation. I did not realize that she hoped Michael would move in with her. I later learned they lived together while we were separated.

Dr. Kaiser: What did you do during the separation?

Newhall: I slept in my office, worked hard and exercised hard. I wrote Marsi love letters every evening since she would not answer the telephone.

Dr. Kaiser: I do not think it was an accident that Marsi did not destroy her diaries. It is related to the reason she shot herself between your house and her parents'. Her choice of location showed her anger at you and her parents. Sometimes manic-depressives unconsciously will try to hurt the people they love when they commit suicide. Marsi clearly succeeded.

Freud said that suicide was a way of murdering your parents or your husband and children—an elemental shout of anger. Others say it is a way to communicate total misery or isolation—a shout of pain. Marsi said in her letter to you that she was eliminating herself because she was an impediment to the future of you and her boys—a shout of love. There is probably some truth in all three statements, but do not accept any one of them as the truth. Do not take it personally even though it hurts so much. It is just another manifestation of the disease—bipolar disorder. Is there anything you have not told me about Marsi or why she picked this place to die?

Newhall: About 10 years into our marriage, Marsi and I were sitting on our terrace drinking wine, talking and watching fireflies dance across the pasture behind our home. We were listening to Dionne Warwick's mournful "Walk on By" and enjoying our firefly-induced display when Marsi went silent and looked across the woods in the direction of her parents' house. She looked back to me and started speaking in a clear, sober, muted voice.

"I was 13 years old," she began. "My mother was just starting to prepare lunch. I decided to walk down towards the Caves Valley where there was a pond filled with trout. I used to go there to watch the fish jump." She paused.

"I felt an arm grab my throat and a hand on my mouth. I started to choke until he turned me around and looked me in the face. He said, 'Scream and you'll die.'"

In language far more vulgar than I'd ever heard Marsi use, she described in vivid detail how a strange, filthy, foul-smelling man raped her, then knocked her unconscious.

The next thing she remembered was her mother standing over her, furious. Her mother was worried that her friends would hear about the rape and that would damage the reputations of Marsi and the family, the perfect family. That night, Marsi said, her mother locked her out of her room. "I stood outside her room pleading to be allowed back to my bed," Marsi said. "She could not hear me because she was shouting at my father. Somehow she thought he was to blame for my indiscretion. I went back to my door and lay on the carpet, crying myself to sleep."

I didn't remember the relevance of the rape until you asked the question. Marsi did not refer to it in her diary and I think I chose to not remember. But then it clicked. Marsi chose to kill herself 300 yards from the spot where she'd been raped. If it had not been for the trees she could have seen it.

Dr. Kaiser: This is important and something does not ring true for me. Rape is a violent, physical attack; a crime that any parent would prosecute to protect the welfare of their child. It is inconceivable that her mother would have reacted in this way under any circumstances. Could Marsi have been ashamed to tell you the truth? That her mother was actually punishing her that night for disobedience? For meeting up with an older boy she had been told not to see? Did you have any sense that she might be lying to you?

Newhall: I have never thought about it until now. Her story was so disturbing that I only tried to listen and understand what she was telling me at the time. I told her that it must have been devastating to keep this secret all these years. I felt close to her and very sad. You may be right, but I believe the story Marsi told me.

Dr. Kaiser: Remember, single traumatic events do not always kill people. Manic depression is a disease that kills when it is stirred up with what we call our life's experience.

Newhall: Marsi knew me too well. Knew how to get to me. We had spent so many hours talking about the nature of love and she knew that physical love was my obsession. Marsi was my only lover. Without her, I am empty and alone.

Dr. Kaiser: How are you right now?

Newhall: It is especially difficult to be around other women, other women to whom I am attracted. Life for me is a series of unending fantasies about women who might be able to give me the love I sought.

Dr. Kaiser: Did Marsi ever apologize to you?

Newhall: Not during her lifetime but as I have told you I came across an apology in her diary.

Dr. Kaiser: Did that help?

Newhall: Yes it did. I even called Michael the day Marsi died and told him what happened.

Dr. Kaiser: What did he say?

Newhall: It was awkward. He blurted out that he was getting married in three weeks. He had never intended to take Marsi away from me. He was really saying that Marsi was just a good lay. He thought that would make me happy but it made me so mad. Marsi risked everything for someone so unworthy of her. But I guess he was afraid. Towards the end of their affair I guessed something was wrong. I took to running around the house and in our fields scaring up rabbits. I would shoot them with an Uzi on the run. He took the hint and stopped coming to the house. I thought about vengeance but he wasn't worth it. I pity his wife.

Dr. Kaiser: What did you do then?

Newhall: I tried to transform the diaries into a book, a worthwhile book edited carefully and published posthumously. I thought if I did so I could put my grief behind me. It would be a way to remember her. It would be like Sylvia Plath's "The Bell Jar." Marsi interlaced her favorite quotations in her diaries. She read "Anna Karenina" seven times, underlining the same Tolstoy sentence in seven different volumes, "All happy families are like one another; each unhappy family is unhappy in its own way."

I spent hundreds of hours preparing this document. There were boxes of notes, diaries, short stories and college papers. I did not change any fact or idea that she was expressing but I edited them for spelling and to clarify meaning. The words are hers; I merely gathered entries made at different times together when they covered the same subject. I reread her favorite books to see what she underlined. I added more quotes that described her life throughout the diary and put them together in chronological order. It took me four months.

The Millers did not want me to publish it. They say Marsi was just expressing unhappiness about her life with me, a man obsessed with business. That made me furious. They refused to admit any responsibility for Marsi's death. They put the blame on me. They are in the process of creating the atmosphere of divorce. This is after I have done everything to keep Marsi's anger at her parents hidden.

Dr. Kaiser: What do you mean?

Newhall: I edited the diary and removed passages that showed Marsi's anger with her parents. I had to do this. Marsi would not want me to hurt them. I had them over for dinner. I did everything I could to help them. I showered them with gifts that were memories of Marsi. I tried to make the boys a part of their life. I gave them an anniversary party and invited their friends. They said no one from their family should talk to me. I paid for the party even though I gave the credit for co-hosting the party to their children. They refused to contribute one cent, and did not give a hand in serving it. The children arrived to drink my wine and eat my food. I served them in quiet like a waiter.

At moments like this, I remember April 1982. Marsi had not been dead for three weeks. The Millers invited me down to Gaymcrest Farm, their place on the eastern shore of Maryland. Marsi and I dreamed of owning that farm someday. If you read Michener's "Chesapeake," the history of that complex part of the world, frozen in time, comes alive. The houses all face the water, because the water is the road on which you travel, not the land. Beautiful Georgian brick houses still face the byways of the tidewater.

When Ashton, Adair and I drove down that driveway of crushed oyster shells there were so many memories. The noise of the tires over oyster shells brought them back. That night we had cocktails with the Millers, their other daughter, Gaye, and her husband, Rick. Mrs. Miller asked me to go to the living room for a talk while everyone else cooked dinner. I sat down, and her personality changed in front of me. This was the woman that

Marsi described, that I had only seen once before. She was a fire-breathing monster.

She said I was wrong to have encouraged Marsi to continue her education. Marsi was not suited for education—books and literature caused her mood swings. My selfish absorption with music, art and literature were sirens that drew Marsi to her fatal end. She said I was a selfish monster—I killed her daughter by my self-absorption. I do not know where this came from. I thought she loved me as one of her own children. I started to shake. A noise exploded in my head and then I could not hear. I excused myself. I packed the sleepy children and paid my respects, and said I must return home. I was shaking all over. I got lost three times driving home, even though I could drive that route in my sleep. After the children were put to bed I cried. Never again did I visit Gaymcrest Farm. I only visited the Millers' home once again in my life. I was exiled from the family I loved and whom I thought had adopted me.

I had only seen this side of Mrs. Miller once before when Adair was born. She had given us a picture of herself as a child. We had it in the dining room but it was too small. Marsi moved it to a bedroom. Mrs. Miller demanded it back immediately. She was like a hurricane that forms over an island or a tidal wave that strikes without warning and leaves nothing in its wake.

Dr. Kaiser: How do you feel about her now?

Newhall: That is the greatest pain. At one time I called her Mom. For me she was a mother who taught me how to survive. When we were married, Marsi's mother knew I was shy and insecure among the people who would ultimately constitute our world. She chose to help me. She brought me out. By her praise, she gave me the confidence to dare. My parents had for years tried to destroy my confidence—not intentionally but effectively. I owe something of what I am to Marsi's mother.

Dr. Kaiser: Why did she turn upon you?

Newhall: She is a survivor. She has survived many difficult times. She survived by finding herself blameless of any and all guilt. She thinks so little of herself, that an acknowledgement of guilt would prick her fragile balloon and she would be gone in a quick rush of air. I'm sure she felt guilt for some role in Marsi's death but escaped that feeling by dumping all the guilt upon someone else's shoulders. That guilt now endangers my survival, and that of the children. I cannot let her destroy me. I am raising her grandchildren. To survive I must harden my heart against her. My parents never were my family. Now Marsi and my second family are gone. All that remains is my love for my boys, the Army and NEA, my second band of brothers.

Dr. Kaiser: As you know, I recommended you keep a superficially pleasant relationship with her. Invite her over for holidays with the boys and take her to dinner. I now think you should separate and keep your distance. You would become too upset by something she would say to make you feel guilty. You would lose your rationality and become ineffective as a father. No, stay away. Let her grandchildren visit her but keep a written record of every visit.

29

Another War

> So on we worked, and waited for the light,
> And went without the meat, and cursed the bread;
> And Richard Cory, one calm summer night,
> Went home and put a bullet through his head.

> — Edwin Arlington Robinson, "Richard Cory"

1 June 1983
Owings Mills, Md.
1400 hours

D r. Kaiser: Does Vietnam have any relationship with Marsi?

Newhall: There is a bit of Vietnam in most of my days—but especially the days after Marsi's death. Marsi and Vietnam are inextricably linked. When I left Vietnam in 1969, I thought that I was normal and that war had no lingering effect on me. I was wrong. Marsi's suicide put me back into the A Shau Valley. I immediately started wearing my old combat fatigues. In Vietnam, I had slept with a loaded weapon for a year. It was the only thing that made me feel safe. On Sundays, I would practice assaulting stone bunkers with my 6-year-old, firing live ammunition at paper targets. My 3-year-old would watch and play with toy soldiers.

The dreams come so often; the greater the stress I am under, the worse the dreams. Do the ghosts of those you have loved and lost appear beside you in the night? I can tell you yes, for it has happened to me. What is worse, they do not come with gentleness but often to accuse. They come at night. Night is the worst of times to receive incoming rounds. Artillery always makes me feel helpless. Where is it coming from? How do I fight back? In Vietnam I saw the rifle flashes, the flame of a mortar. Only then did I know where to seek cover. But with the dreams I hear the shots, hear the bullets whiz by, but there are no flashes. I cannot breathe.

The night begins; I go to sleep. I am in the A Shau again, back in a time when the mortars and the bullets come. Each night I start to sweat. I wake up. I go to sleep. The ghosts come. They seek their revenge for the life I took from them. They are all around me. I look into the face of hell. The smell is the worst. It is what I smelled on the A Shau plain; the smell of fear, rotting vegetation, blood, guts and the hollowness of death. The Uzi protects. It is then that I awake. I am bathed in sweat. My night shirt is wet. The problem is that I have been fighting. I try to block a knife to my throat. I throw my arm up and flip the forearm to the left. It is a perfect block.

I never leave the battlefield. Firing a CEO, appeasing the ego of a prima donna and trying to save a company from failure are today's battlegrounds. I am always short of breath. I am tired. My hands shake. Move from right to left, swing, follow through, pull the trigger—kill.

Dr. Kaiser: Don't you think this an overreaction to a business problem?

Newhall: Where does business begin and survival end? Everything is a fight to the death.

Dr. Kaiser: You really are something. Don't you realize the war is over? This is business, not life or death.

Newhall: You are wrong. Everything is war. My hopes and dreams have faded into never-ending pain and soul-eating remorse. It is war, war, continuous war.

Dr. Kaiser: No, Mr. Newhall, you are wrong. You are one of Skinner's rats, or Pavlov's dog. You suffer from a conditioned response. You receive an injustice, an affront, in civilian life and you are back on that jungle trail in Vietnam. You react as if your survival is in doubt. You become alive; you start to swing right to left, so you can keep the target, the enemy, at bay. You expect no quarter and you will give none.

The Army is the secret of your success and of your failure. Within a few seconds you analyze the alternatives, prepare for each contingency, plan for attack or retreat. But you overreact. Your heart races, you do not sleep. You enter a twilight zone where you do not communicate with others, especially those you love. You keep your feelings hidden from everyone. That creates stress that will kill you if you do not change.

The psychiatric term for what you are encountering is called post-traumatic stress disorder. Your nature complicates it. You are so anxious you can almost see the future at times, but it can be a curse. You are hell to live with because you shut everyone out by being so preoccupied. Your anxiety is like a volcano that erupts, overflows, and whose molten lava smothers all life around it. You are a deadly enemy, a troubling friend, and most of all a dangerous man to love.

You are also severely depressed. This is not genetic; it is event-caused depression. Your medicine will help if you give it time. It will be better than the alcohol that you are self-medicating yourself with today.

Newhall: That's encouraging. I have been ridden hard and put up wet.

Dr. Kaiser: Yes, you have been ridden hard. But let me say again, reduce your alcohol consumption. You are destroying yourself. You are using alcohol to self-medicate—your tranquilizer—you drink too much. You know the name of this— it is substance abuse. You say it helps you succeed, that it is your muse. But it is a mirage, the vision of an oasis in the desert that draws the thirsty traveler to his death on the sands. You are destroying yourself. Do not drink when you feel depressed or angry. Alcohol is the black dog's most effective trap. You may think that is your best defense mechanism. It is not.

You know when you are entering a time of crisis. You can make a list of what causes your anxiety reaction: squabbles with your partners, a company in trouble, or firing a man you respect because it is necessary to make a company work.

When you confront these problems, analyze your behavior. Is it appropriate for the boardroom or the battlefield? Your problems will not go away. It is a response conditioned by your childhood, where you were conditioned to have an anxiety attack in order to please parents who could not be pleased. That response became an integral part of you in Vietnam. It saved your life. Why do you think you came back and the others did not? You can anticipate what will happen. But this comes at a high price; you must learn to moderate the response.

Newhall: Great. I disguise what I am feeling in business situations. It is not easy, but no one in a boardroom knows what is going on inside me. But at home it is different. Occasionally, I have fits of anger that are totally inappropriate for the situation. As I age, this happens much more frequently and without reason.

Dr. Kaiser: Let me be very clear. When you feel like you are sliding back into that valley, realize the feeling that wanting to kill the CEO or partner sitting across the table who disagrees with you is an inappropriate response. I want you to try what psychologists call cognitive behavior therapy. Recognize the symptoms of PTSD and change your behavior and your thoughts. Breathe deeply and relax. Then think of the good things in your life. That CEO really made many good decisions with his company. Your partner has made many brilliant investment decisions over his career. Think of your children and how proud you are of them. Think of your gardens abloom in springtime, or the lean contrast of your evergreens and giant beach trees against the snow. Think of watching the sunset when you go to Bermuda. Think of skiing in Utah where you go to the top of a mountain, look out at all of nature's beauty and think you can talk to God. Think of the painting you just bought or the book you just read and what they taught you about life. Yes, you may leave your meeting for 15 minutes, but that is no worse than taking a phone call for 15 minutes. When you leave the meeting and are flying home, focus on all the positive things that are going on in your life. I know this sounds simple but it is not. You will fail much more than you succeed. But do not tolerate defeat. Will yourself out of that valley.

I will prescribe something, but it will not be particularly effective. PTSD is treatment resistant depression. While lithium is still the gold standard for treating bi-polar disease, we have just begun to research the diseases of the mind that create a host of other problems—everything from cardiovascular disease to irritable bowel syndrome. Cure the mind, cure the body.

I know you suffer from these other diseases. There may be a medication that can help, but in the end, the solution to eliminating your pain lies within you—your heart and your mind. Perhaps your brave sons, if they walk down your path may find the magic bullet. They have already encountered more challenges than others men overcome in a lifetime. I have no doubt their success will astound you.

Also, give up your military paraphernalia. Get rid of the loaded Uzi in your bed. Do not use military time with your boys: Say 1 p.m., not 1300 hours. Do not wear Army fatigues on the weekend or assault bunkers with the boys. Now I want to test you. What do you think caused your relationship with Marsi to deteriorate so fast?"

Newhall: I actually can answer that question. When Marsi started to aggressively criticize me all the time, it reminded me of my parents when they told me I was not good enough or my mother told me I looked like a girl. It reminded me that they never came to any swimming meets to cheer me on. So I tried to please them but always failed. That criticism made me more anxious. Positive feedback, which my grandmother gave me, is what motivates me.

When Marsi denied me physical intimacy and did not touch me, it reminded me of my parents. They sent me away from them. No one was there when I got an A on a test. We shook hands during the few times when I returned home. The loss of intimacy fueled my anxiety because Marsi and I once had been very intimate.

So how did I react? I totally withdrew from her. I answered her long questions with a word or a sentence. We slept on opposite sides of the bed. I often slept clutching my legs. I became rigid. Nothing could alter my schedule. I was so easily distracted; the only way to finish a task was to stay totally focused it. Even when we went on trips everything was planned to the minute. There was no spontaneity in our lives. I did not take 20 minutes to see a sick child because I would be late for work.

How this must have tortured Marsi. Her emotions were running wild. She took my behavior as a rejection and that collapsed her self-esteem, sending her anxiety to the sky. There must have been 100 other negative side effects. Then along came Michael and for a short time the feeling that she had her hand in an electrical socket went away, but only for a short time. Her anger and contempt for me increased. She criticized all my goals because she knew it would hurt me. She would no longer even kiss me when I went to work.

We were like two people punching each other. The first one would punch and the second would punch harder. And so it would proceed, increasing in violence until both get knocked out, fall to the ground, and cannot get up. We each contributed to the destruction of the marriage.

Dr. Kaiser: I give you an "A" for that self-analysis. Remember the four ways to treat yourself for PTSD. First, when you feel yourself getting angry, depressed and increasingly out of control, realize that is not the real you. It is a disease called PTSD. Seek to return to the real you. Second, use cognitive behavior therapy to focus on the good things in your life. Third, and perhaps the most important, know the hidden triggers to your emotions. To do this you will probably have to meet with a psychiatrist the rest of your life. Do not let the hurt and fears of the child control the man. Fourth, keep developing defense mechanisms. Collecting, gardening, classical music, your love for your pets, your involvement in your son's lives and your travel are all defense mechanisms, When you focus on them, they keep the black dog at bay. You will have to get new defense mechanisms as time goes on and develop new interests when you can no longer hunt, fly fish or ski. Adapting to old age is a game for you to win. Don't get frustrated. Play the game.

Newhall: It is so difficult. I think back to what my grandmother said.

Dr. Kaiser: What do you mean?

Newhall: I told you my grandmother raised me. When I was a child, she would sit before me. "You are special," she would say. "You are different from your father and your mother. Your father is my son but you are so different from him. Listen to your parents—obey them; but know that their concerns are not your concerns. Their dreams are not your dreams. Their demons will not haunt you." This is a difficult message for a 12-year-old. But my grandmother was always there for me—I trusted her completely.

She looked at me and said, "I cannot see what you will become but do not disappoint me. Your friends make fun of you. You are slender and not yet the man that you will be. Let their bitterness run off your back. Be still and listen to what happens around you—do not let minor failures shape your impression of yourself. When your teacher gives you an F and you have worked hard and feel you deserve an A, know in your heart that you have gained knowledge from writing the paper that will stay with you forever because it was so ill received. The world is perverse and does not understand you.

"Most of all relish each defeat, for defeats teach you. Study your defeats so that you will not repeat them. Study defeat so that you can turn it into victory. Defeats are God's way of telling you that you must change course. Those who betray you, the bully, the cheat, they are all lessons. They do not diminish you."

My grandmother ended our conversations like this: "You, by your deeds, will give us something akin to immortality. Your honor, your virtue as shown in your actions, will speak for your family—all of us. That is what allows me not to fear death. If death smiles at me, I smile back. Yes, I may sing with the angels, but if I do not join that choir, you, my angel, will sing for me on Earth. Hold your voice high and when you sing think of your grandmother who believed in you, and will always be with you when you face the trials that are your destiny. But above all, never let your actions show the depth of your troubles. Control your mind and your emotions."

Dr. Kaiser: Well, that's an interesting way to help an emotionally abused, learning-disabled boy deal with the issue of self-esteem. But your grandmother directed you to a dangerous path—excellence in everything. You always see the next risk. You cannot be content with what you have accomplished.

Newhall: But she sent me down that path.

Dr. Kaiser: Perhaps, but if you wish to walk that path for much longer, moderate your response.

Newhall: But I enjoy the intensity of my response so much. I'm addicted to the passion. Will you give me more wisdom?

Dr. Kaiser: The wisdom is within you. I only listen. My job is to help you open the doors.

Newhall: I am so tired of opening doors. They are heavy oak and they have tigers behind them.

Dr. Kaiser: Well, it is time to open another. Try that solid oak door in front of you and face your tiger. What do you think Marsi felt? She was a manic-depressive—the highs and the lows. How do you think she felt being married to you? You were so close to her, perhaps she thought that by destroying you she would destroy herself and at last find peace? You cannot sit still. You move at a run around the house because you chase the impossible dream. Being busy is a good defense mechanism, but your impossible dream is everything—the furniture, the garden. It is as if every little detail is necessary to express the meaning of your soul. That practice helped destroy your marriage and alienate Marsi—the woman who only wanted to sit beside you and discuss what the children did during the day. The woman who found your presence, that which centers her universe, her reality. Don't let your defense mechanisms become obsessions. If they do, it destroys their value.

The best thing in life may be to know that you will spend eternity in heaven. But Marsi felt she would spend eternity in hell. Her life in her mind was a failure. She was an unfaithful wife, she beat her children. She lied and tried to convince the world that she was the goddess of beauty and light. This was the greatest pain—to pretend that she was good when she believed herself to be the ultimate evil.

To Marsi, when she was depressed, there was no evil like her. She existed. She hid. She pretended but beneath the pretty face, the overwhelming self-confidence, the manners, the grace, the style—she was a woman who hardly had the strength to put one foot in front of another every day.

What do you think now? Did you appreciate the courage of the woman who slept beside you? She gave you support at T. Rowe Price. She supported you when you started your own company, NEA. But she was fragile. She supported you with courage while knowing her own fatal flaws. Fatal flaws—we all have them. For Marsi to support someone like you was hell. Everything you did emphasized her own inadequacy. When you conquered, in her mind, she was defeated. Yet she conquered her fears and her pain for a time. Then it was too much. She felt like hell's bait. Her life was a sin. She stood in the way of you, Chuck Newhall. She thought you could only find happiness if you were free from the curse that she had put upon you. Most of all, she feared for the children. She had beat them. She was damned to perdition. You cannot imagine the torment, the hell of feeling absolute self-worthlessness, that every suicide victim embraces. In her mind, she chose the devil as her husband to free you of her.

You must appreciate her pain and her sacrifice. You must realize that she is not alone. Marsi's fate is yours and mankind's. Remember what she taught you. Life is an accident of events that you do not control. These events change the chemistry in your mind and the nature of your soul. You must deal with unexpected change if you aspire to be a survivor. Do you feel betrayed by Marsi?

Newhall: Yes, I suppose so. You remember that song: "You picked a fine time to leave me, Lucille, with two hungry children and the crops in the field." Even after everything, I love her too much. Too well.

Dr. Kaiser: Do not be too hard on her. Remember Dante reserved the ninth level of hell for those that betrayed the trust of people who have loved them or who are traitors. They are doomed to suffocate and run buried in mud until the devil eats them, which he does again and again for all eternity. I do not think God wants those plagued by bipolar disease to suffer like that. They have suffered enough during their lives. Remember anger. You must let it slide off your back like rain off a rubber poncho in a downpour. You must do the same thing with your grief and your guilt or you will not survive and be able to fulfill your dreams. Leave the anger, guilt and grief behind. They are yesterday's news. How are you feeling today?

Newhall: My mind plays tricks on me. The harder the armor, the more fragile the flesh. My chiton shell is impervious to the world. But my flesh is jelly. When the shell is breached, I have few defenses. I have difficulty dealing with anger—Marsi's anger, my mother's anger, or my partners' anger. Yet give me an affront against my family, my honor, or most important of all do something that is morally wrong, and I will be your enemy. I may look calm, but such affronts send me back to the A Shau Valley for my soul is the soul of a warrior. I seek peace in battle and peace in destroying my enemy. Battle is the place I feel most secure.

Dr. Kaiser: That's an impressive story, but let's end our session with a very serious warning: You are a narcissistic obsessive-compulsive workaholic and you have to change. You have sole responsibility for the lives of two very fragile children. You have responsibility for a company that is important to the future of the country. The children are jeopardized by their genetics. The children are at risk for developing bipolar disorder and both have attention deficit hyperactivity disorder. This combined with the post-traumatic stress disorder caused by their mother's suicide is a potentially lethal mixture. Their odds of survival are 5 percent. Do you understand?

Newhall: All too well. If they overcome this challenge, and many others, they will be heroes who will change the way the world is.

Dr. Kaiser: Good. I want you to abide by two rules: If you are ever remarried, I do not want you to have any additional children. You face a tremendous challenge handling the responsibility you have; to add another would lower the chance of raising your two boys to successful adulthood to almost zero. Do you accept that?

Newhall: Yes, but if I find a new wife, won't she have something to say about that?

Dr. Kaiser: Of course, but you must convince her of why this is absolutely necessary. Secondly, you must raise your children at home. You must immerse yourself in their lives. This will demand a lot of your time. I know this will be hard given the demands of NEA, but it is the only way you can succeed. You went to a boarding school and liked it, but I'm afraid that is totally out of the question for your sons.

Newhall: Then I must totally change course.

Dr. Kaiser: You know that PTSD leads to depression and

the black dog. You have been savagely bitten by the black dog. You will recover but you will never be the same. In your youth, you will see him in the distance, just a glimpse of him running between the trees. In your middle age, the black dog will become bolder. He will sit on the lawn in full sun only 20 feet away, his jaws open and his saliva dripping to the ground. If you do not fight as you age, that rough beast will run behind you biting your legs, taking the food out of your hands, and destroying the relationships with those you love most. He will haunt your every move. His breath is as fetid as the hell he comes from. Then one day, if you let him, he will grab you by the throat and drag you to a smoldering hell and no one will come to your funeral.

Remember, you make your own fate, good or bad. In a sense you must be reborn. As your grandmother would say, "Get over it." For I know you will not hide and put yourself out of harm's way. You will always pursue your great dreams. You will develop defense mechanisms and create a minefield to keep the black dog at bay. Some days you will only get 2 hours of sleep. When you are not working, you will be focused on the other passions of your life—the gardens, travel, art and museums. Your business will be an army mission for you with a daily calendar and copious notes about what you have to do. You will no doubt exhaust everyone around you with your obsessions, but you'll make no time for the black dog.

If you choose any other path, I know you will continue to immerse yourself in—what did Conrad call it—the destructive element. It is the path your grandmother sent you down. Let me put it in her words. It is not honorable to let PTSD and the black dog defeat you.

I have no doubt that you will write extensively about Vietnam, Marsi and the rest of your experiences. You will chew on your book like a dog chews a bone. My hope is that when you are finished, you will burn it all—the drafts, the diary, everything and focus solely on the next chapter and the people who will now be standing beside you every day for the rest of your life. It may be decades before this is realized, but taken one at a time, each day will bring you closer to a realization of a full and satisfied life.

So, become a teacher to your children and a mentor to your associates. Find a second wife who will love you unconditionally and can help you be a better parent. Build close relationships with your sons. Work at developing friendships and travel together. And learn to control your anger, manage your grief and avoid toxic people and environments to chase the black dog away every day of your life.

You faced and overcame fearful odds in Vietnam and now you are facing them again.

Beat those odds.

Afterword

"Victory is sweetest when you have known defeat."
— Malcolm Forbes

So you think "Fearful Odds" is a story of defeat? It is not. I did not let PTSD and the black dog of depression win. My grandmother told me each crisis is the stepping-stone to the next victory. For you to survive an attack, the wound must make you stronger. Each crisis will give you the strength to conquer the next defeat. It is a far better fate than slipping into the quicksand and disappearing forever. I was saved in Vietnam by Marsi. I climbed a rope back to her from the place where the black dog rules. I was saved from Vietnam and Marsi's suicide by Amy, my second wife. Again, I climbed a rope back to Amy and my children from the place where the black dog rules. I am going to rate myself on a scale of 1 to 10 in my pursuit of making the world a better place.

I was a poor father and husband when I was married to Marsi. One hundred percent of my emotional energy went to chasing impossible dreams. I was never home for a dinner with my wife and children and traveled six days a week. Marsi spent most of her time alone.

Amy taught me how to be a parent. When Marsi committed suicide, the psychiatrist we saw said that with post-traumatic stress disorder and severe ADHD the boys had a 95 percent chance of ending up in jail by the time they were 21. Amy forced me to come home for dinner at 6 p.m. and engage in serious dinner conversations with the boys. We took them on family vacations. I became a teacher. I created my own parable of the talents: Three boys were given 10, five and one talent. The boy with 10 came back with 10, the boy with five came back with seven, and the boy with one came back with 10. It does not matter what you do or how many talents you have, the important thing is to increase them. My goal for the boys is that my ceiling will be their floor. My children, Ashton and Adair, have increased their talents tenfold.

The boys are my heroes. They have faced fearful odds and have overcome them. The psychiatrist who said they would fail now lectures around the world about how they overcame PTSD. Ashton started his own venture capital firm at age 26 and now manages more than $3 billion. Adair played a role in getting two biopharmaceutical companies started, both of which were sold for more than $500 million. He now is working at one of the best health care venture capital firms in the United States. Who knows—he may cure cancer. Amy and I get a grade of 10 for the boys.

NEA, the venture capital firm I founded with Frank Bonsal and Dick Kramlich in 1977, has raised more than $14 billion and has helped to start 800 companies with more than half a trillion in revenues. The companies that NEA has helped entrepreneurs build have created balloon angioplasty, interleukins, chirally pure pharmaceuticals, Medicare and Medicaid case management, epigenetics, the Internet, the ethernet, high-speed data communications, and software as a service, to name only a few. The companies I helped create have revenues of more than $160 billion. NEA has changed the world for the better. Many of the great companies were generated by my partners, but the founders of NEA created the platform. NEA gets a grade of 10.

While at NEA, I co-founded the Mid-Atlantic Venture Association (MAVA) with Frank Adams of GroTech (another Maryland venture firm). The association served the area from Northern Virginia to Delaware, which is similar in size to the greater Boston area. When we started, there were three venture capital firms in the region. When I left MAVA, there were 120. We attracted tens of billions of dollars to the region through public and private financings. MAVA gets a grade of 7.

The venture capital industry was almost destroyed over the last 12 years. Over its 150 years of life, the venture industry has created 70 percent of the economic success this country has enjoyed. Gulf Oil, Carborundum, General Reinsurance, Alcoa, Walmart, IBM, 3M, Thiokol and Eastern Airlines were venture deals. Over the past 12 years with help from Pete Bancroft (a famous California venture capitalist), the National Venture Capital Association, and the Harvard Business School (Felda Hardiman, Tom Nichols and Dr. Josh Lerner), we have recorded the oral histories of 70 venture capitalists that would otherwise have been lost. Harvard is writing a history of venture capital that will hopefully educate our country on the industry's importance. This effort now deserves a 5, but it could go higher if the book is published.

One reason the venture capital industry was almost destroyed was the demise of the capital markets. I helped found a company called Inside Venture with the hope of correcting the problem. It failed and was sold to Second Market, a company founded to make a market for the secondary sales of private companies' shares. As a result of my work on Inside Venture, I met a former senior officer of NASDAQ, David Wield. David provided the data, and the data showed the effects of capital markets' demise on small companies. This data was used by Kate Mitchell of Scale Ventures, whom Timothy Geithner had picked to form a task force that would recommend a cure for small company capital markets. The result was the Jobs Act, which has done much to improve small companies' access to capital. I give myself a grade of 7 for this effort.

Over the years, Amy and I have created four houses filled with art collections. The beauty of the houses and the art collections has sheltered us from life's storms. During our 31 years together we have also created a garden with 54 formal garden rooms that has approximately 750 visitors a year. I am writing three books, a process that will take at least 15 years. Our creative life gets a grade of 7.

The Baltimore Museum of Art is a great institution built more than 100 years ago, but Baltimore is becoming Detroit. I have served as a trustee for 35 years raising money for this institution. I am apprehensive about its future over the next 30 years because companies and the wealthy are fleeing the state. The BMA gets a 3.

Over the past 31 years, I have had four more life-shattering crises, and each crisis is another war; each crisis dragged me back to the A Shau where Marsi hunts me with an AK-47. Each battle takes three to four years. Fortunately, the intensity diminishes over time. In Vietnam, I thought it took wolves to make the caribou strong. Not true. In my dreams, wolves and the black dog devour me.

One battle was the scandalous collapse of a company I helped to build for 20 years. Another battle was during the tech bubble of 2000. Some of my partners wanted to fire the health care team. Their effort was thwarted and health care is now an important part of NEA. The third battle was my separation from Amy. We are now happily reunited. The fourth battle was the unfortunate circumstance surrounding my self-imposed exit from NEA. I am now happily working at Greenspring Associates, Ashton's venture capital firm. Of the last 31 years, 16 years have been spent in the A Shau Valley, where I was totally focused on survival. God bless Amy, for she has suffered much. I have successfully battled PTSD and have made important contributions to both our country and the world. My average grade is 7. Not bad for someone who has battled the black dog for 16 years. Best of all, if I meet my grandmother again, I will say, "Like Lord Nelson, I have done my duty."

There are two types of casualties in Vietnam, Iraq, and Afghanistan—those who lived and those who died. Post-traumatic stress disorder haunts the living until they die. Have I survived? Can I see the sun and flowers, and smell the sweet salt smell of the ocean? Does it register in my heart? Can I see my grandchildren and love their smiles, or must I frown all the time and be haunted by my past? Do I jump when a car backfires? Am I able to love Amy, or am I a hollow shell who destroys intimacy and her self-confidence with never-ending demands to fight the next war and my pursuit of perfection in all things? Can I adhere to my central tenant of life, which is to give far more than I get to anyone I meet? Can I cry or can I stop crying? If I can do these things, I will survive; otherwise I am nothing but the chaff left after the wheat is harvested. The question has yet to be answered.

Why is this relevant today? I had a 12-month tour of duty in

Vietnam. I can only imagine what the warriors of Afghanistan and Iraq faced—four or five years of combat tours with brief returns to home. I remember parting with Marsi on R&R in Hong Kong. I doubt I could have done that four or six times. Suicide rates in the military are at all-time highs because the troops are macho and warriors do not cry. I believe the suicide rates reflect only a small fraction of those affected by PTSD. Given a hundred-year war, school shootings, and the economy's effect on those who have lost homes and jobs and who stand in food lines, and the violence engulfing society, I believe we face an epidemic of PTSD.

Over the past 40 years the government has systematically destroyed the mental health industry by reducing reimbursements for psychiatric hospitals, outpatient clinics and physicians. We are ill prepared to face the epidemic we will face over the next 30 years.

There are two other aftermaths of war other than PTSD. The first is physical damage. When I resigned my commission, I seemed to be in perfect health, but it was an illusion. For months, weighing 120 pounds, I carried a 140-pound load over torturous terrain, rappelled down cliffs, jumped 15 feet off a ridgeline with the pack, and climbed many a steep slope, slipping and crashing 30 feet down the hill. About 10 years after my return, my chronic back problems started. Today, they hamper my ability to walk. Was my back damaged in Vietnam or did I just have a disintegrating skeletal frame? Who knows?

Over the past 30 years, I have paid at least $30,000 a year to treat PTSD and my back. Insurance paid some of the bills. My psychiatric problems are not covered by insurance today. The country can ill afford to pay for problems that arise 10 years after you leave the service. I was lucky. I had the insurance and enough money to pay my bills out of my own pocket. Think of the veterans who are not as fortunate as I was.

The final aftermath of war is more difficult to measure. It is what the military does to your mindset. Since the age of 8, I was trained to anticipate the good, the bad and the ugly—and have pre-planned responses for each of the three situations. The plans had to be perfect. This training kept me alive in Vietnam and in business. It was the behavior I carried into my personal life—gardens, collecting, my charitable activities and a host of other things.

My military training is still hard-wired in my civilian brain. I spend time preparing how to defeat adversity, ignoring love and the beauty of the sunrise. I have high goals when I go to business meetings. My companies must change the way the world is. My wife and I argue continually over my obsession to erase adversity and pursue perfection, which conflicts with her desire for a normal, peaceful life. Recently, I met Nate Fick, a young Marine officer and now a civilian. He wrote a compelling book, "One Bullet Away." We were discussing this behavior trait. He said, "My wife always tells me I am great in a crisis but hard to live with on a day-to-day basis." Amy would say: "Hell to live with on a day-to-day basis!"

Warriors were trained to create hell for our enemies, and that can spill over into civilian life. We can be hell to live with— there is no doubt.

Postscript

March 12, 2015
Owings Mills, MD
4:21 p.m.

Following numerous personal and professional submissions leading up to the publication of Fearful Odds, I received many constructive and insightful comments that have been incorporated into the final version. I sincerely value each comment. Thank you for making this work better and more relevant.

With this publication, it is my intention to redouble efforts and collaborate with organizations to help others understand the issues addressed here have on individuals and their families. Our website at: www.fearfulodds.com is rich with information about Operation Somerset Plain, the brave men I served with in Vietnam and those whose death was the supreme consequence of war. The website is also a reservoir and resource for more information on the warning signs of post-traumatic stress, treatment locations, partner organizations and an up-to-date reading and reference list on related developments in these areas.

I am deeply indebted to Dr. Solomon H. Snyder, M.D. for his support and endorsement of Fearful Odds which follows in its entirety.

Chuck Newhall

JOHNS HOPKINS
UNIVERSITY

**The Solomon H. Snyder
Department of Neuroscience**
School of Medicine
Baltimore, MD 21205

Solomon H. Snyder, M.D.
Distinguished Service Professor of Neuroscience,
Pharmacology and Psychiatry

March 4, 2015

Mr. Charles Newhall
Owings Mills, MD 21117

I am writing to convey some additional thoughts about your book "Fearful Odds".

Fearful Odds can be conceptualized as a treatise on PTSD based on your personal life experiences. You have overcome myriad stresses since childhood highlighted by difficulties during school years and, most importantly, the vividly depicted, terrifying but illuminating episodes of your time in Vietnam. You then recount the difficulties with Marsi and the aftermath of her death.

There have been many books written on PTSD. They are largely "how to" manuals incorporating prescriptive "lessons" on what to do about one or another type of emotional stress. Too often, these volumes render problems in black-and-white with comparably simple-minded remedies.

Your volume is far better than the great majority of PTSD books. You let the reader appreciate the psychological pain of a wide range of traumatic episodes. In describing how you managed to confront these challenges with largely successful outcomes, you enable the reader to empathize with what you experienced and to apply your insights into his/her own problems.

The illuminating depictions of sessions with your psychiatrist Dr. Kaiser can be regarded as almost a manual for understanding PTSD and learning how to overcome it. However, unlike the majority of books on the subject, you explain how PTSD can be addressed via depictions of how your own efforts have succeeded to varying extents. Readers will learn far more from your book, which is "real life," than from others.

I never met Marsi, but the portrait you convey of her is so eloquently presented that I feel like I know her -- a sentiment that will likely be espoused as well by your readers, heightening the book's impact. Besides your description of Marsi as a personality, you bring forth many clinical characteristics that one could almost employ to pinpoint a diagnosis.

One lesson all of us learn in psychiatry is to eschew making a diagnosis based on something written down on paper, especially in a book that is not designed as a clinical treatise but as a creative depiction. Bearing in mind such caveats, I think the image you depict of Marsi is of an entrancing personality who is nonetheless notably disturbed. She appears to be subject to fits of serious depression and overall instability, which of course you appreciate far more than me.

What propels people to suicide? The most simple minded explanation is that individuals who kill themselves are seriously depressed and thus qualify for labels from the Diagnostic and Statistical Manual(DSM5)along the lines of major depressive disorder. However, I don't think that this approach adequately conveys what goes on in the minds of the victims who, as you aptly convey, "annihilate" themselves. A good bit of research fits with the notion that suicidal iduation and actions are not simply products of depression but represent a unique impulsive activity, which has a 'life' of its own. The 'Bell Jar' by Sylvia Plath describes Ms. Plath's encounter with a powerful suicidal drive that she cannot escape. She talks about walking down the street and seeing every rooftop as a vehicle for death. Every movie she views suggests diverse means of ending her life. All of this takes place in the absence of obvious, serious depression.

In your chapters on Marsi, you describe a series of events that lead inexorably to her suicide. These episodes roll on and on in a relentless parade that resists efforts to place roadblocks that might prevent the emerging tragedy. In my estimation this portion of your book enables the reader to appreciate the overwhelming forces that concatenate in the minds of the future suicide victim. You tell the story of Marsi's end as the inevitable termination of long series of emotional traumas. You do this with greater persuasive power and elegance than I have seen in any other comparable writings, even those of Plath herself. Your book is a valued contribution to the literature on this important area.

Congratulations on a splendid opus.

Solomon H. Snyder

Charles W. "Chuck" Newhall, III

Charles W. Newhall III co-founded New Enterprise Associates (NEA) in 1977. Prior to founding NEA, Chuck was a Vice President of T. Rowe Price. He played a major role in formulating NEA's investment strategy with partners Dick Kramlich and Frank Bonsal, and he has been instrumental in financing the dramatic changes in both the health care services and pharmaceutical/biotechnology industries. NEA helped to start over 800 companies with revenue in excess of $500 billion. He was also a start-up investor in several companies that helped to change the health care delivery system. One such success was Amerigroup, the leading independent Medicaid HMO, which Chuck helped to start in 1994. He also helped to start BRAVO, a company that case manages the frail elderly in the last three years of life.

In 1988, Chuck co-founded the Mid-Atlantic Venture Capital Association (MAVA) to encourage the growth of venture capital in the region, and is Chairman Emeritus of MAVA. In 2010 Chuck was honored by National Venture Capital Association with the American Spirit Award for his sponsorship and guidance of a project chronicling the achievements of venture capitalists and the evolution of the industry by producing oral histories, archiving early documents and establishing research outlets for academics wanting to understand the industry.

Chuck has served on the board of numerous charitable and community institutions including the Greater Baltimore Committee, as well as the Baltimore Museum of Art, where he was involved for over thirty years and served a term as Chairman of the Board.

Chuck served in Vietnam commanding an independent platoon including an initial reconnaissance of Hamburger Hill. His decorations include the Silver Star and Bronze Star V(1st OLC.) He received an MBA from Harvard Business School, and an honors degree in English from the University of Pennsylvania.

Source: Venture Capital Greats: Charles W. Newhall, interview by Carole Kolker, April 18, 2013, National Venture Capital Association, Arlington, VA 2010.

Acknowledgments

I wish to thank the following people who have helped me with this book. Some gave me encouragement and some spent hundreds of hours editing my work. The list includes Dr. Theodore Kaiser, the physician who guided Amy and helped me defeat the black dog, as well as the other psychiatrists who worked with my family for 40 years. I also want and need to acknowledge the support and encouragement of Barbara Dryer, Marc Blum, Dr. Ellen Reeder, Dr. Kay Jamison, Wayne Rogers, Mark and Mauree Jane Perry, Roger Frisky, Nate Fick, Joseph Galloway, John Neely, Jim Blair, Jim Swartz, Brian Libby, Nick Stoneman, Nancy Dorman, Stan Maseroff, Trudy Brown, Dr. Carolee Barlow, Tom Clancy, Dr. Sol Snyder, Lt. Col Steve Bauer, Lt. Col Peter Quirin, Rachel Weller, Alan and Nancy Gilbert, Barrett Friedlander, Patrick Donnelly and Jack Pollard. I want to also thank Ed Tracy, Robert Hodierne, Linda Hansen, Linda Monroe, Christine Vande Voort, John Makowski, Ph.D. and John Koehler for their expertise in preparing the manuscript for publication.

My deepest appreciation goes to my extraordinary family, my wife Amy and sons Ashton and Adair, for their understanding of the importance of telling this story and the hope and promise that it represents to the generations of families dealing with the complex issues surrounding post-traumatic stress.